Francis Frith's

# ISLE OF WIGHT
## LIVING MEMORIES

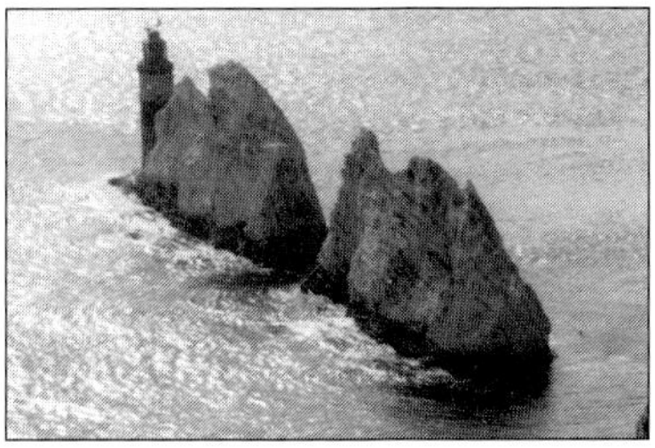

photographs of the mid twentieth century

Francis Frith's

# ISLE OF WIGHT
## LIVING MEMORIES

Robert Cook

FRITH BOOK Co

First published in the United Kingdom in 2001 by
Frith Book Company Ltd

Hardback Edition 2001
ISBN 1-85937-304-6



British Library Cataloguing in Publication Data

Francis Frith's Isle of Wight Living Memories
Robert Cook

Frith Book Company Ltd
Frith's Barn, Teffont,
Salisbury, Wiltshire SP3 5QP
Tel: +44 (0) 1722 716 376
Email: info@francisfrith.co.uk
www.francisfrith.co.uk

Printed and bound in Great Britain

*Front Cover:* Ventnor, The Promenade c1950 V1004

SPECIAL THANKS TO LOIS BOWN, RUTH HALL, MURIEL ADKINS AND JOHN NEWBY

AS WITH ANY HISTORICAL DATABASE THE FRITH ARCHIVE IS CONSTANTLY BEING CORRECTED AND IMPROVED AND THE PUBLISHERS WOULD WELCOME INFORMATION ON OMISSIONS OR INACCURACIES

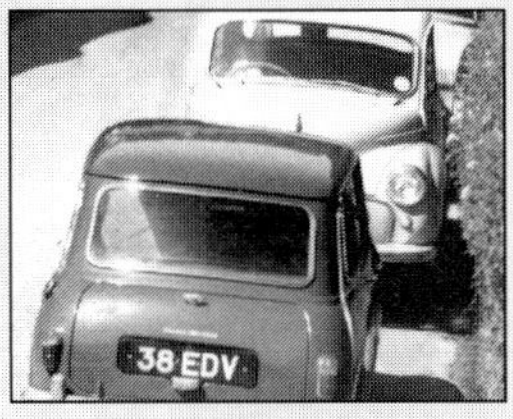


# contents

# Francis Frith: Victorian Pioneer

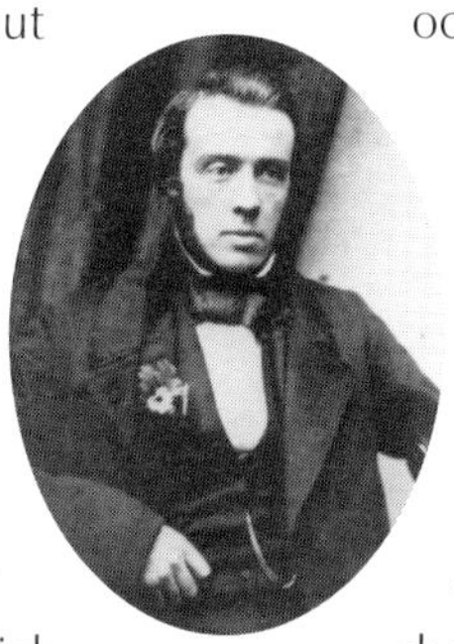

FRANCIS FRITH, Victorian founder of the world-famous photographic archive, was a complex and multi-talented man. A devout Quaker and a highly successful Victorian businessman, he was both philosophic by nature and pioneering in outlook.

By 1855 Francis Frith had already established a wholesale grocery business in Liverpool, and sold it for the astonishing sum of £200,000, which is the equivalent today of over £15,000,000. Now a multi-millionaire, he was able to indulge his passion for travel. As a child he had pored over travel books written by early explorers, and his fancy and imagination had been stirred by family holidays to the sublime mountain regions of Wales and Scotland. 'What a land of spirit-stirring and enriching scenes and places!' he had written. He was to return to these scenes of grandeur in later years to 'recapture the thousands of vivid and tender memories', but with a different purpose. Now in his thirties, and captivated by the new science of photography, Frith set out on a series of pioneering journeys to the Nile regions that occupied him from 1856 until 1860.

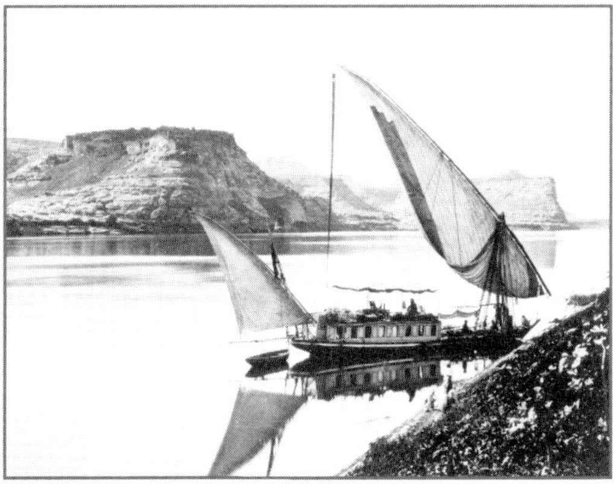

## Intrigue and Adventure

He took with him on his travels a specially-designed wicker carriage that acted as both dark-room and sleeping chamber. These far-flung journeys were packed with intrigue and adventure. In his life story, written when he was sixty-three, Frith tells of being held captive by bandits, and of fighting 'an awful midnight battle to the very point of surrender with a deadly pack of hungry, wild dogs'. Sporting flowing Arab costume, Frith arrived at Akaba by camel seventy years before Lawrence, where he encountered 'desert princes and rival sheikhs, blazing with jewel-hilted swords'.

During these extraordinary adventures he was assiduously exploring the desert regions bordering the Nile and patiently recording the antiquities and peoples with his camera. He was the first photographer to venture beyond the sixth cataract. Africa was still the mysterious 'Dark Continent', and Stanley and Livingstone's historic meeting was a decade into the future. The conditions for picture taking confound belief. He laboured for hours in his wicker dark-room in the sweltering heat of the desert, while the volatile chemicals fizzed dangerously in their trays. Often he was forced to work in remote tombs and caves where conditions were cooler. Back in London he exhibited his photographs and was 'rapturously cheered' by members of the Royal Society. His reputation as a photographer was made overnight. An eminent modern historian has likened their impact on the population of the time to that on our own generation of the first photographs taken on the surface of the moon.

## Venture of a Life-Time

Characteristically, Frith quickly spotted the opportunity to create a new business as a specialist publisher of photographs. He lived in an era of immense and sometimes violent change. For the poor in the early part of Victoria's reign work was a drudge and the hours long, and people had precious little free time to enjoy themselves. Most had no transport other than a cart or gig at their disposal, and had not travelled far beyond the

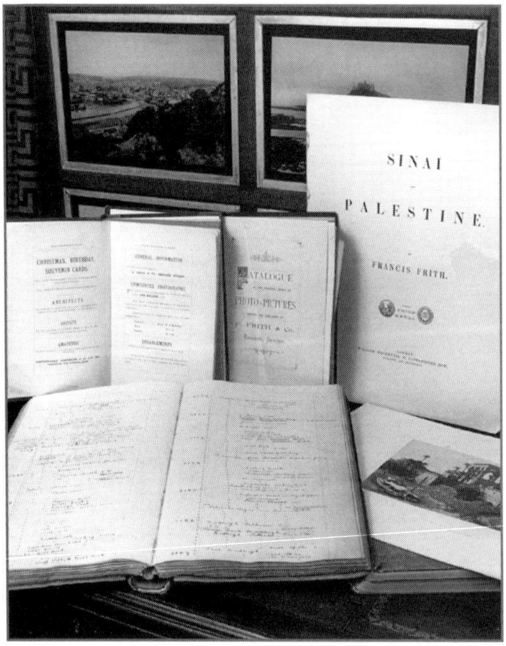


boundaries of their own town or village. However, by the 1870s, the railways had threaded their way across the country, and Bank Holidays and half-day Saturdays had been made obligatory by Act of Parliament. All of a sudden the ordinary working man and his family were able to enjoy days out and see a little more of the world.

With characteristic business acumen, Francis Frith foresaw that these new tourists would enjoy having souvenirs to commemorate their days out. In 1860 he married Mary Ann Rosling and set out with the intention of photographing every city, town and village in Britain. For the next thirty years he travelled the country by train and by pony and trap, producing fine photographs of seaside resorts and beauty spots that were keenly bought by millions of Victorians. These prints were painstakingly pasted into family albums and pored over during the dark nights of winter, rekindling precious memories of summer excursions.

## The Rise of Frith & Co

Frith's studio was soon supplying retail shops all over the country. To meet the demand he gathered about him a small team of photographers, and published the work of independent artist-photographers of the calibre of Roger Fenton and Francis Bedford. In order to gain some understanding of the scale of Frith's business one only has to look at the catalogue issued by Frith & Co in 1886: it runs to some 670 pages, listing not only many thousands of views of the British Isles but also many photographs of most European countries,

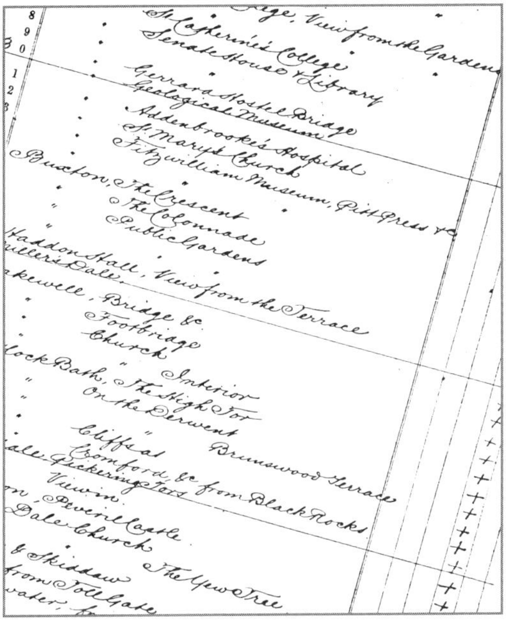
...ege, View from the Gardens
St Catherine's College
Senate House & Library
Gerrard Hostel Bridge
Geological Museum
Addenbrooke's Hospital
St Mary's Church
Fitzwilliam Museum, Pitt Press &c
Buxton, The Crescent
The Colonnade
Public Gardens
Haddon Hall, View from the Terrace
...llers Dale
...kewell, Bridge &c
Footbridge
Church
Interior
...ock Bath, The High Tor
On the Derwent
Cliffs at
Brunswood Terrace
Cromford &c from Black Rocks
...ale Pickering Tor
View in
...n, Peveril Castle
Dale Church
The Yew Tree
& Skiddaw
from Toll Gate
...water, ...

and China, Japan, the USA and Canada – note the sample page shown above from the hand-written *Frith & Co* ledgers detailing pictures taken. By 1890 Frith had created the greatest specialist photographic publishing company in the world, with over 2,000 outlets – more than the combined number that Boots and WH Smith have today! The picture on the right shows the *Frith & Co* display board at Ingleton in the Yorkshire Dales. Beautifully constructed with mahogany frame and gilt inserts, it could display up to a dozen local scenes.

## Postcard Bonanza

The ever-popular holiday postcard we know today took many years to develop. In 1870 the Post Office issued the first plain cards, with a pre-printed stamp on one face. In 1894 they allowed other publishers' cards to be sent through the mail with an attached adhesive halfpenny stamp. Demand grew rapidly, and in 1895 a new size of postcard was permitted called the court card, but there was little room for illustration. In 1899, a year after Frith's death, a new card measuring 5.5 x 3.5 inches became the standard format, but it was not until 1902 that the divided back came into being, with address and message on one face and a full-size illustration on the other. *Frith & Co* were in the vanguard of postcard development, and Frith's sons Eustace and Cyril continued their father's monumental task, expanding the number of views offered to the public and recording more and more places in Britain, as the coasts and countryside were opened up to mass travel.

Francis Frith died in 1898 at his villa in Cannes, his great project still growing. The archive he created continued in business for another seventy years. By 1970 it contained over a third of a million pictures of 7,000 cities, towns and villages. The massive photographic record Frith has left to us stands as a living monument to a special and very remarkable man.

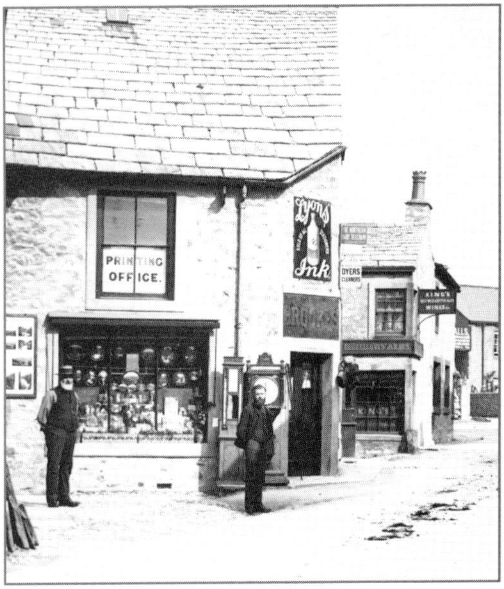

# Frith's Archive: A Unique Legacy

**FRANCIS FRITH'S** legacy to us today is of immense significance and value, for the magnificent archive of evocative photographs he created provides a unique record of change in 7,000 cities, towns and villages throughout Britain over a century and more. Frith and his fellow studio photographers revisited locations many times down the years to update their views, compiling for us an enthralling and colourful pageant of British life and character.

We tend to think of Frith's sepia views of Britain as nostalgic, for most of us use them to conjure up memories of places in our own lives with which we have family associations. It often makes us forget that to Francis Frith they were records of daily life as it was actually being lived in the cities, towns and villages of his day. The Victorian age was one of great and often bewildering change for ordinary people, and though the pictures evoke an impression of slower times, life was as busy and hectic as it is today.

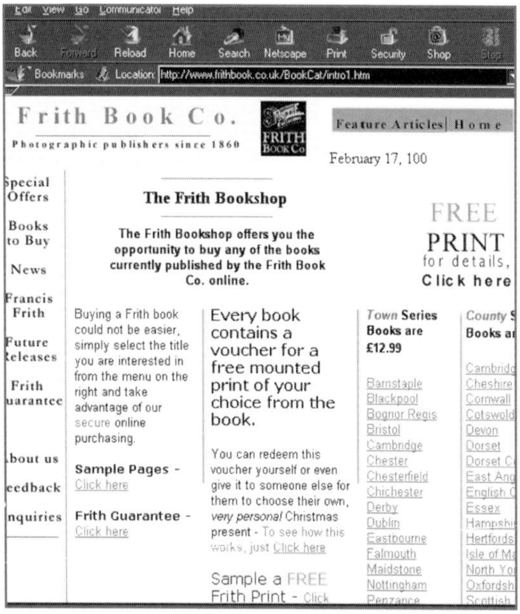


**See Frith at www. frithbook.co.uk**

We are fortunate that Frith was a photographer of the people, dedicated to recording the minutiae of everyday life. For it is this sheer wealth of visual data, the painstaking chronicle of changes in dress, transport, street layouts, buildings, housing, engineering and landscape that captivates us so much today. His remarkable images offer us a powerful link with the past and with the lives of our ancestors.

## Today's Technology

Computers have now made it possible for Frith's many thousands of images to be accessed almost instantly. In the Frith archive today, each photograph is carefully 'digitised' then stored on a CD Rom. Frith archivists can locate a single photograph amongst thousands within seconds. Views can be catalogued and sorted under a variety of categories of place and content to the immediate benefit of researchers.

Inexpensive reference prints can be created for them at the touch of a mouse button, and a wide range of books and other printed materials assembled and published for a wider, more general readership - in the next twelve months over a hundred Frith local history titles will be published! The day-to-day workings of the archive are very different from how they were in Francis Frith's time: imagine the herculean task of sorting through eleven tons of glass negatives as Frith had to do to locate a particular sequence of pictures! Yet the archive still prides itself on maintaining the same high standards of excellence laid down by Francis Frith, including the painstaking cataloguing and indexing of every view.

It is curious to reflect on how the internet now allows researchers in America and elsewhere greater instant access to the archive than Frith himself ever enjoyed. Many thousands of individual views can be called up on screen within seconds on one of the Frith internet sites, enabling people living continents away to revisit the streets of their ancestral home town, or view places in Britain where they have enjoyed holidays. Many overseas researchers welcome the chance to view special theme selections, such as transport, sports, costume and ancient monuments.

We are certain that Francis Frith would have heartily approved of these modern developments in imaging techniques, for he himself was always working at the very limits of Victorian photographic technology.

## The Value of the Archive Today

Because of the benefits brought by the computer, Frith's images are increasingly studied by social historians, by researchers into genealogy and ancestory, by architects, town planners, and by teachers and schoolchildren involved in local history projects.

In addition, the archive offers every one of us an opportunity to examine the places where we and our families have lived and worked down the years. Highly successful in Frith's own era, the archive is now, a century and more on, entering a new phase of popularity.

## The Past in Tune with the Future

Historians consider the Francis Frith Collection to be of prime national importance. It is the only archive of its kind remaining in private ownership and has been valued at a million pounds. However, this figure is now rapidly increasing as digital technology enables more and more people around the world to enjoy its benefits.

Francis Frith's archive is now housed in an historic timber barn in the beautiful village of Teffont in Wiltshire. Its founder would not recognize the archive office as it is today. In place of the many thousands of dusty boxes containing glass plate negatives and an all-pervading odour of photographic chemicals, there are now ranks of computer screens. He would be amazed to watch his images travelling round the world at unimaginable speeds through network and internet lines.

The archive's future is both bright and exciting. Francis Frith, with his unshakeable belief in making photographs available to the greatest number of people, would undoubtedly approve of what is being done today with his lifetime's work. His photographs, depicting our shared past, are now bringing pleasure and enlightenment to millions around the world a century and more after his death.

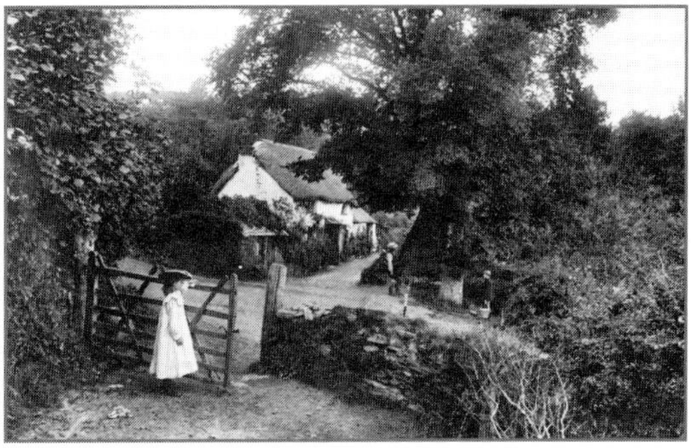

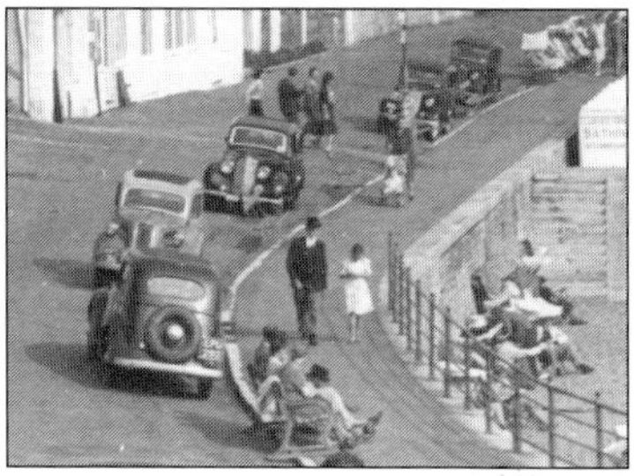

# Isle of Wight Living Memories
# An Introduction

Barely two miles from the mainland and extending merely 23 miles east to west, with 60 miles of coastline, the Isle of Wight has enjoyed exceptional importance in England's history. This is because it controls the approaches to the Solent and the ports of Southampton and Portsmouth. It is a place rich in seafaring history. Noel Pycroft, a retired Hayling Island brickmaker, recalls: 'On 24 March 1878 my grandfather, a boy of 12, was playing cricket in the family's Portsmouth brickyard when his father saw a storm cloud coming up over Portsdown Hill, north-east of them and travelling fast. By the time they had covered their bricks up there was three feet of snow.

The 'Eurydice' was coming up the channel with cadets on board. She was close in under Dunose Point, near Bonchurch. She never saw the storm, and it struck her as she was coming in close-hauled under the land against the north-east wind on the port tack. She was driven so fast under the water that her bow was badly damaged (her four foot broke off the long stem). Only one sail, the main sheet, was carried away. She was lost with a crew of over 300 boys. Only 2 survived'. The event is commemorated in Sir Arthur Conan Doyle's poem, 'The Homecoming of the Eurydice' from his 'Songs of Action' anthology.

Geologically, the Isle of Wight is an outlier of

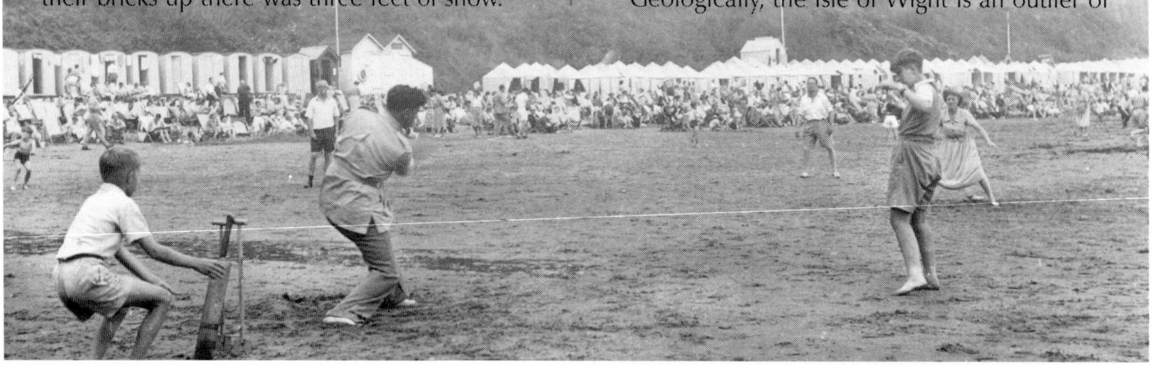

southern England's chalk downland and occasionally gravel-capped heathland. It extends east to west, with the peak at Brighstone and St Boniface, dwindling westward toward the Needles. The chalk backbone supports an area of rolling fields and intensive arable farming. To the south-west, the undercliff presents a remarkable 7 miles of old coastline where massive chalk blocks and upper greensand strata move against the underlying clay. There have been few fatalities, but this instability presents problems: in 1928 part of the coastal road at Gore Cliff near Blackgang was destroyed - a 2-mile diversion via the village of Niton had to be made.

Short, steep valleys - chines - slice through the southern landscape, damp, densely-wooded and thick with willow scrub and ferns. Unstable rocks have revealed a wealth of fossils; brachiosaurus bones have been found at St Catherine's, the southernmost point.

To the north and east, on the lower land, there are denser hedges, and smaller fields for pasture and horticulture. Yarmouth and Cowes are primarily major ports catering for industry; their role as tourist havens is secondary, except during Cowes week, when elegant yachts and pretty girls abound. Conspicuous wealth is the hallmark of this famous regatta.

Ever since the Victorians popularised the island, there have been vulgar elements; even Queen Victoria's son King Edward VII could be crude. The 16-stone monarch was affectionately known as 'Tum Tum', owing to his passion for 12-course meals. He refused to help his grocer friend Sir Thomas Lipton, whose racing yacht 'Shamrock II' lost its mast on the Solent in 1901. Lipton, a self-made millionaire, spent over half a million pounds on four Shamrock racing yachts in a 32-year bid to win the Americas Cup. For his fruitless efforts the Americans awarded him a presentation cup inscribed 'To the gamest loser in the world'. Queen Victoria spoiled the young Edward. When she died at Osborne House in 1901, Henry James wrote: 'We are to have no more little mysterious Victoria but instead fat dreadful Edward'.

The Isle of Wight's rise as a holiday resort began when Queen Victoria and Prince Albert rebuilt Osborne House to Albert and Thomas Cubitt's Italianate design. It had large gardens with rare trees, and a Swiss chalet for the children. Victorian day trippers and holidaymakers were encouraged by the royal enthusiasm, regarding the island as a toy England. It was just the place for healthy bathing and boating. Ryde's population grew from around 500 at the end of the 18th century to over 3000 by the 1820s. As Tennyson observed, 'the ringing grooves of change' brought the railways, with the first line from Ryde to Shanklin opening in the early 1860s; there were

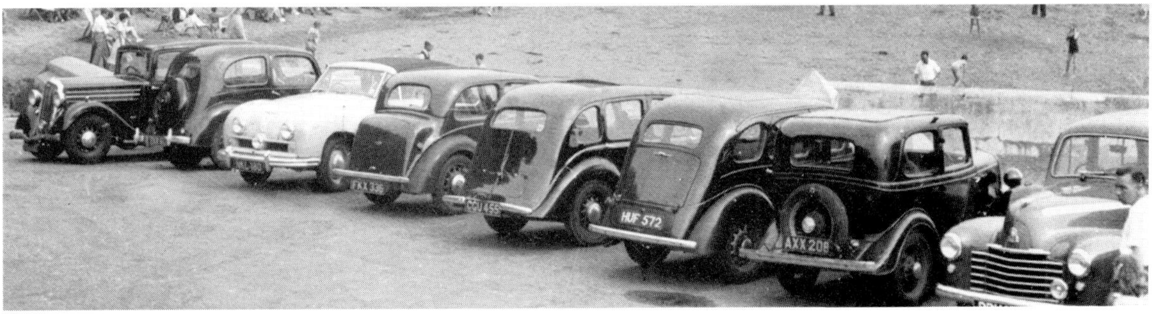

lines linking all the major towns by the 1880s. Nowhere was far from a station - there were once 30 - and there were 50 miles of track; there were even plans for a tunnel under the Solent. Fortunately for the ferry companies, it never materialised, but in those early days it would have been welcome. Ferry competition was fierce. In 1899 the London and South Western Railway's steamer 'Stella' was wrecked while racing a Great Western Railway vessel.

The number of foot passengers going to the island doubled in the period from 1937 to 1948 to 441,000, and the number of cars increased tenfold to 20,000. These days, the ferry and hovercraft crossings could not be safer. Red Funnel, operating from Southampton to East Cowes, completed a £25 million investment programme with their new flagship 'Red Eagle' in 1996, setting new standards of comfort. The company continued its tradition of buying Clyde-built craft. Originally known as the Royal Mail Steam Packet Company, they once operated the romantically-named 'Lorna Doone', a 427-ton side-paddle steamer, Clyde-built in 1891 and bought second hand in 1898. Gladys and Ken Eacher recall the pleasure of popping across from their Southampton home. Ken said: 'The ship was very manoeuvrable, because the crew could vary the paddle speed on either side'. Gladys observed: 'It was very relaxing watching the paddles going round'.

The Solent may not be wide, but it is wide enough to contribute to the island's romance; the sub-tropical climate helps the romantic atmosphere too. The surrounding water increases the light intensity, and the lowest recorded temperature is minus 9 degrees centigrade. In recent years, sheltered sites and sea breezes have been exploited for vineyards. Not surprisingly, the Isle of Wight has been the inspiration for many literary figures. Alfred Lord Tennyson (1809-92) had a favourite walk named after him; a wooden bridge led from his garden to the cliff tops. He only left when summer visitors overwhelmed him. Queen Victoria frequently visited the Tennysons at Farringford, and the Poet Laureate urged other writers to join him in paradise. Longfellow brought a party of 10, who enjoyed the fare at the Crab Inn in Shanklin Old Village before taking the path through Shanklin Chine. Lewis Carroll and Edward Lear were also among Tennyson's distinguished guests. Even the previous Poet Laureate, William Wordsworth, discovered the island's charms. Algernon Swinburne used to visit Farringford from his Bonchurch family home. Given his then outrageous views, his burial in 1909 at St Boniface 'new' church caused outrage. Still, his teenage admirer Edith Sitwell came to make homage. Charles Dickens spent his Isle of Wight mornings writing episodes of 'David Copperfield'; his afternoons were

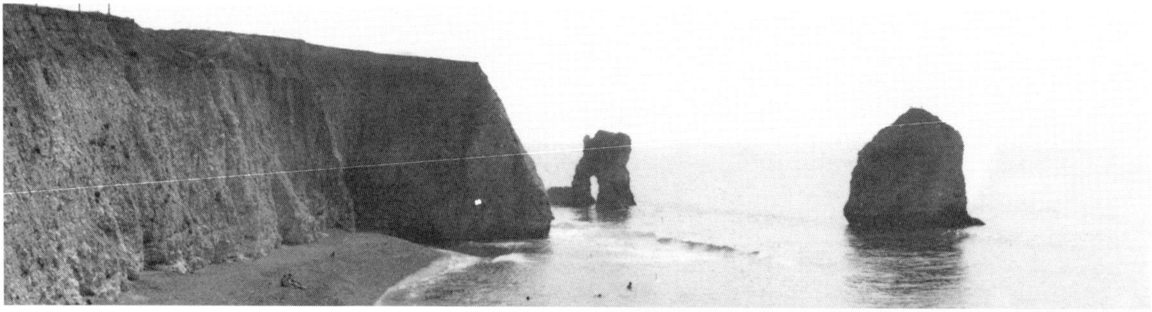

spent struggling up St Boniface down, playing rounders or taking tea with Lady Swinburne.

In 1902 Edward VII gave Osborne House to a grateful nation. Siegfried Sassoon, who had written some of the most moving war poetry of his time, was among a few writers who came to recuperate during their time as officers in World War One. J B Priestley was another writer sickened by his experiences in that great war to end wars. Spending intermittently over 25 years on the island, he moved to a mansion overlooking the bay facing Farringford. A restless spirit, he found something of the peace he craved.

Fifty years ago, the island was a quaint land with ancient hunting forests and developing attractions like the zoo. Newly-qualified district nurse and midwife Lois Bown came to West Wight, and was allocated her own district and a car. Many patients lived in remote rural areas. It was usual for babies to be born at home, unless there were complications. 'We were usually called out by telephone, but I remember talking to an 80-year-old retired midwife. She said that in her day the husband of one of her mothers had a different scheme. He and his wife lived in an isolated wooded area. He was a good rabbit catcher, using his shotgun. He would fire his gun as a signal, and the blast would wake the midwife a mile away. She would then set off on her bicycle to bring yet another baby into the world. In those days the father took time off work for the event. He would run the household and be on hand to keep kettles of water boiling for the midwife during the confinement, and when everything was over he would make tea for the mother, the midwife and possibly the doctor. We used to take the 'little black bag' containing everything we needed, and our first job on returning home was sterilising it all. Nowadays the midwife takes everything needed in a box, and it is all disposable. We used to take a large gas and air machine to relieve pain - one little boy asked the doctor why I brought my gramophone. I still see my ex-mothers and hear all about their children, most of whom are now married with children of their own. My work was very enjoyable; it was a great privilege to be able to drive around the lovely garden isle, as it is often called'.

Before the Victorians created that holiday paradise, the island's role was one of defence. As it was the first landfall from across the channel, the Romans called the island Vectis or Ictis, meaning 'from the sea' (the local bus company commemorates the name). The Solent is peculiar in having two high tides, crucial to the mainland port at Southampton and the three island harbours of Newport, Cowes and Yarmouth. The Normans were the first to spot the military potential of the island, and built Carisbrooke Castle, which was highly important

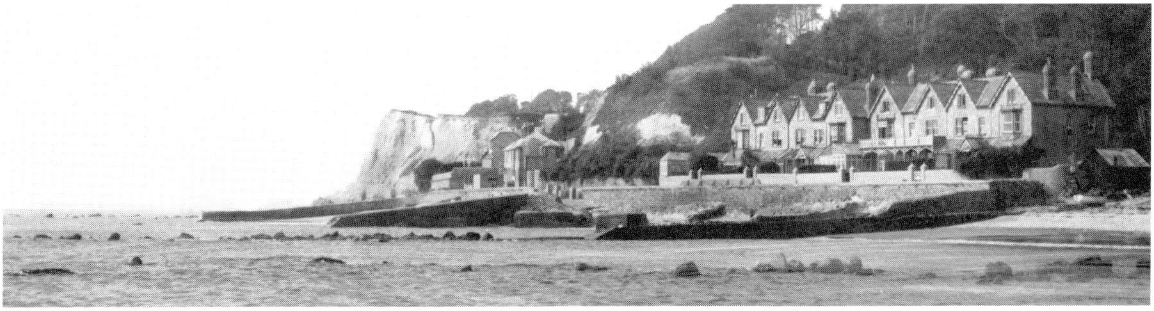

to Portsmouth's defence. Later, Henry VIII exploited the natural landscape, building forts at each end of the island to control the approaches across Spithead in the east and the Needles in the west. The Freshwater redoubt was built to prevent the French landing, and the military road was constructed along the south-west of the island: it follows the cliffs from Niton to Freshwater Bay, offering outstanding views inland to the downs and cliffs below. It was built in 1860 for garrisons faced with a possible French invasion. Palmerston's era of gunboat diplomacy and the imperial and naval rivalry with Germany created the massive brick structures of Fort Victoria, near Yarmouth, and Fort Albert, at Cliff End. World War Two underlined strategic concerns. Shanklin was particularly busy with the construction of the Pluto pipe line, which was to carry fuel under the Channel for the D-Day invasion.

Peace brought new hope to the nation. Sad to say, the steam railways were closed in an age obsessed with motor cars, but a small section was preserved for tourists. The austere 1950s gave way to the 60s, and the island did its share of swinging. It was perhaps not as popular with the hippies as Cornwall, but in 1969 it was the venue for protest singer Bob Dylan's first paid public performance for four years. A quarter of a million idealistic young fans, some coming all the way from Los Angeles, waited until 11.00pm on the last night of the Isle of Wight pop festival for their hero. Dylan said he came because the island had been Tennyson's home. He earned a reported £335,000 for under an hour's work, speaking only five sentences in the process. Eventually it dawned on the public that the stars were a grossly materialistic contrast to their followers, and ageing hippies gave way to a new pop culture, all wanting the glamour life based on money.

A recent report, 'Sea Changes: Creating World Class Resorts in England', warns that traditional resorts may go into terminal decline unless they think about what makes them distinctive, and market themselves accordingly. Beach holidays have also changed from long stays to short breaks. Purists might argue that pressures to modernise will destroy the very thing that sets the island apart. Others might say that a tourist economy needs diversity: Blackgang Chine can boast some garish pleasures, and why not? Other changes on the island include the pressure of numbers. The local population of 130,000 is growing, for the 8-minute hovercraft service to Portsmouth and Southsea makes the island attractive to commuters. During the summer, the island teems with around 2 million people. Success always has a price.

Maybe prices have gained precedence over values. In March this year the island's banks ran

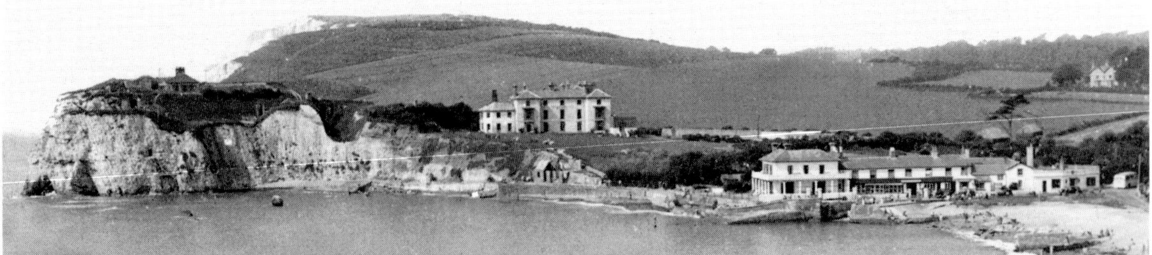

short of money when a pyramid scheme led many customers to remove £3000 from their accounts. Apparently they were urged to do so by a caller to the local radio station: a group called Women Empowering Women claimed to generate £24,000 for each person who invested £3000. (Howard Moreton, the island's trading standards officer, said that the scheme would only benefit those joining at the beginning). So the island is no haven of so-called traditional values. We all want to get rich quick now, and are perhaps a little susceptible to marketing gimmicks. Unemployment is around 9% and wages are below the national average, which is not surprising in an area dependent on tourism.

Against this hustling workaday backdrop, the beauty of the island is a joy to see. I do not know whether the poet William Henry Davies visited the island, but his words are most appropriate: 'What is this life, if full of care, we have not time to stand and stare?' Visitors come from far and wide to enjoy the beauty. Trinidadian visitor Vernon Church compared the Isle of Wight with his homeland: 'It's very nice for a holiday, not only during Cowes week when all the toffs arrive in their fancy yachts. One thing struck me was how large it seems after being told how small. One expected to stand at one end and see the other. My home island is 15 times bigger and we've got 14 times more people. Trinidad is a bit hotter but it has a similar feel, especially with good weather'.

The island is so exotic that it even has an ancient hunting forest complete with red squirrels; and yet it is so near. It is well worth a visit, as this photographic collection from the 1950s and 60s reveals. By dividing the island into four sections, these pictures take us on a clockwise journey through the past, from East Cowes to Cowes.

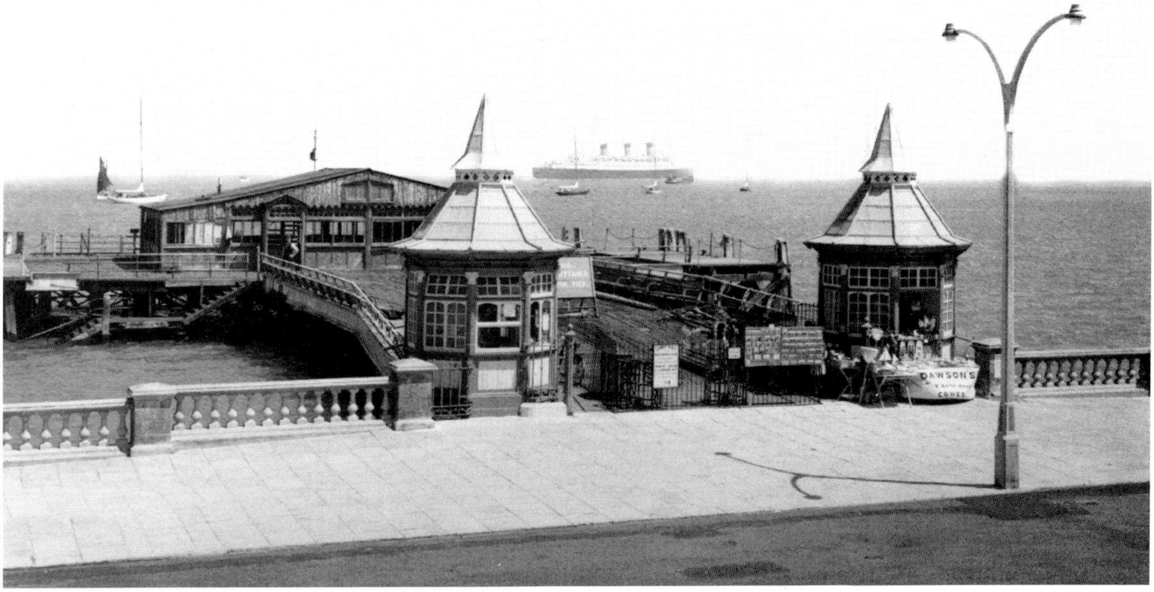

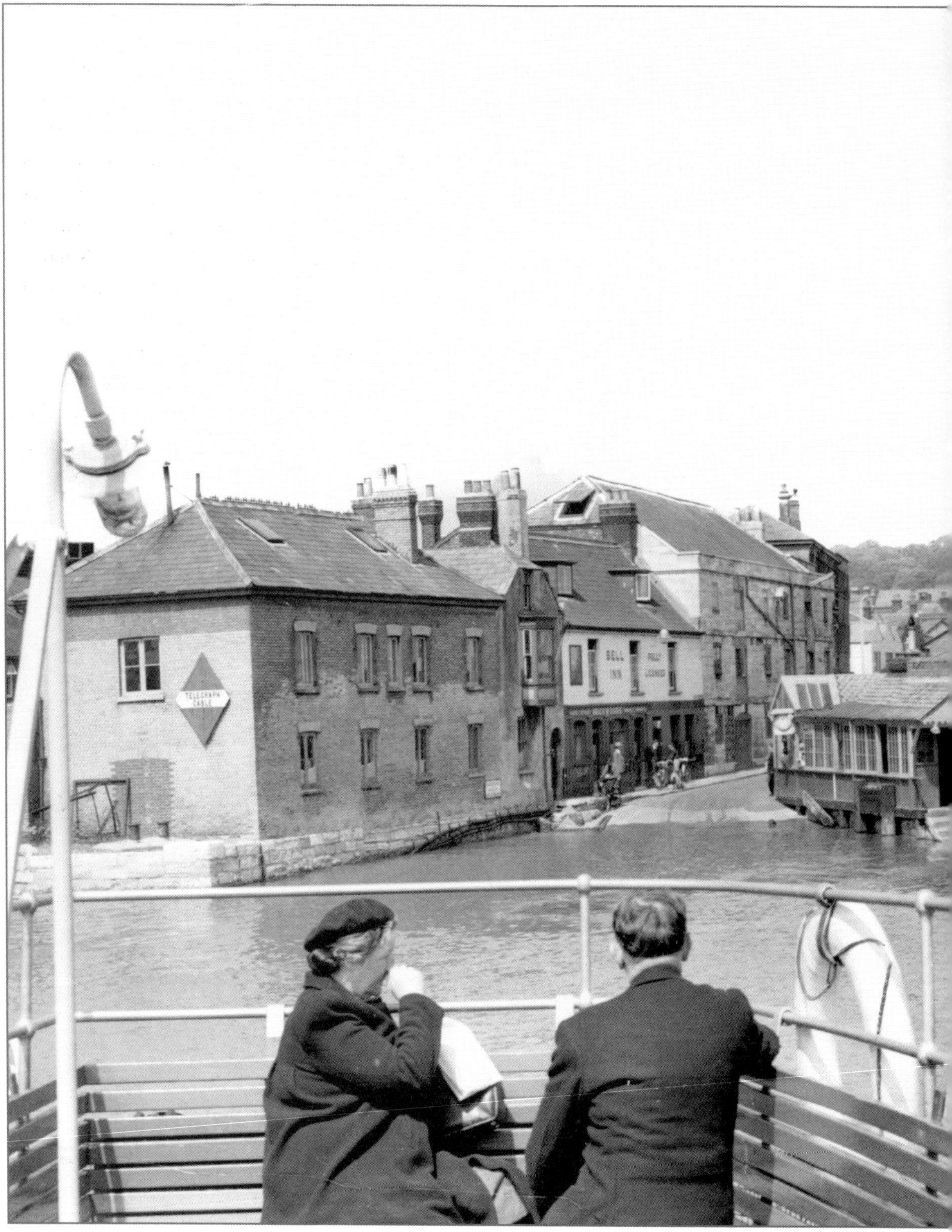
TELEGRAPH CABLE
BELL INN
FULLY LICENSED

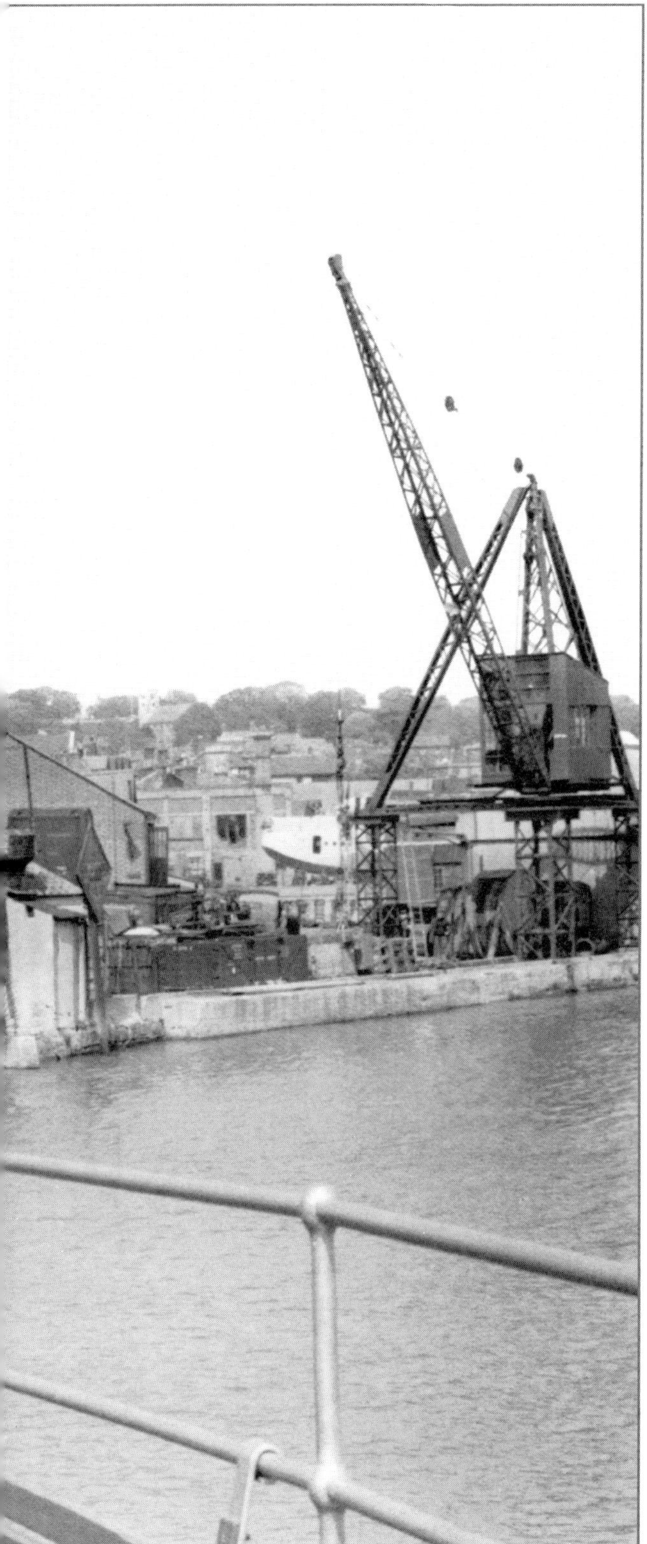

# Around Ryde

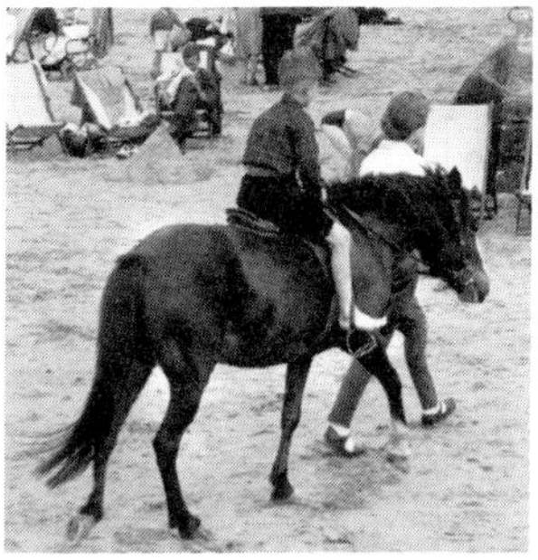

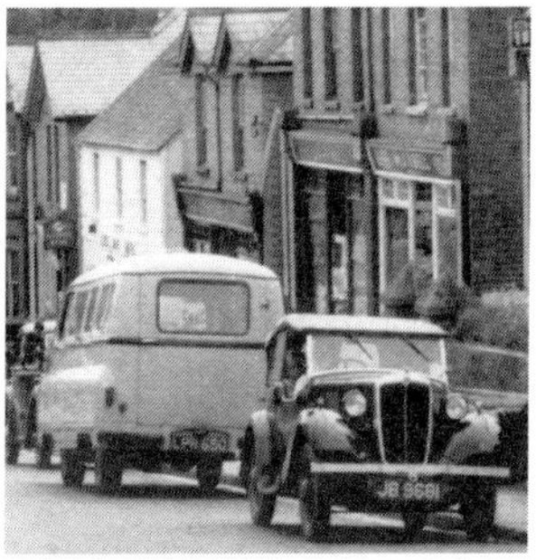

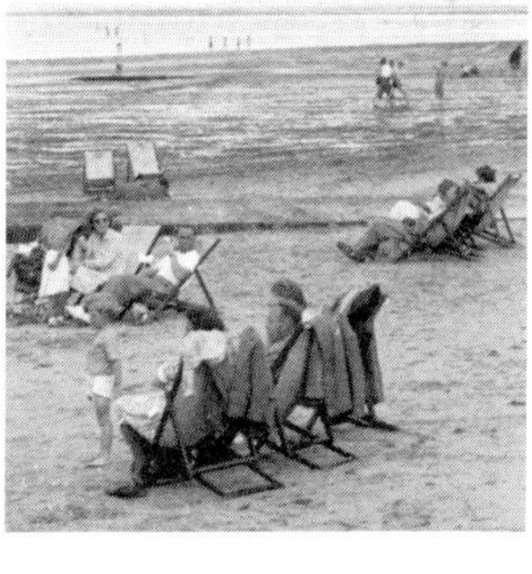

**East Cowes, From the Ferry c1955** E139008
East Cowes is the ferry port for Red Funnel from Southampton. Today's ferries are much larger than the one seen here, but the port retains its charm. Separated from the glamorous yachting centre by the Medina, it is an industrial centre with busy boatyards and cranes.

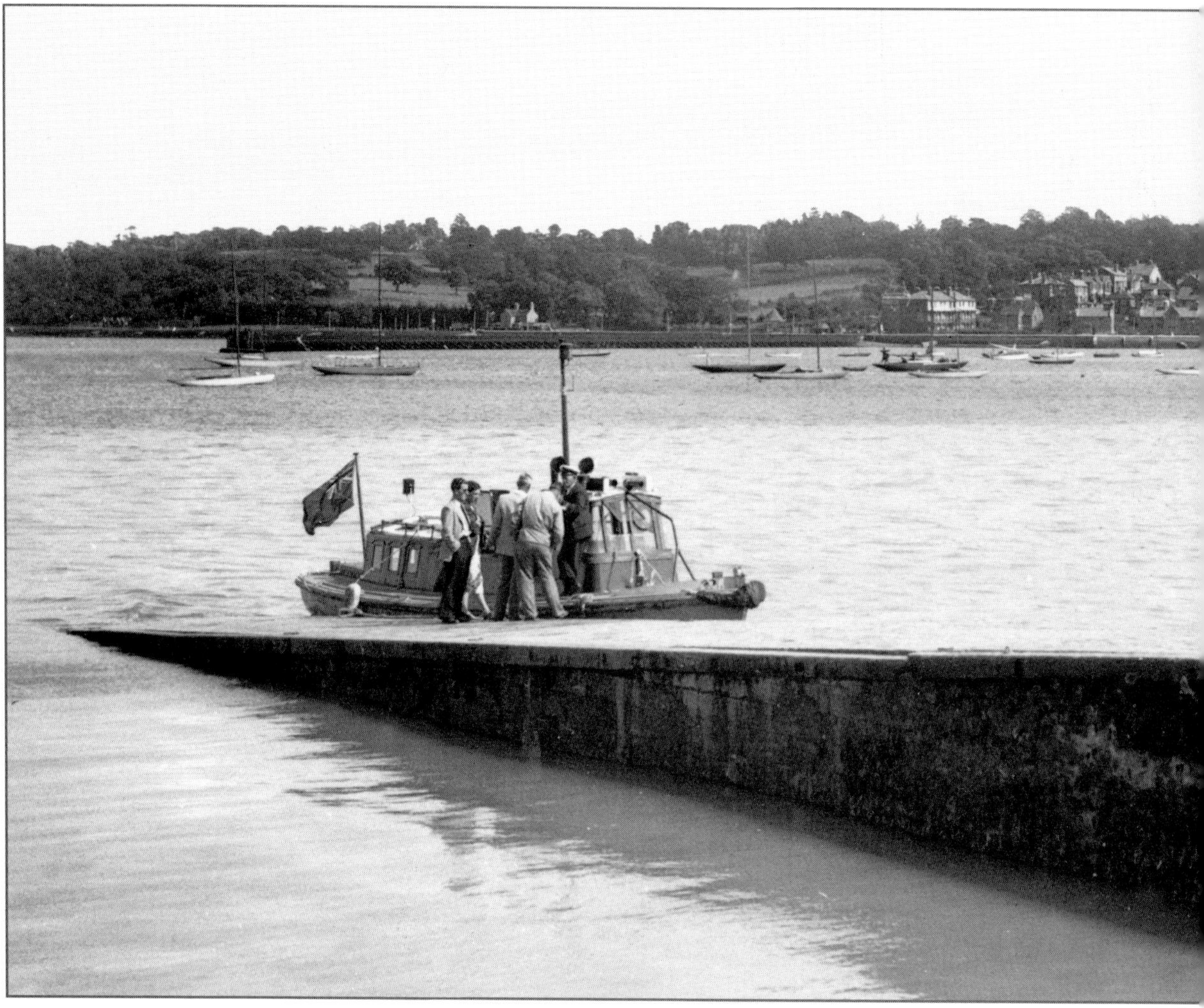

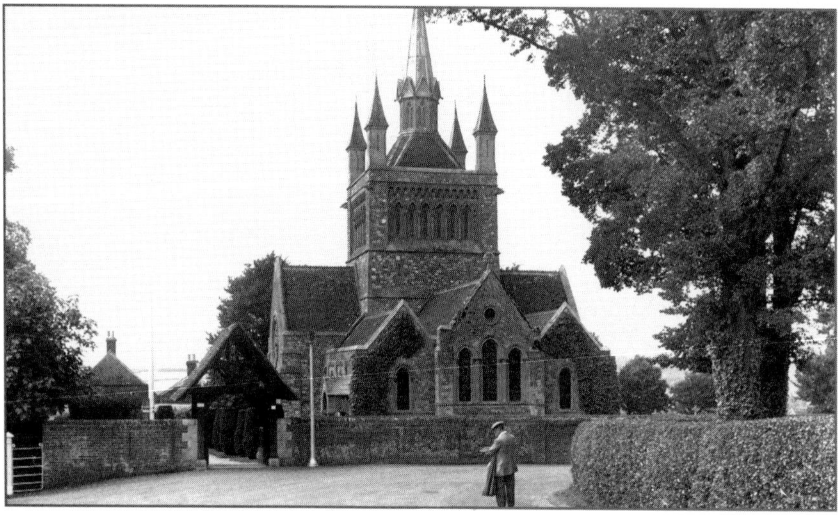

◄ **Whippingham**
**The Church c1955**

W79014

The church stands close to Osborne House, and its fairytale design by Prince Albert is in Romanesque Gothic style. The tower has five pinnacles and an Early English-style spire. The rose windows in the transepts are impressive, and there is a large marble tomb for Prince Henry and for Queen Victoria's youngest daughter in the Battenberg Chapel.

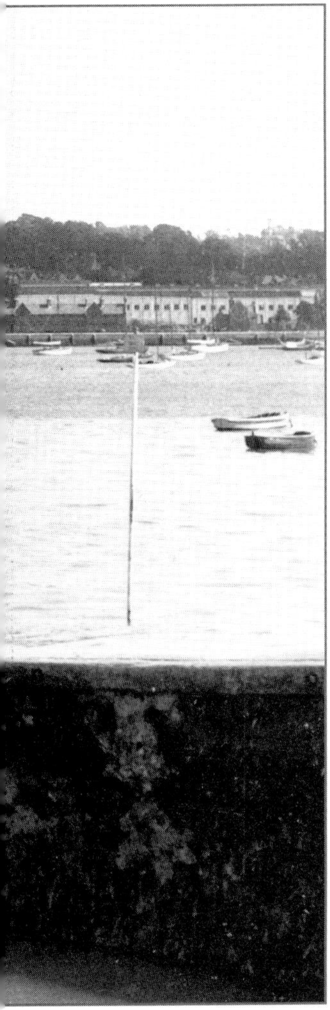

◄ **East Cowes, From West Cowes c1960** E139022
An official launch flying the Royal Ensign waits by a slipway. Perhaps it is waiting for VIPs, to take them to see a demonstration of the new hovercraft being developed at East Cowes by Saunders Roe.

▼ **Whippingham The Post Office c1955**
W79007
This is a rather splendid and fancy post office for such a small cluster of houses. Perhaps the post box is full of letters telling of lazy days on the banks of the River Medina. Whippingham grew along with the Osborne estate. Barton Oratory was established here in the 13th century; it was rebuilt by Queen Victoria.

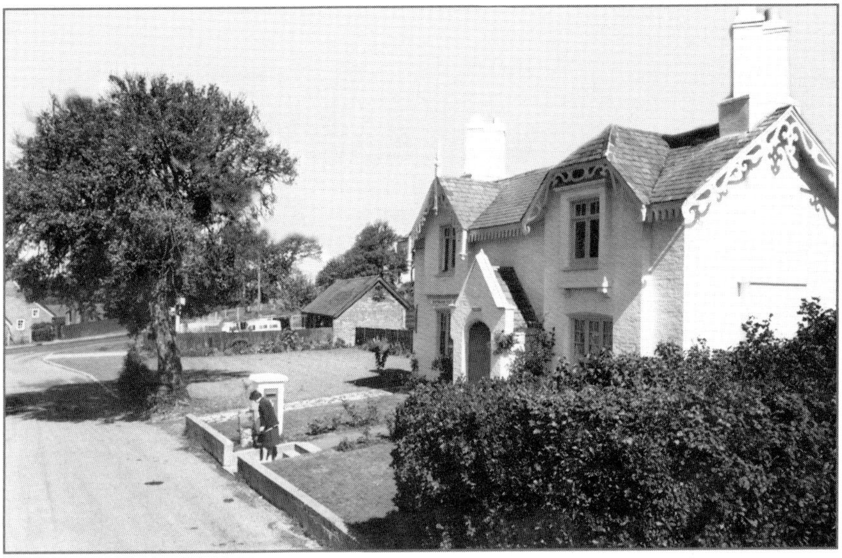

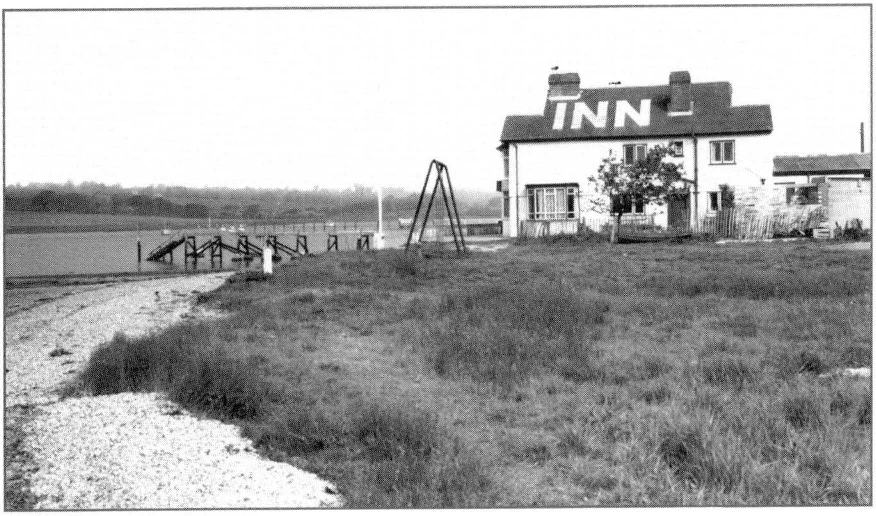


◄ **Whippingham The Folly Inn c1955**
W79003
This pub began as a sloop grounded on the river bank in the 18th century, which was used as an inn. This building advertises itself well, and offers more comfort than a sloop. The terrace is well-placed for views of a river alive with boats. Upstream the river broadens among the water meadows, offering good bird watching, and nowadays a marina.

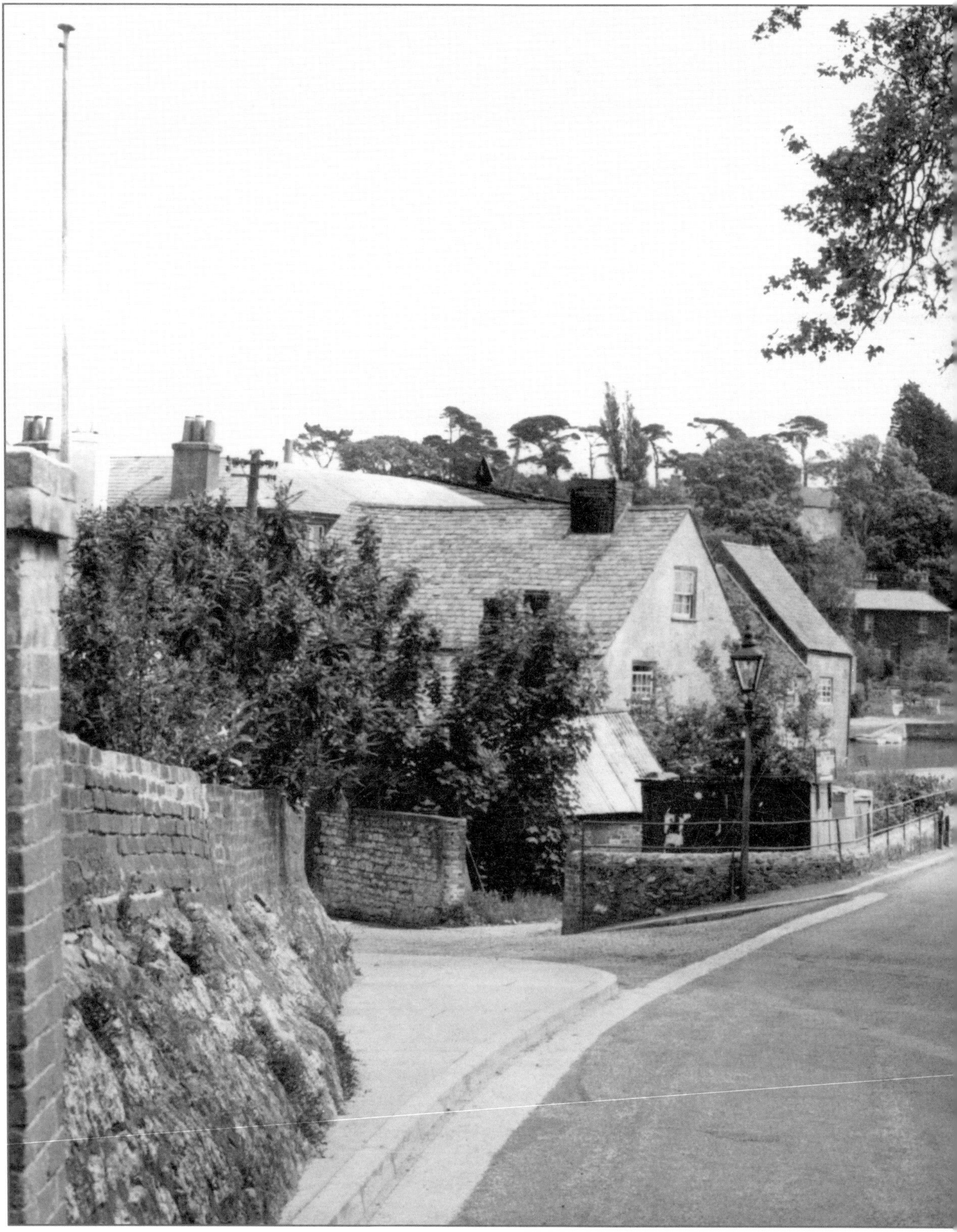

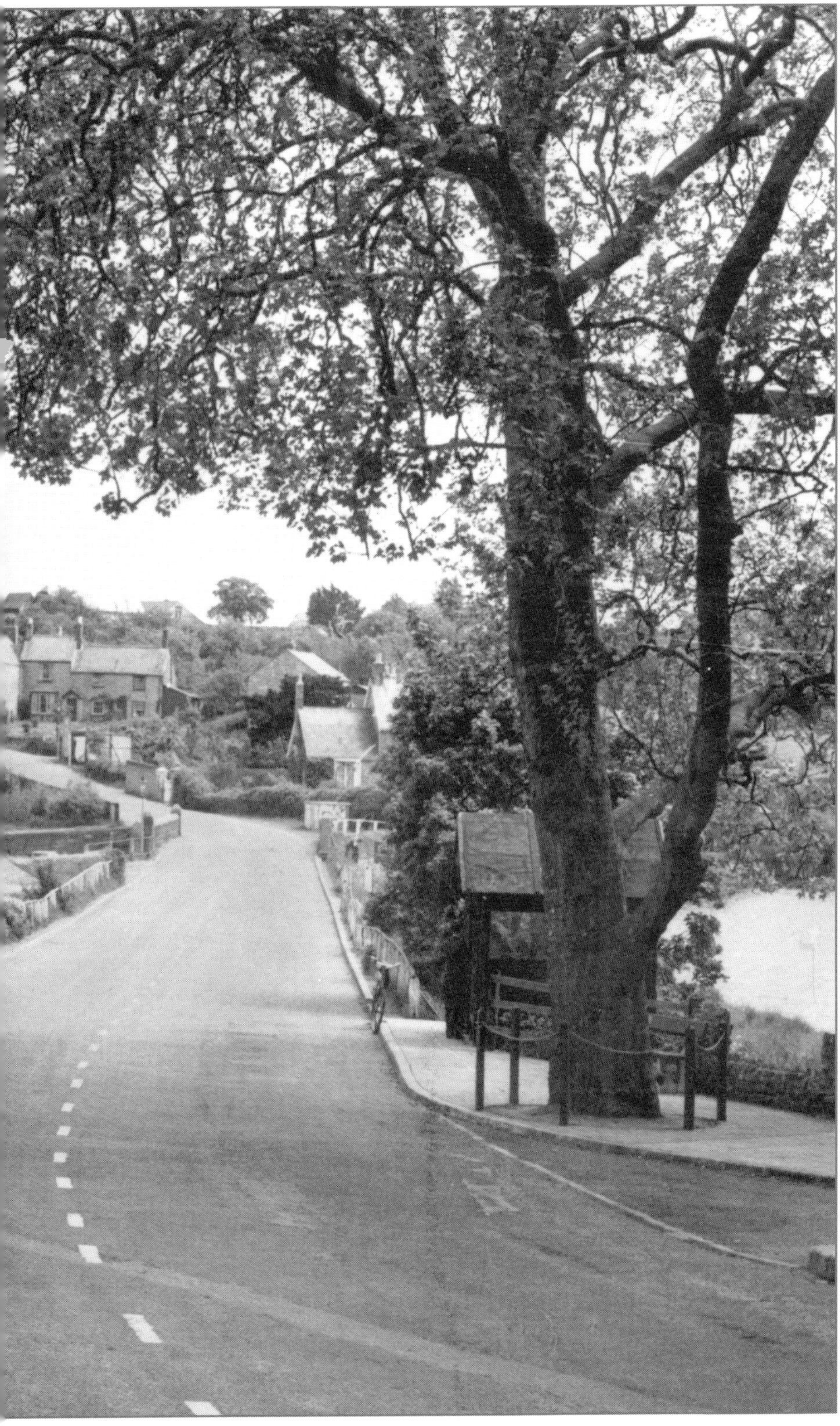

**Wootton Bridge**
**The Bridge c1955**

W282005

This view shows a string of red brick houses along the main A3054 road towards the bridge over the creek. The tide flows up here to an old water mill. The main road bridge is the causeway of the dam that controlled the mill pond. There is also a small 11th-century church here, with later additions.

**▼ Wootton Bridge, The Village c1960** W282035

The road toward Ryde, heading up Kite Hill, is quiet; the foliage is abundant, and there are only a few dark clouds to trouble the scenery. The bridge over the creek completes a pretty picture.

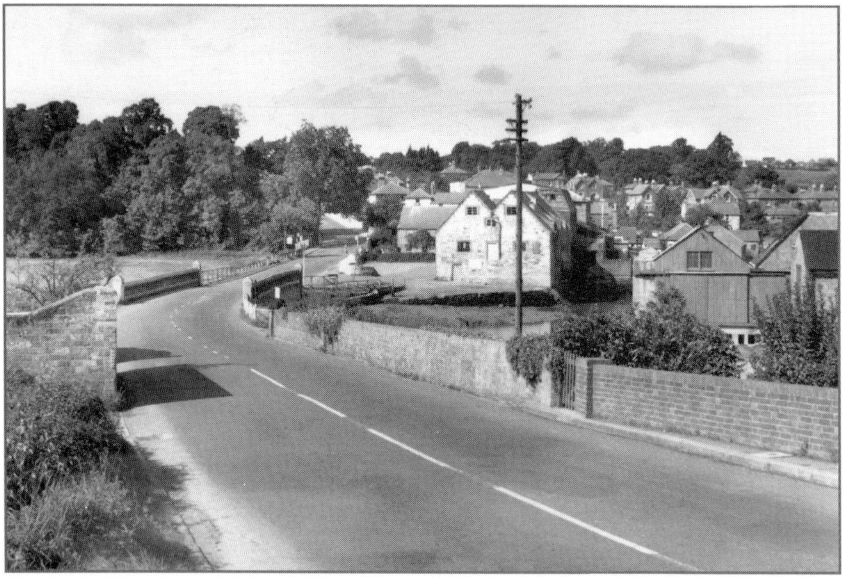

**▼ Wootton Bridge, The Bridge c1955** W282003

The creek ripples under the bridge. One can imagine the scene at night illuminated by the old gas lamp. As the boat at its moorings suggests, this is just the place for messing about on the river. State-of-the-art traffic is represented by a box-shaped delivery van and a drab black car.

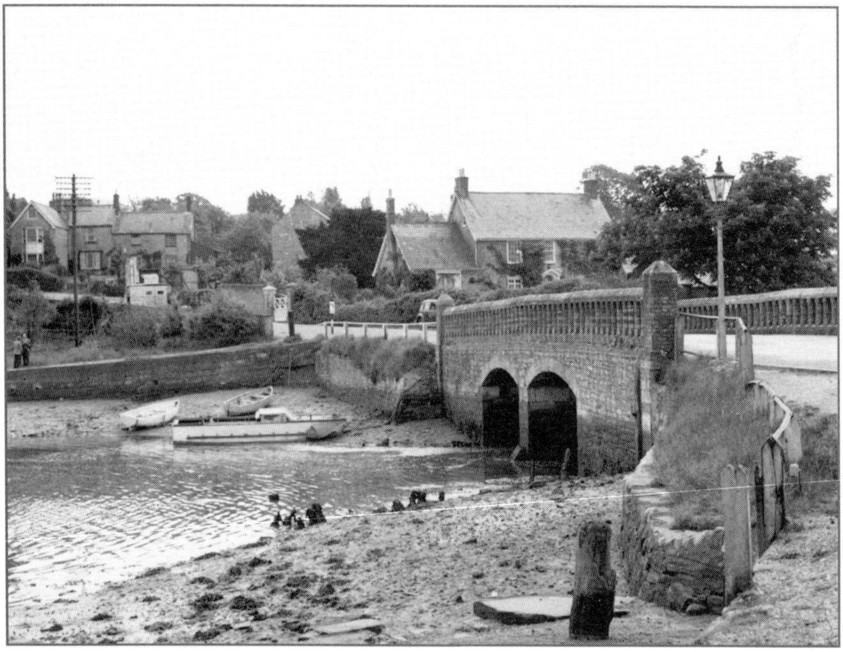

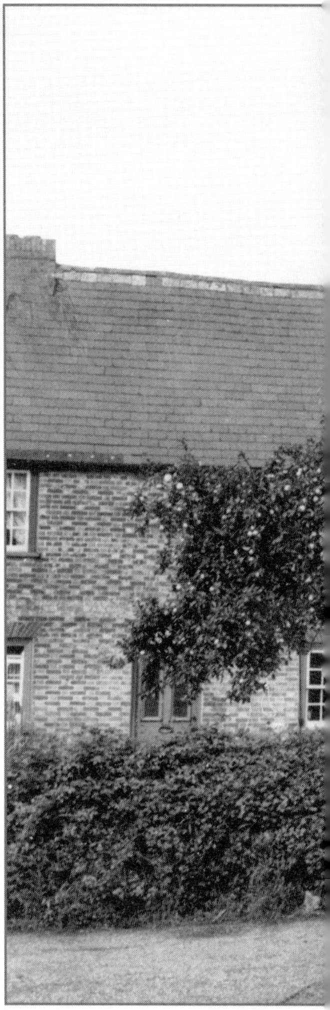

**▲ Wootton Bridge The Sloop Inn c1965** W282043

What tales must have been told by locals and tourists in the little inn. A stately Triumph Mayflower is parked by the stone wall; it may belong to the taxi firm advertised on the wall ahead.

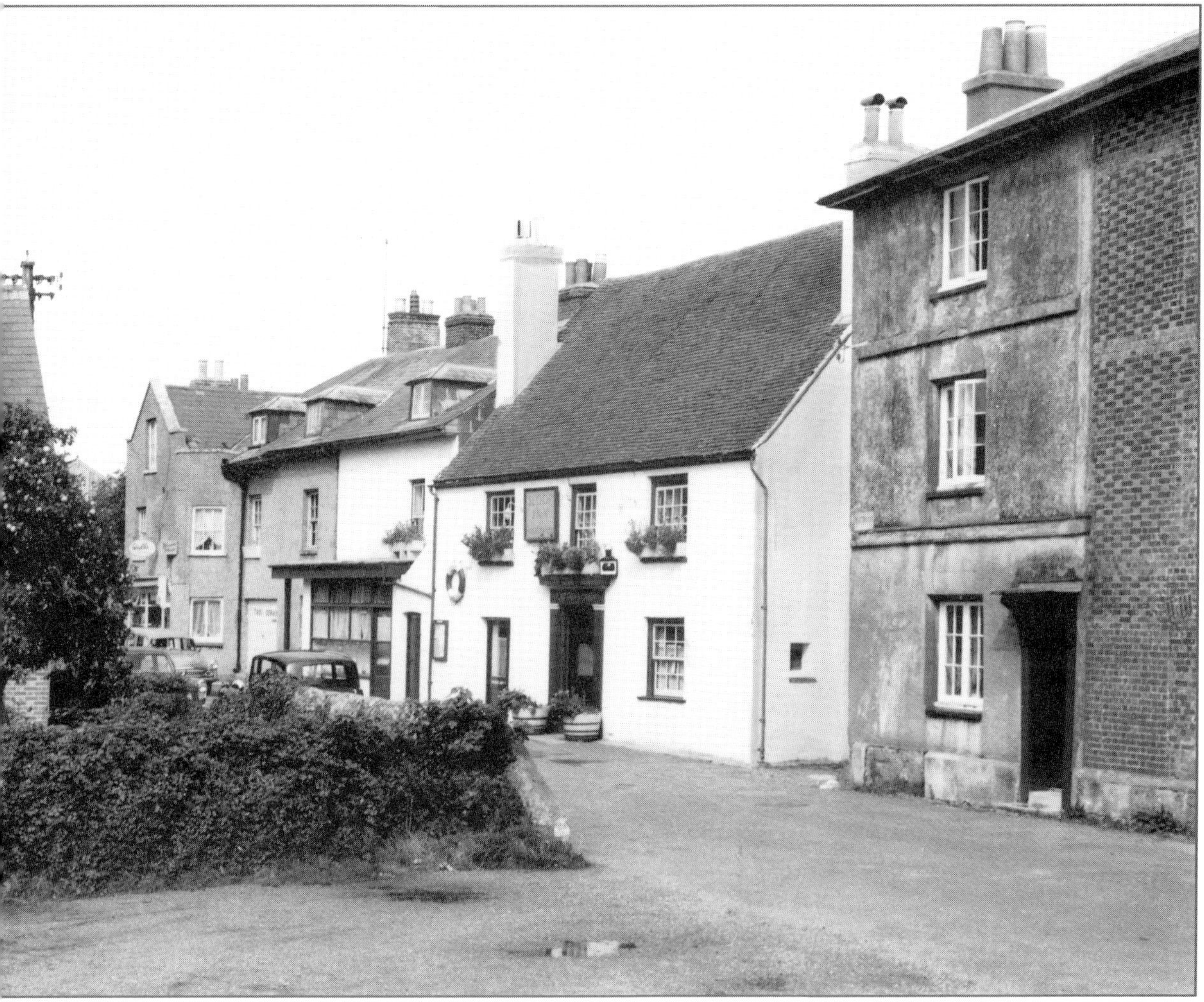

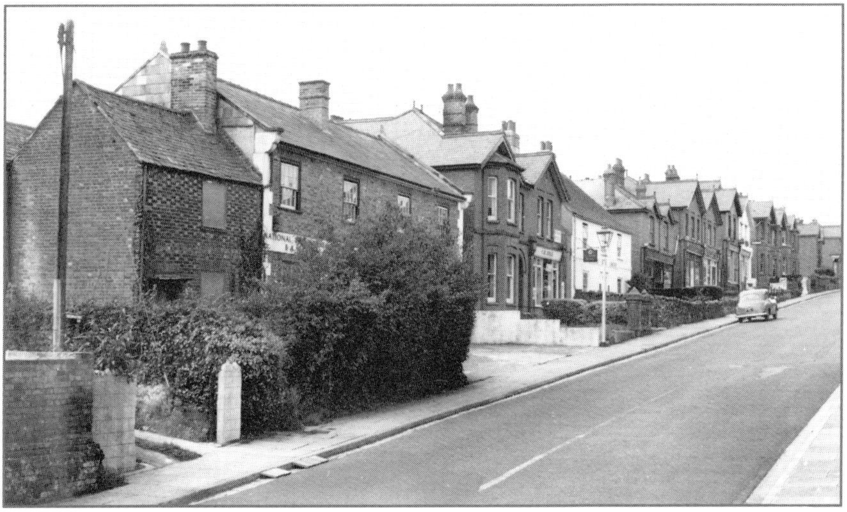

◄ **Wootton Bridge High Street c1960**

W282039

These were the days when having a car parked out front was something to boast about. The house boarded up in the foreground would not be left like that for long nowadays; it would be worth too much money. F M Hale and C Archer, Chemist, are pre-eminent in the High Street.

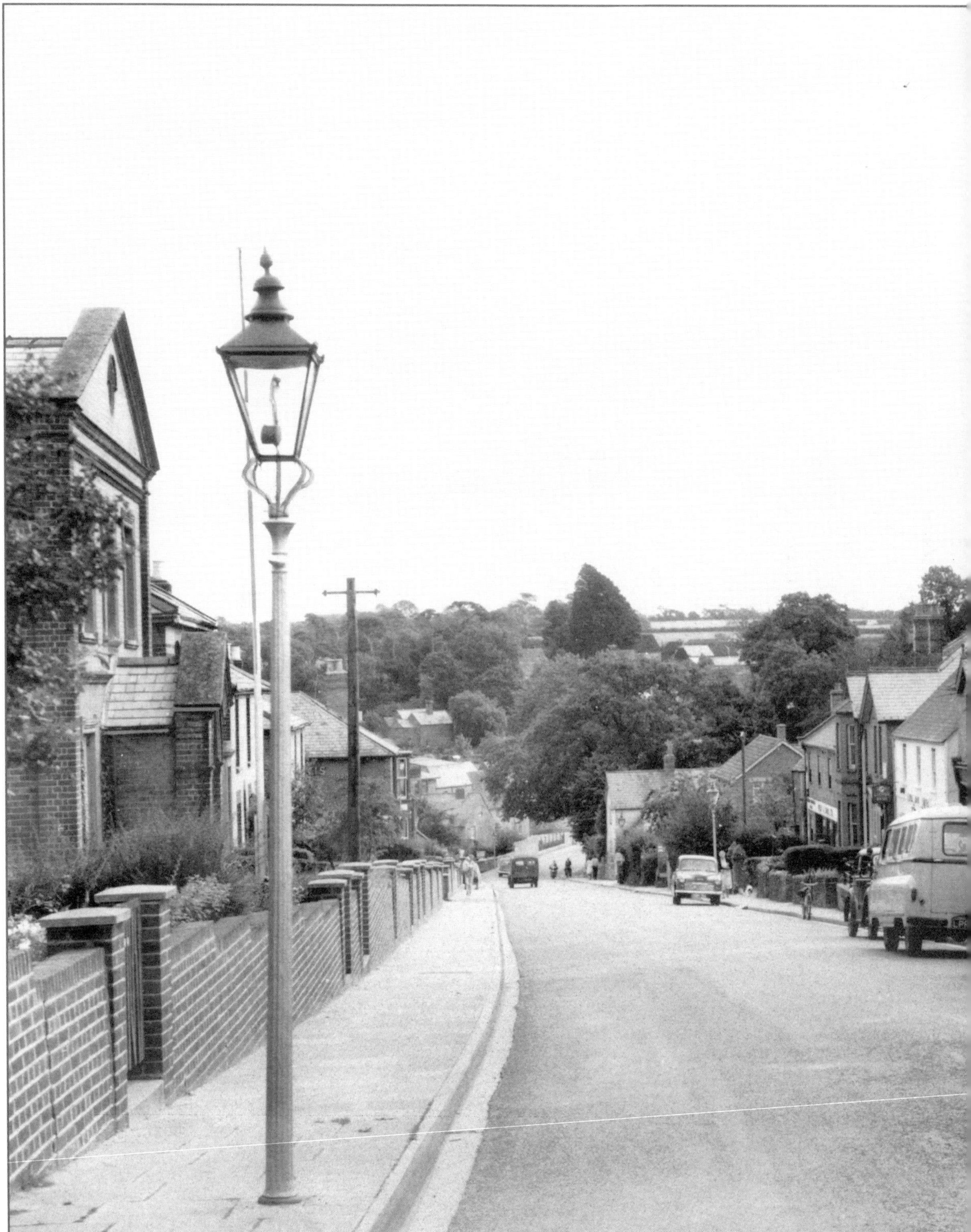

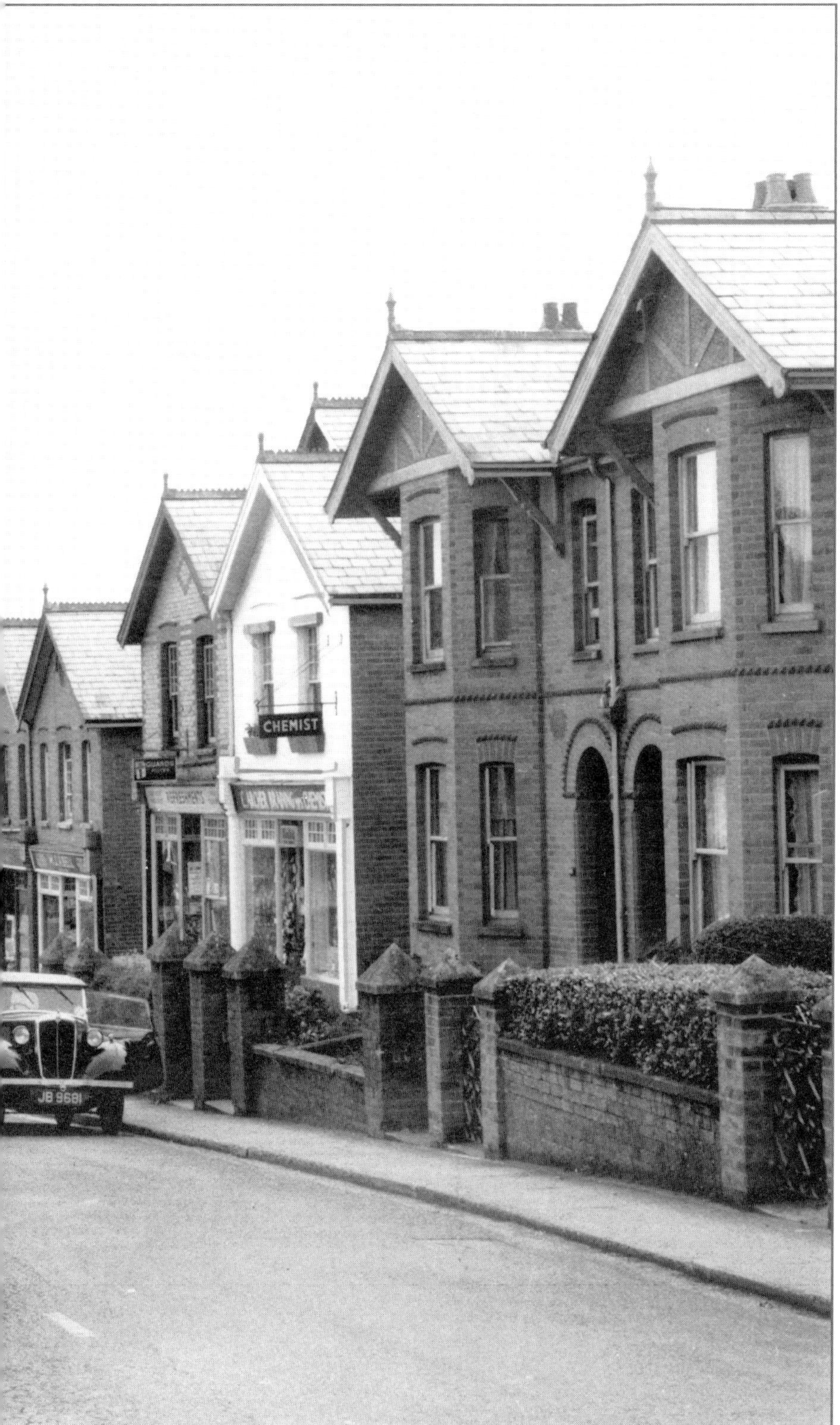


**Wootton Bridge High Street c1960**
W282040
We are looking downhill, eastwards toward the creek. An elegant gas lamp takes pride of place in the foreground. A grand old roadster is parked in front of a modern looking BMC J-type mini-bus.

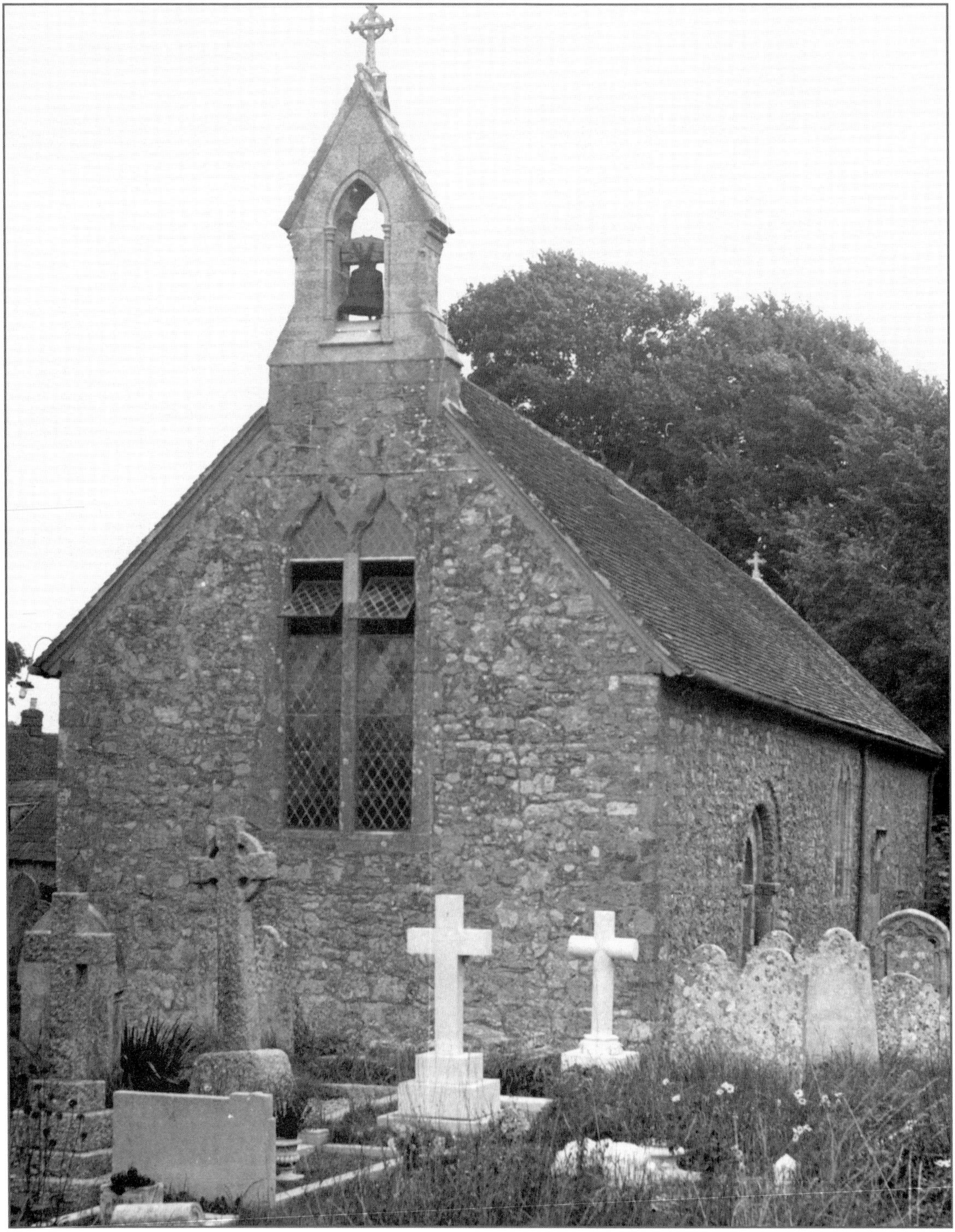

**Wootton Bridge, St Edmund's Church c1955** W282014
This is a simple building with origins in the 11th century. The nave and chancel is all in one, with a chapel for the organ. Kempe's east window represents the crucifixion. King Edmund the Martyr's arms are in the chancel window. The four evangelists are in four lancets. The reredos has pillars and background of coloured marbles.

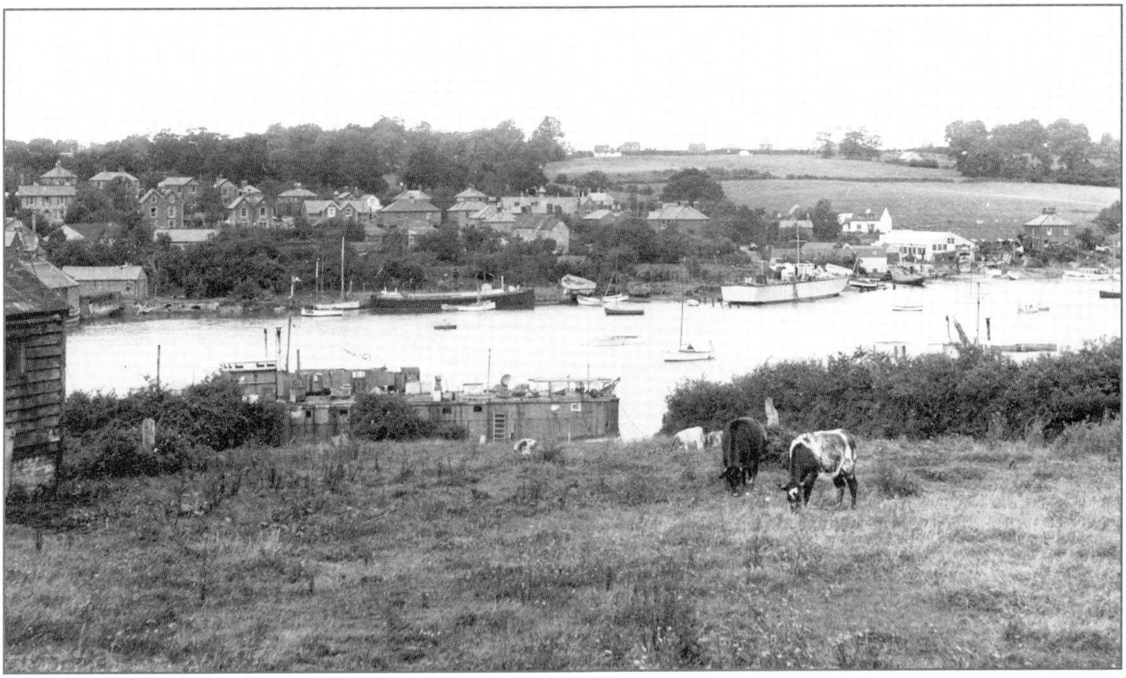

**Wootton Bridge, The Village c1960** W282006
Wootton Creek is busy with boatyards; little copses slope down to the water. Cattle graze peacefully in the foreground, although an outbreak of foot and mouth disease was only 8 years away.

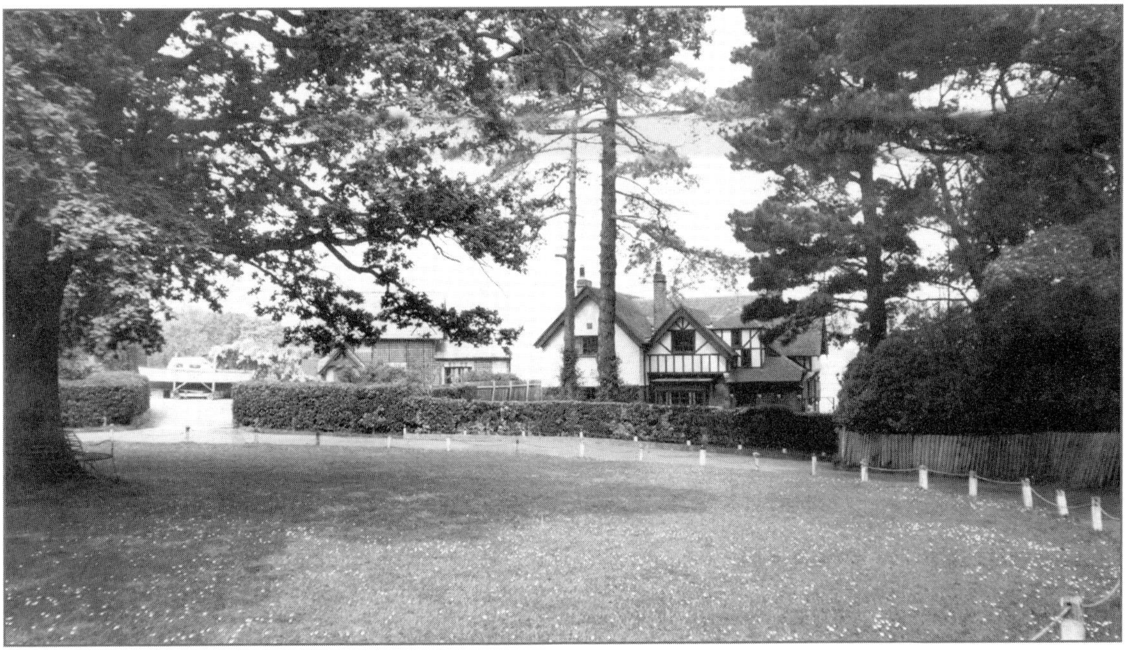

**Fishbourne, The Green c1960** F140001
This is old Fishbourne, just beyond the Portsmouth ferry terminal. A very old tree is surrounded by a circular green, and we can spot a little boat on a trailer ready for the Solent just out of sight. Here is boat house country for the aspiring or well-to-do.

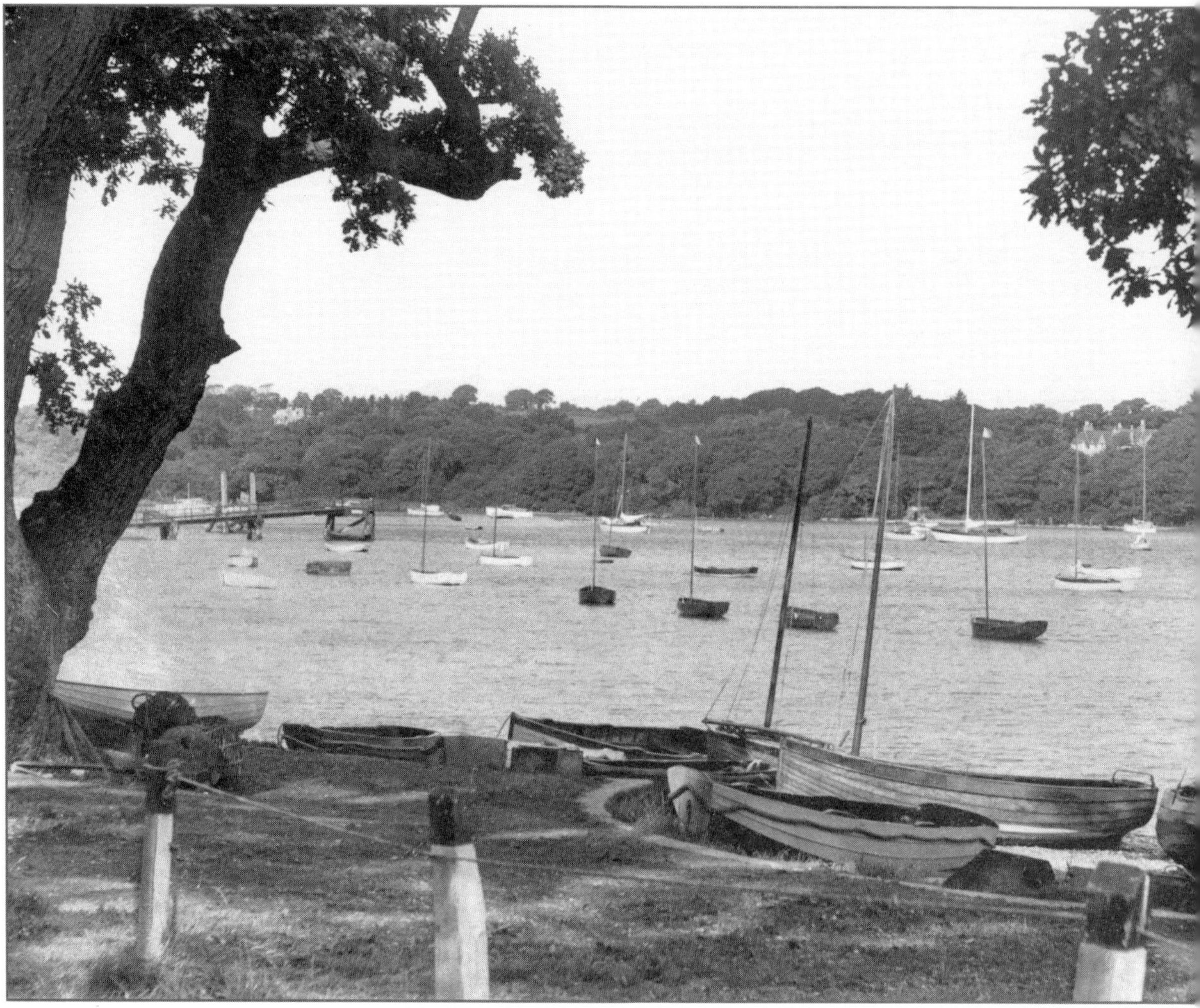

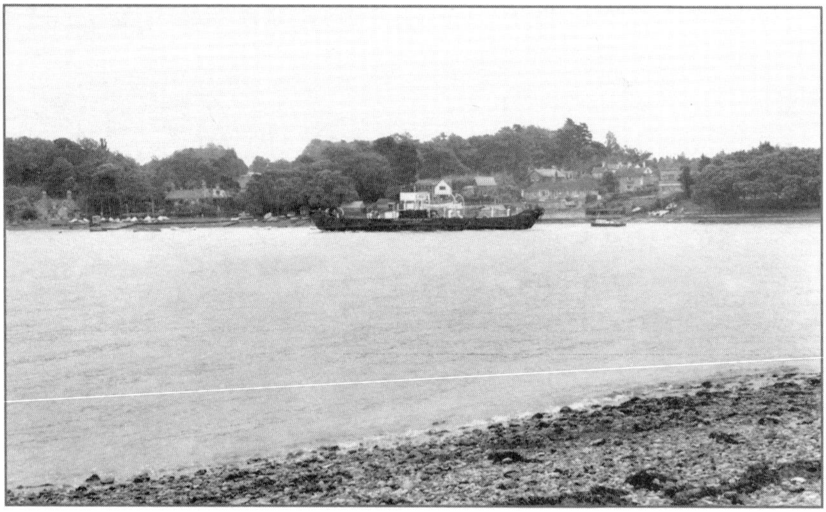

◄ **Fishbourne, The Car Ferry c1955** F140007

Portsmouth harbour lies almost in a straight line from here, and the crossing was well used by the monks of old. This picture shows the new-fangled car ferry, which appears rather small by today's standards. The woodlands are abundant, adding mystery to the river bank. Boats are drawn up until their owners can take them out on this pleasant water. Houses and bungalows mark several eras of development on what must be a popular sight-seeing spot.

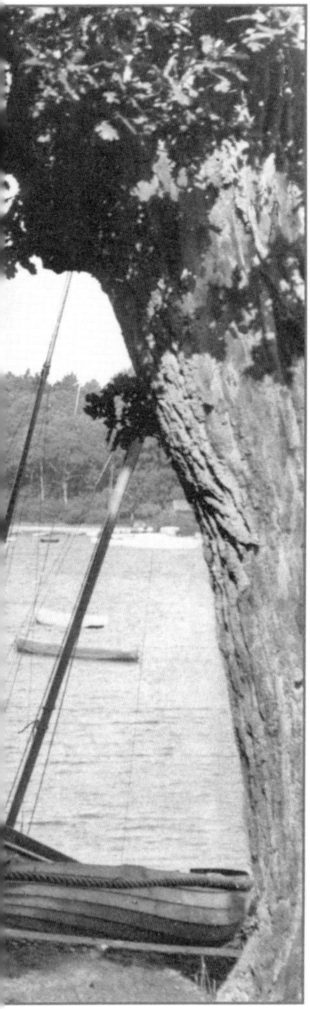

◄ **Fishbourne**
**The Creek c1960** F140014

The Abbot of Quarr built fortifications here in the 14th century. Then came the Watch House and the coastguard station. Wootton Creek boasts a yacht club, and has launched some fine boats. The foreground of this scene, facing the northern shore, displays humbler fishing and rowing boats, with little fishing baskets for the catch. The bigger boats are further out, with intriguing woodland marking the horizon.

▼ **Fishbourne**
**The Fishbourne Inn c1960** F140004

This interesting half-timbered building looks snug and inviting. Nice big chimneys assure us of a cosy fireplace in winter-time, and there are the tea gardens to sit in in summer. The little shop and post office is just the place for those postcards home.

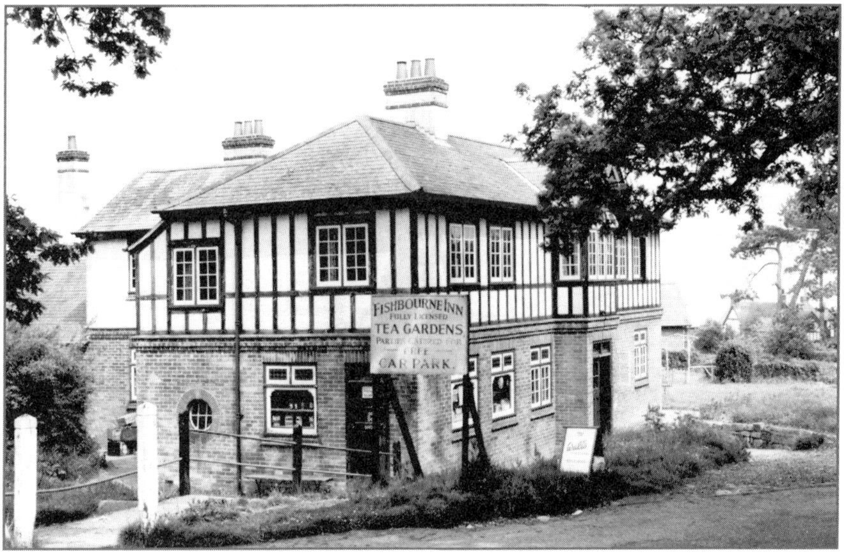


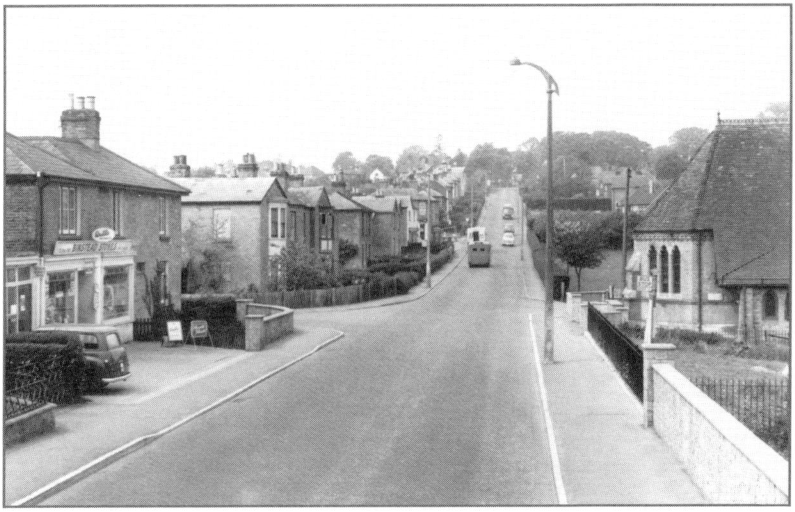

◄ **Binstead, The Village c1960**
B772002

Binstead's proximity to Ryde meant the inevitable spreading urban sprawl, but this street looks a little less busy back in the fifties than it does now. Binstead Stores supplied the neighbourhood with its immediate needs, including old favourites like Walls Ice Cream; the Players Please sign reminds us that smoking was still cool - and that good manners were not sneered at! The Hillman Husky on the forecourt was then the nearest thing to a hatchback, and ideal for deliveries to less mobile customers in outlying areas.

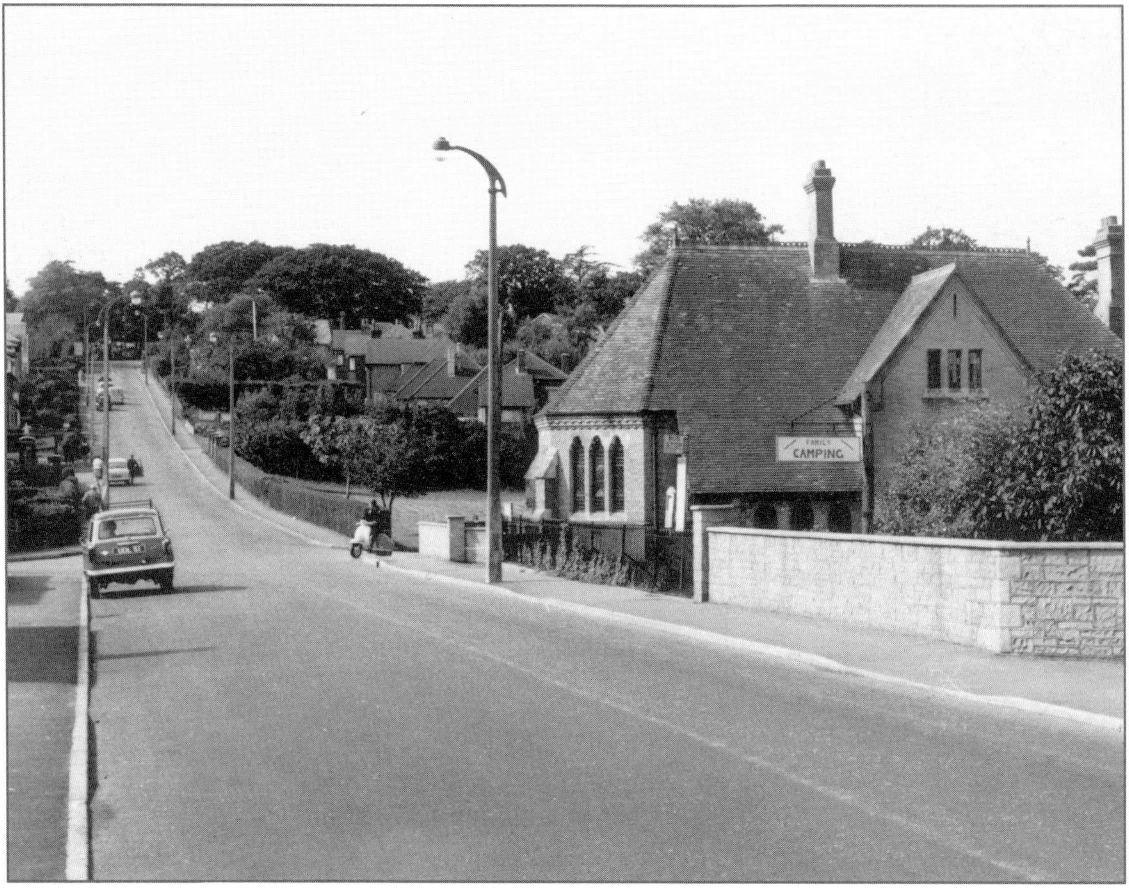


**Binstead**
**The Village c1960** B772009

Binstead's population was 2,689 in 1960, and housing estates have proliferated. An unusual limestone quarried here was used for Winchester Cathedral, Chichester Cathedral, Beaulieu Abbey and Romsey Abbey. Binstead is close to the original Quarr Abbey, which was founded in 1132; the neighbouring oak woods were a haunt of Druids. Henry VIII dissolved the abbey, and only ruins remain in the sea meadows. A new one was built in 1907, using Flemish bricks. Stonework dominates the domestic architecture in this scene, with family camping offered in the paddock. One of Gilbert Scott's classic red phone boxes stands just along the road, crucial in a pre-mobile age, while a trendy young girl on a motor scooter shows some modern style.

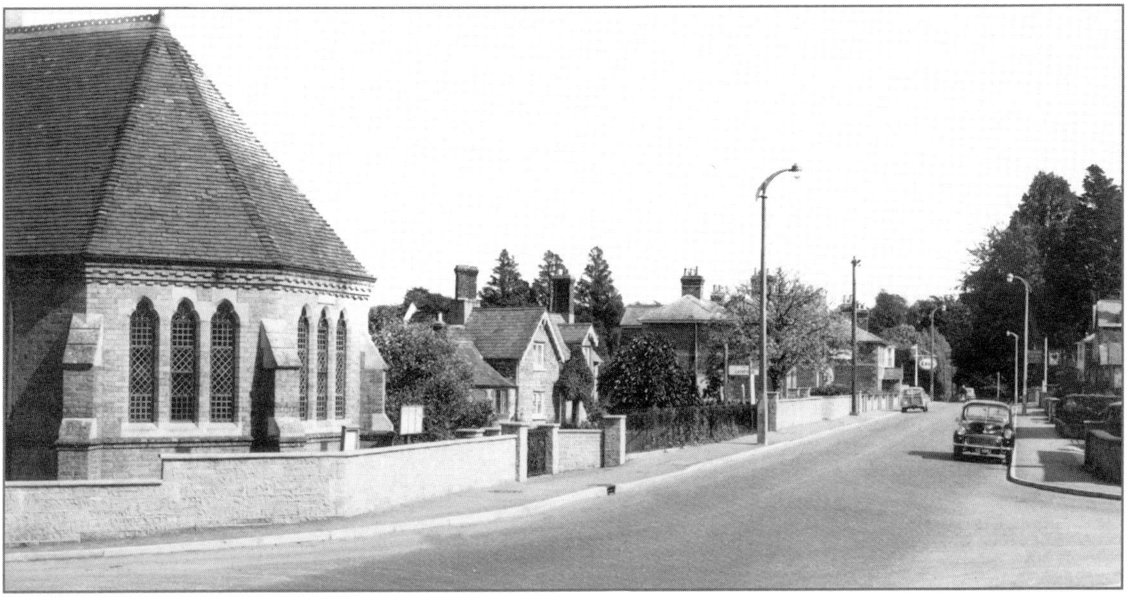

**Binstead, The Institute and Forge c1960** B772012
This view looks in the opposite direction to picture No B772009. It shows the old forge, reminding us that we are not far from Brickfields horse country. By this time, forges are becoming fewer; many converted to garages as blacksmiths developed their skills to suit the motor age. The Esso sign - said to mean happy motoring - proclaims the motorists' cause, and the split windscreen Morris 1000 has its sister, the Morris 1000 Traveller, parked on the opposite roadside.

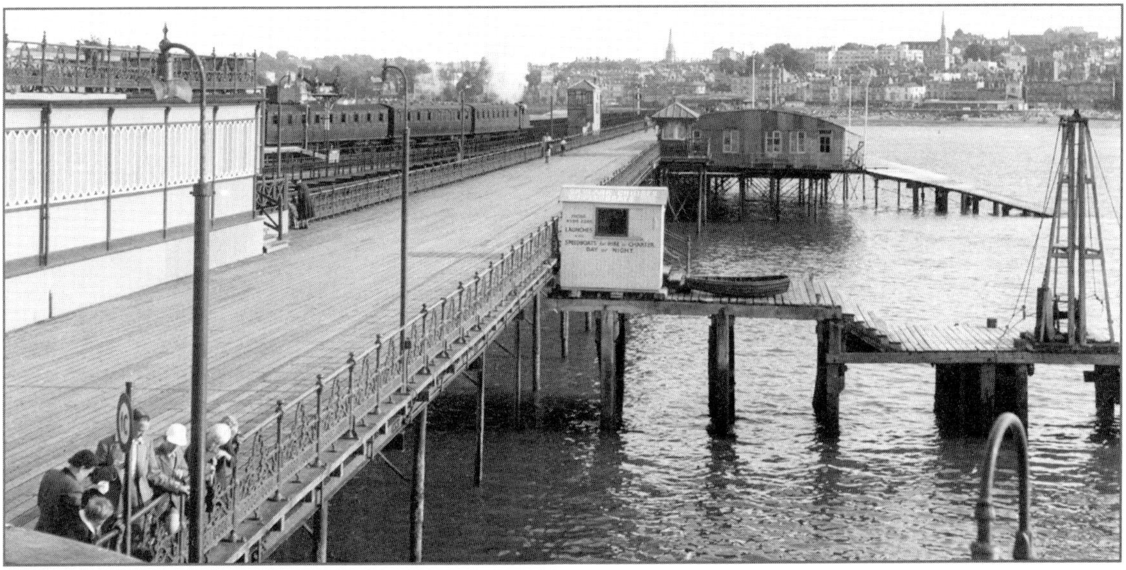

**Ryde, The Pier c1955** R76012
The pier was completed in 1824 as a pier for boat passengers, avoiding the long stretch of sand and mud. The tramway and railway were later additions. The steam train would have been much in demand, with the railways carrying 3 million passengers a year in the 1950s. It is remarkable that such a tourist attraction was closed down; even though Beeching's mandarins admitted that the roads would not be able to cope with the summer influx, they recommended complete closure in 1964. Luckily the route from Ryde to Shanklin was saved, though sad to say it offers a rather rush hour-like atmosphere - it is worked by ex-London Underground stock.

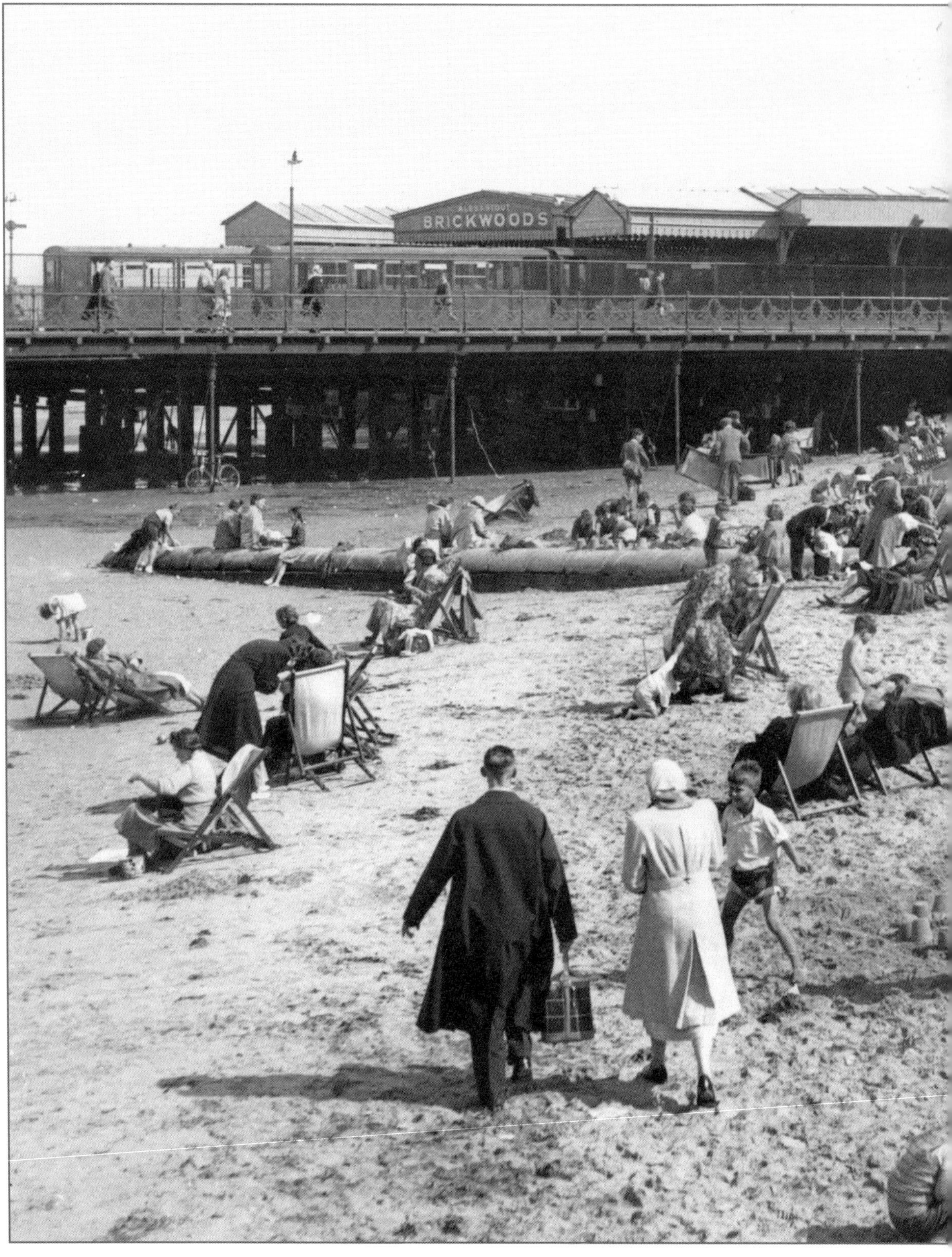
BRICKWOODS

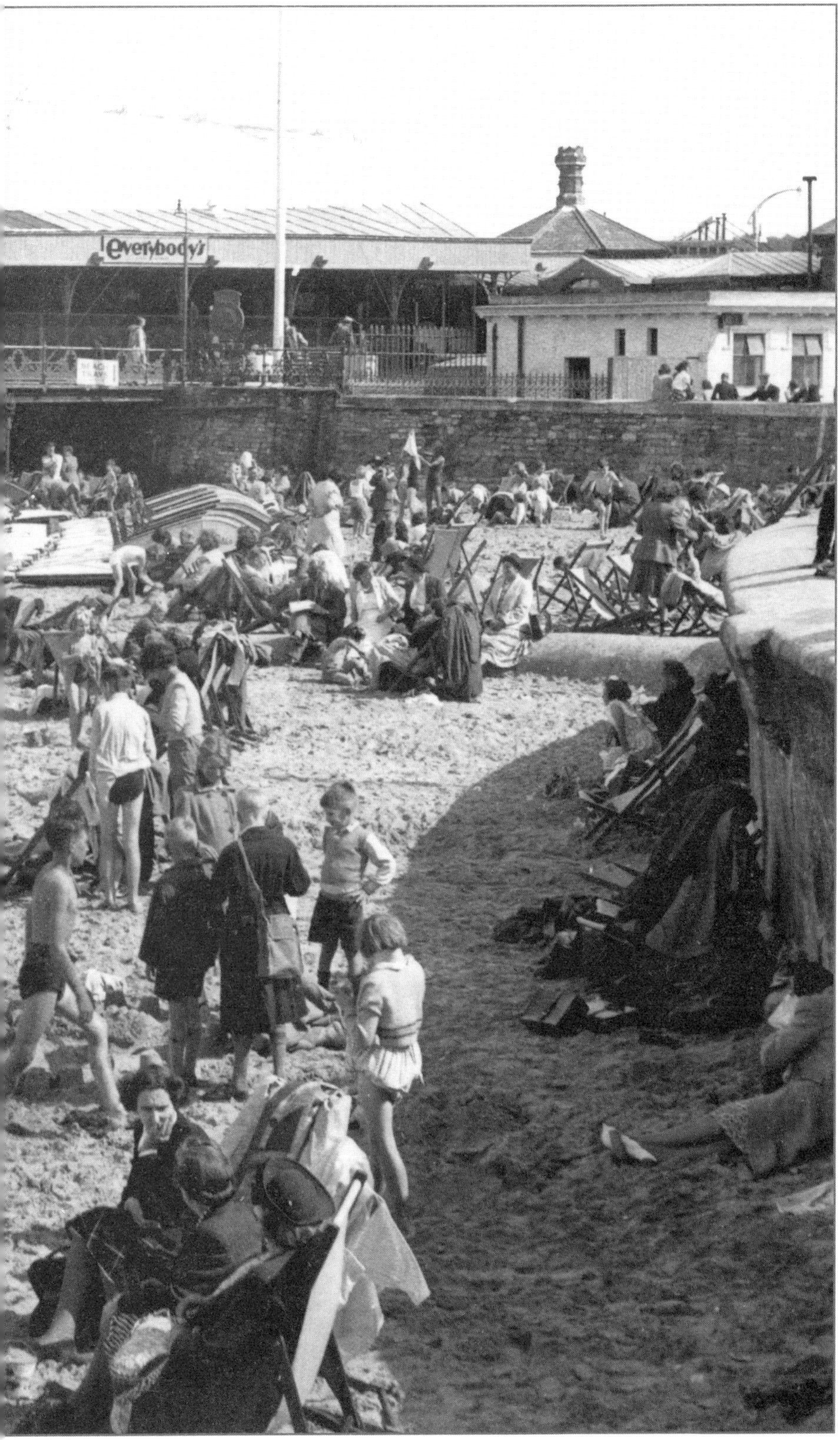


**Ryde, West Beach c1950** R76023
The pier was built to span half a mile of golden sands. The little train disgorges more visitors onto the pier, while down below it is all very much a family affair. Sand-castles mimic the island's grand old defences, while the absence of bare flesh suggests either the greater modesty of the day or chilly winds blowing across the Solent. Brickwood's ales are advertised on the pier above, so dad can warm himself up a bit!

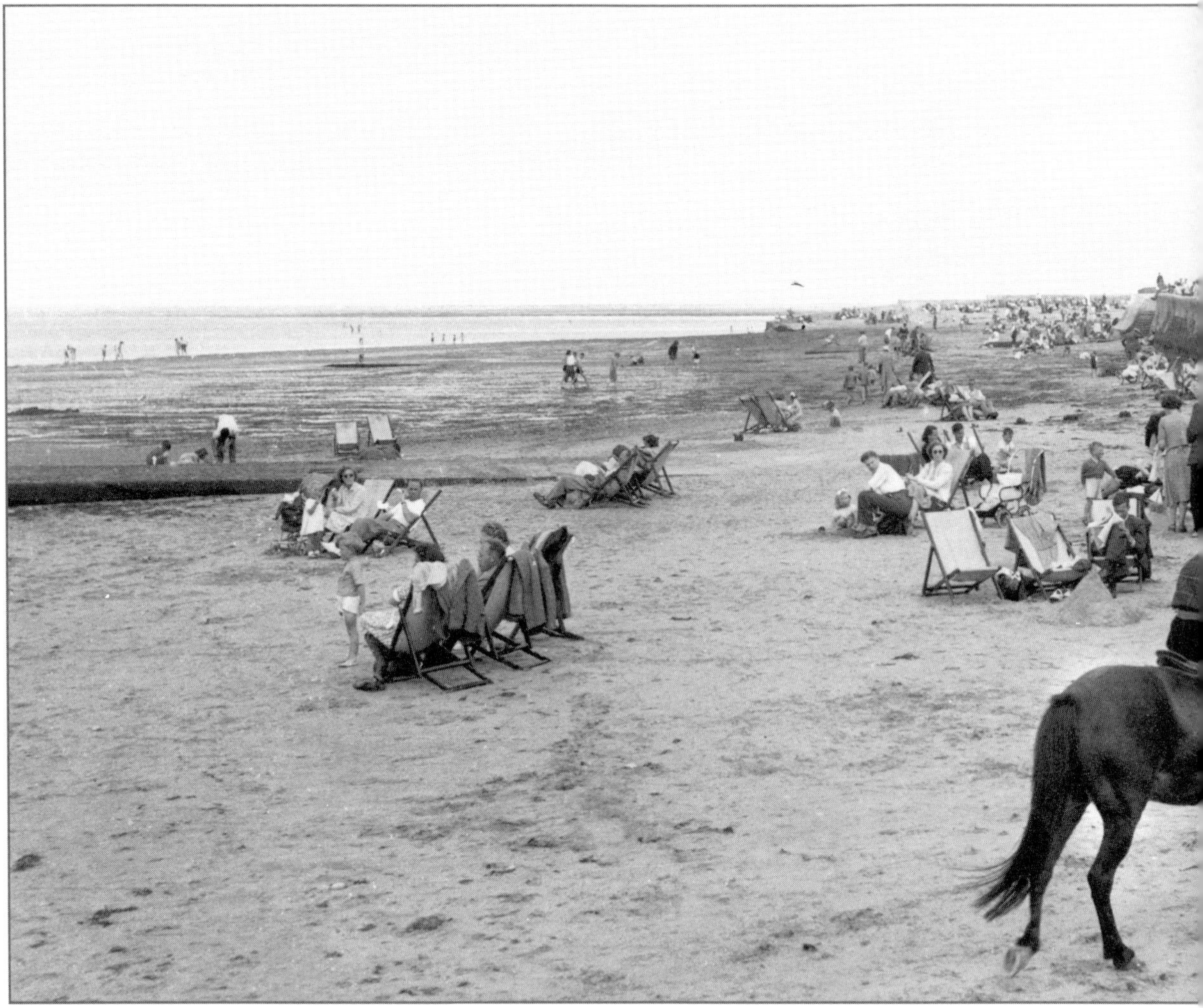

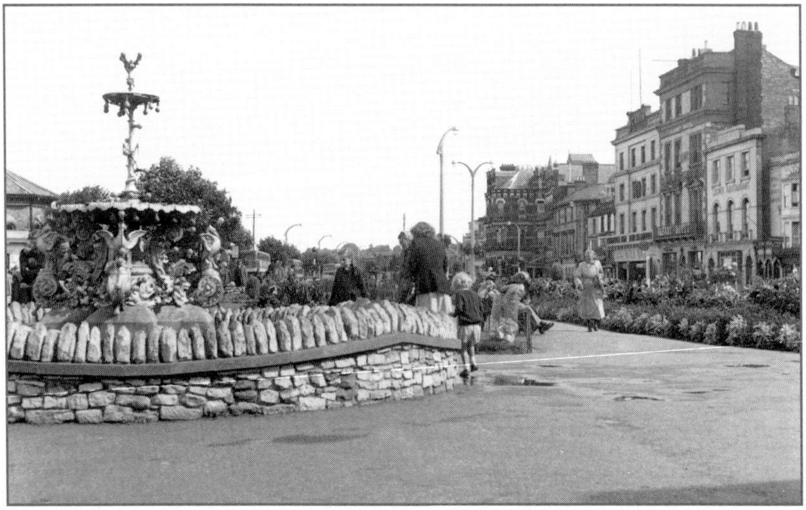

◀ **Ryde, West Esplanade c1950**

R76022

Ryde grew after 1800, when the wealthy came to enjoy their summer houses. Although now boasting some brash entertainments, Ryde still manages to retain its grandeur. In this view we can see a milk bar, the Albany Hotel, Leon's restaurant and Harvey's cafe. Flowerbeds abound, but the children are more attracted to the old fountain. In the background, bus enthusiasts can admire Southern Vectis's Bristol double-deckers. Nowadays they have room to park in the station forecourt.

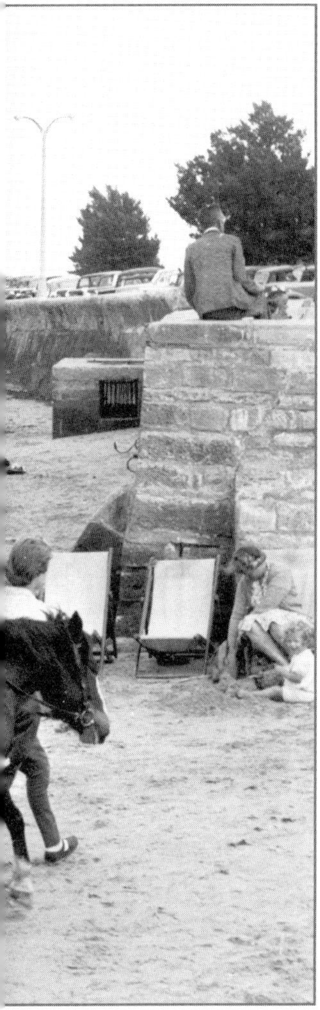

◄ **Ryde, East Beach c1950**
R76006
Cars are ranked along the sea wall, stately old pre-war styles to match the restrained behaviour upon the sand. One wonders what cares these folk were trying to forget, and what joy of anticipation there was for such a holiday as this, where the nippers could enjoy a pony ride. It was the steamers of the 1830s and then the railways that brought the London trade.

▼ **Ryde, Eastern Gardens c1950** R76010
There is a variety of sport displayed in this wide view, and some intensity of interest among the spectators. Whether holidaymakers or locals, there was not the same TV and video distractions to divert their enthusiasm. Look at how much care the parks department have taken over the flower beds.

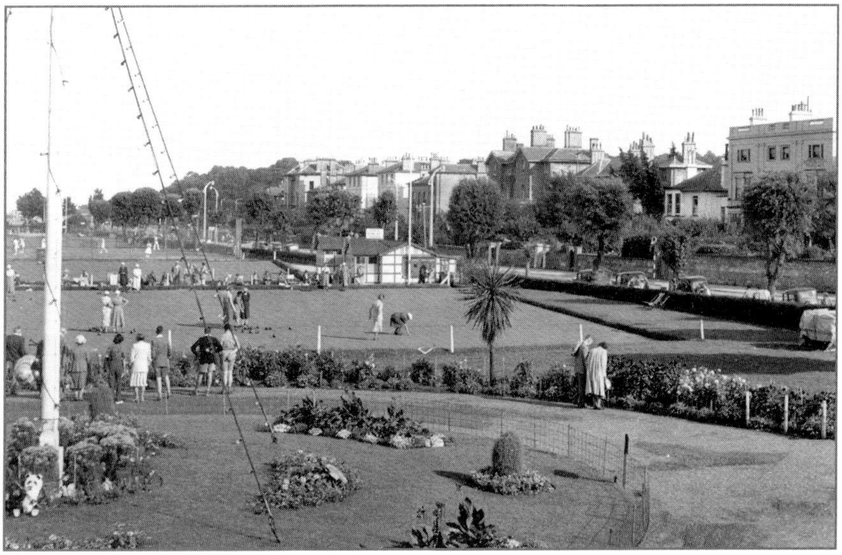

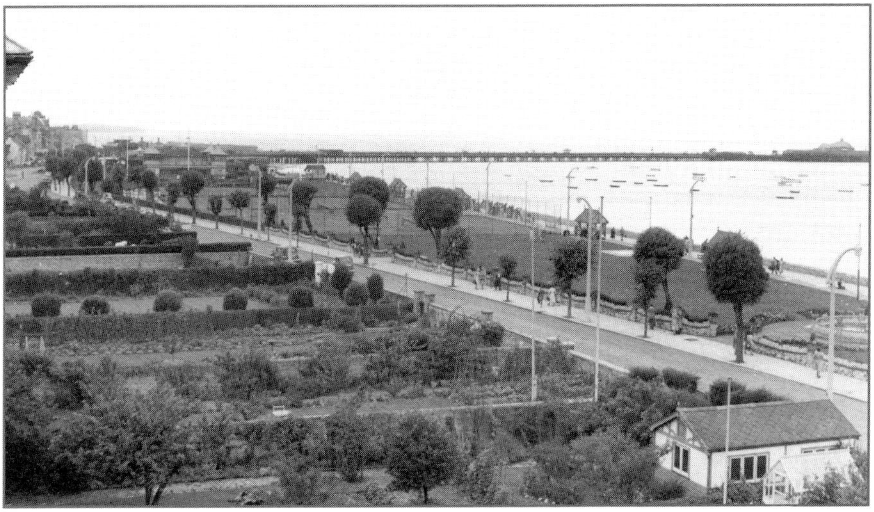

◄ **Ryde, Eastern Esplanade c1950**
R76017
The magnificent pier is almost in silhouette in this magnificent view; the pier extends half a mile out to sea. Before it was built, passengers were transported over the sand and shallows by horse and cart. The pace of life looks easy at this time: couples and groups are enjoying the promenade, while fishermen would have been busy on the far (western)side of the pier.

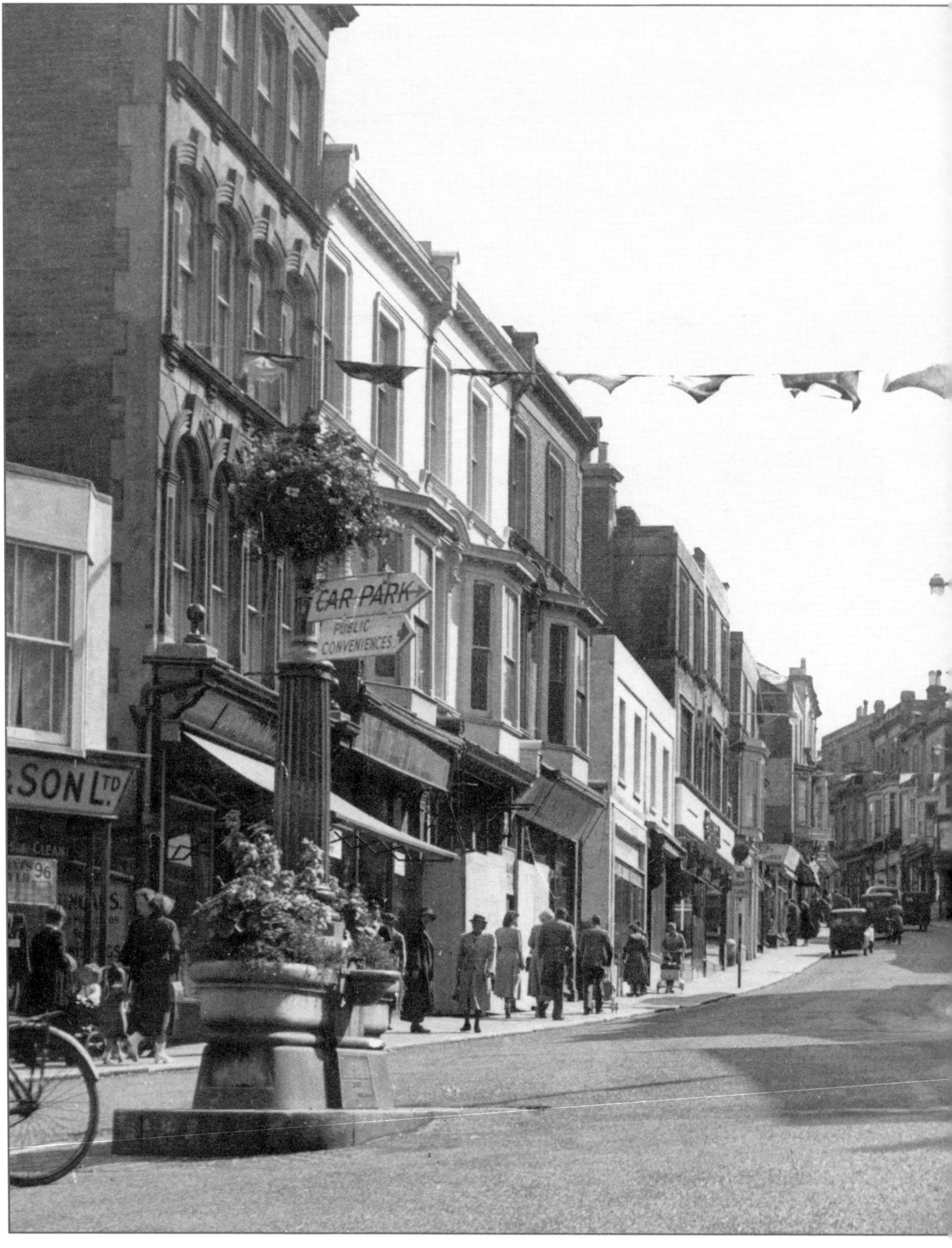
CAR PARK
PUBLIC CONVENIENCES
&SON LTD

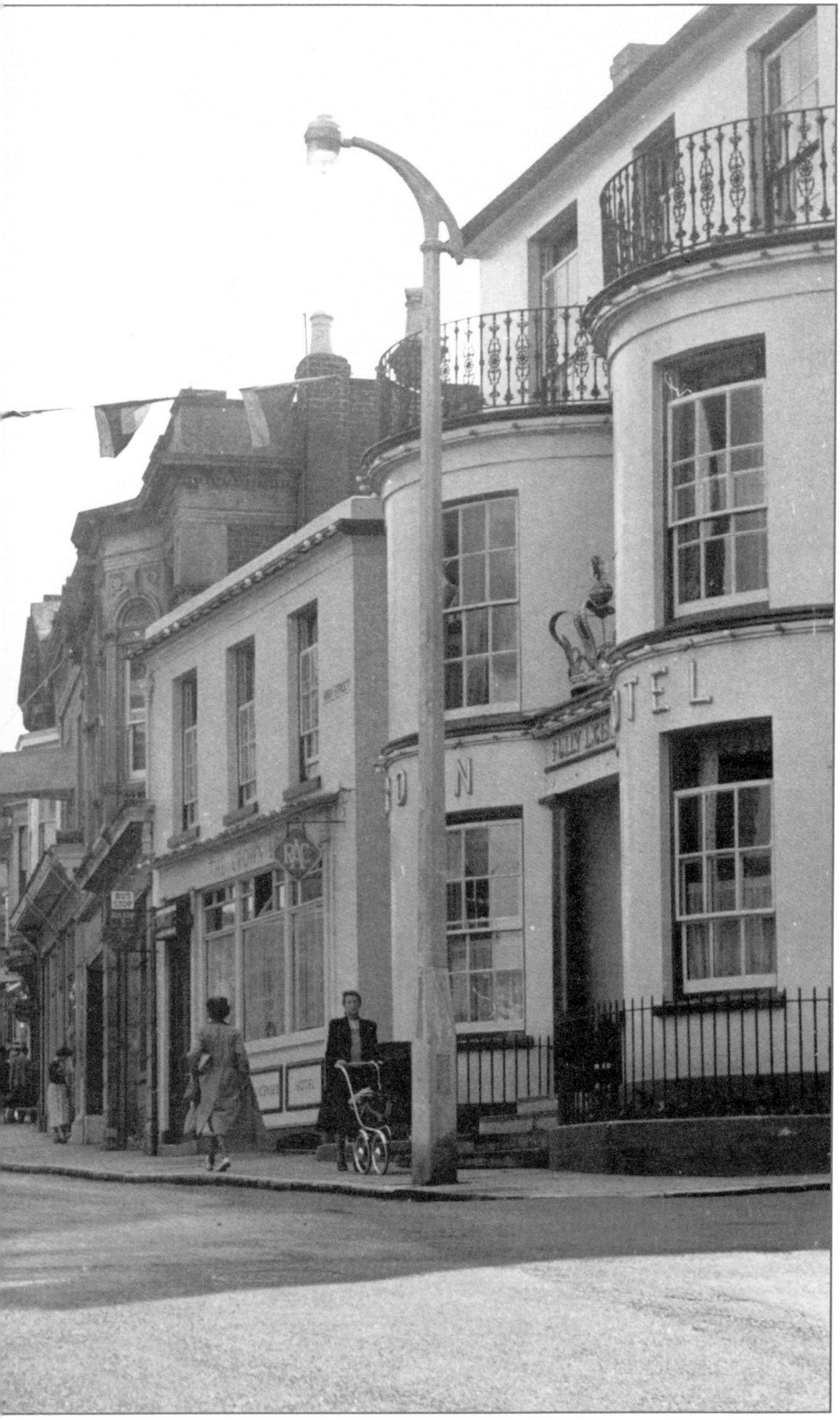


**Ryde, High Street c1950** R76030

It is hard to believe that the town was once a tiny farming village, joined to a fishing hamlet along Union Street. This view looks up a High Street packed with substantial properties and busy shops; perhaps the bunting is out for a regatta. The Crown Hotel looks everything a traveller would have relished. It is ideal for a pleasant weekend, and it offers an excellent view of the town's busy centre.

**▼ Ryde, East Esplanade c1960** R76059

Fortified structures are a keynote of the island. They proliferated especially after the 1859 invasion scare: new defences were constructed, including the rebuilding of Hurst Castle and 10 new forts. This tower reminds us of those patriotic days.

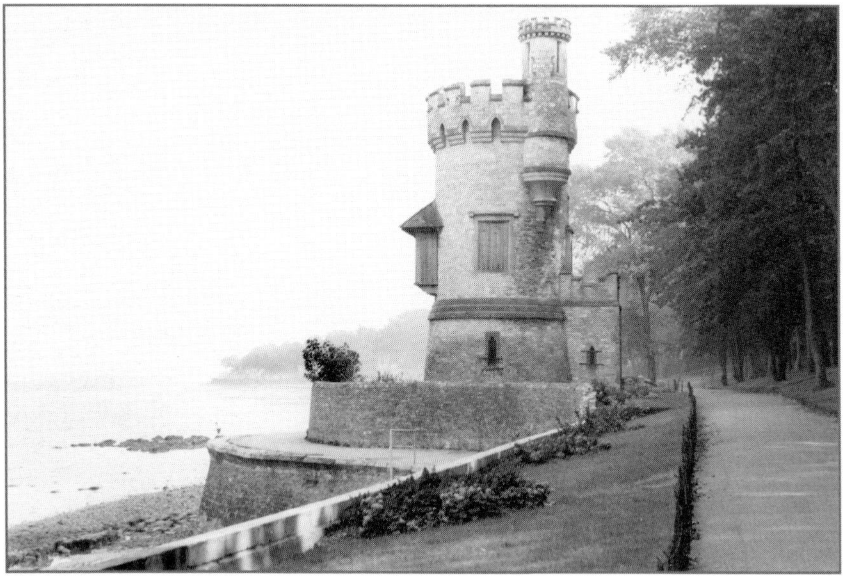

**▼ Newport, General View c1950** N24012

This is a place of hidden riverside quays and curious little streets. Monks built the Priory of St Cross. In this view, St Thomas's Church dominates the building line, though the rolling downs upstage everything. So much life is packed into this little corner of this old market and county town. W H Croucher's wholesale grocers' warehouse (in the foreground) looks rather grim, as does much else in view here. But times change: nowadays one of the warehouses has been converted into a squash club, and another has become the Quay Arts Centre. Tucked away in adjacent woodland are Parkhurst and Albany prisons, but few of the inmates will know what they are missing.

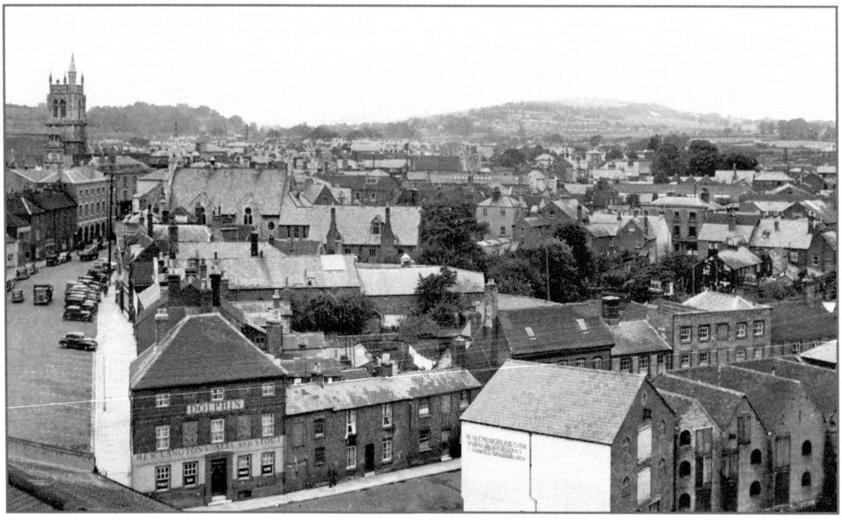


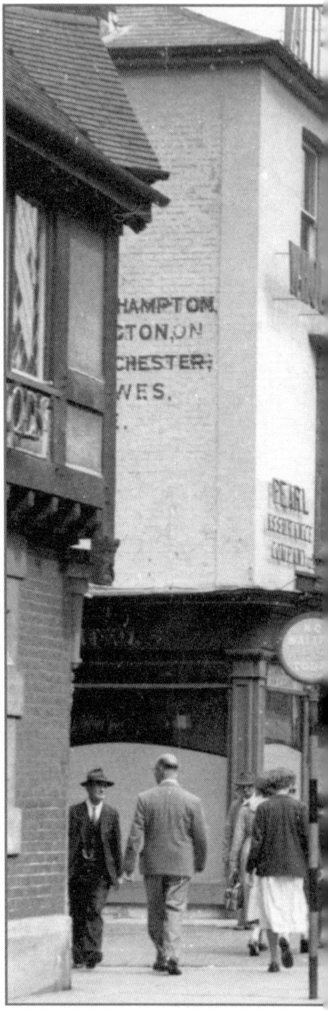

**▲ Newport, High Street c1950** N24007

This is John Nash's Town Hall, with its large portico and Ionic columns, completed in 1816. Watchbell Lane runs close by, where a watchman once announced the hour; now it bustles with little shops. Richard de Redvers founded the town in 1180. It was burned by the French, but flourished during the Napoleonic Wars. This was a planned town, well placed for trade and communication and as a port for Carisbrooke, on the tidal limit of the Medina.

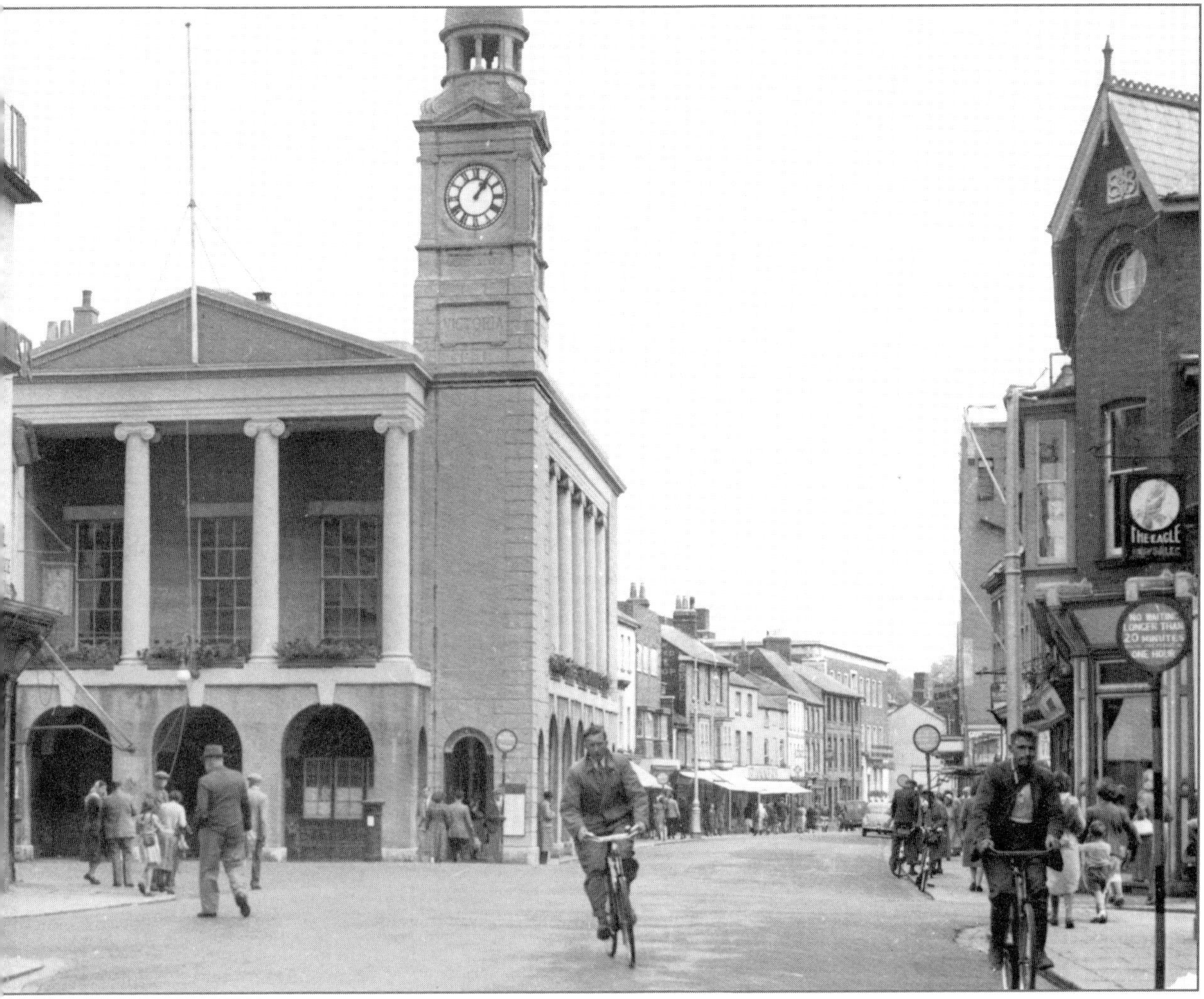


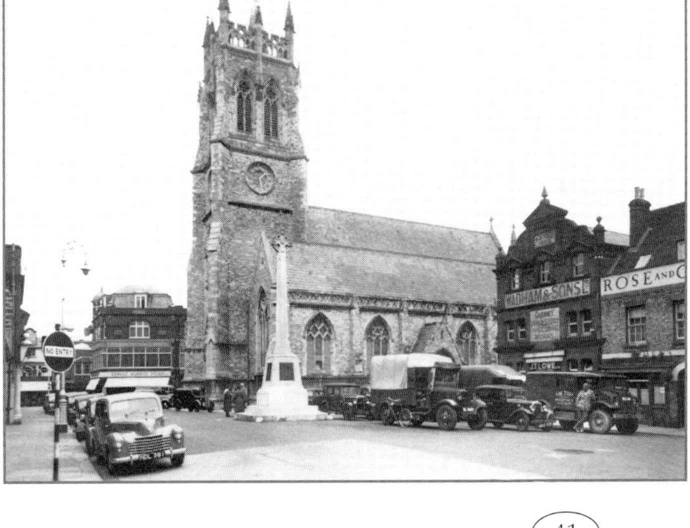


**Newport, St Thomas's Square c1950**

N24016

The war memorial reminds us of those who sacrificed themselves for freedom. S M Tidy of Brighton has his own wartime souvenir, far right - it is an ex-army truck. Though these were austerity years, someone has managed to afford a new Vauxhall Velox, and has parked it by the No Entry sign. This square was the corn market. The church was built in 1824 on the site of an older church containing the tomb of Charles I's daughter Elizabeth. The Rose and Crown, far right, took its name from when King Charles was escorted through Newport to prison at Carisbrooke, and a girl ran from the crowd to hand him a rose.

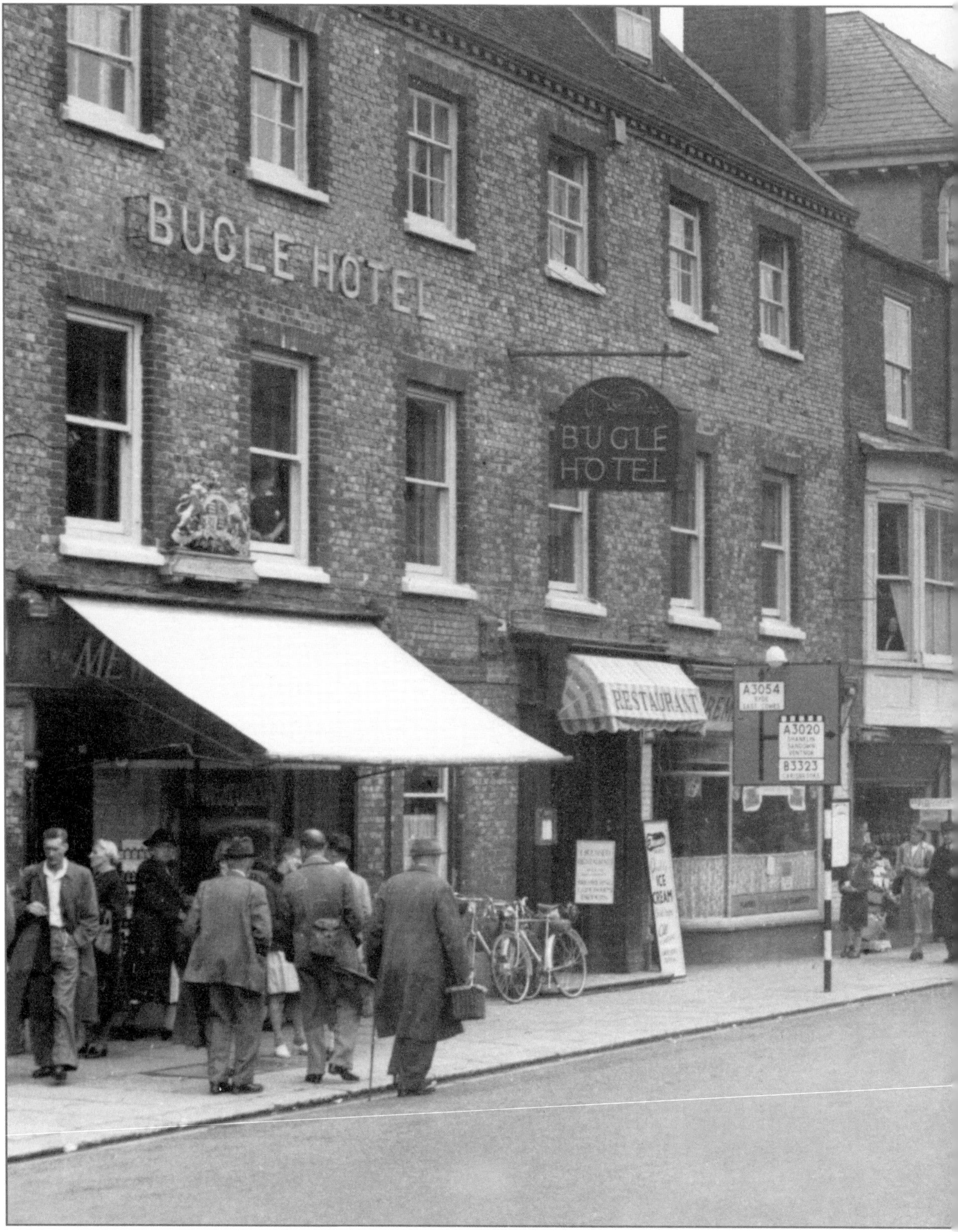
BUGLE HOTEL
BUGLE HOTEL
RESTAURANT
A3054
A3020
B3323
ICE CREAM

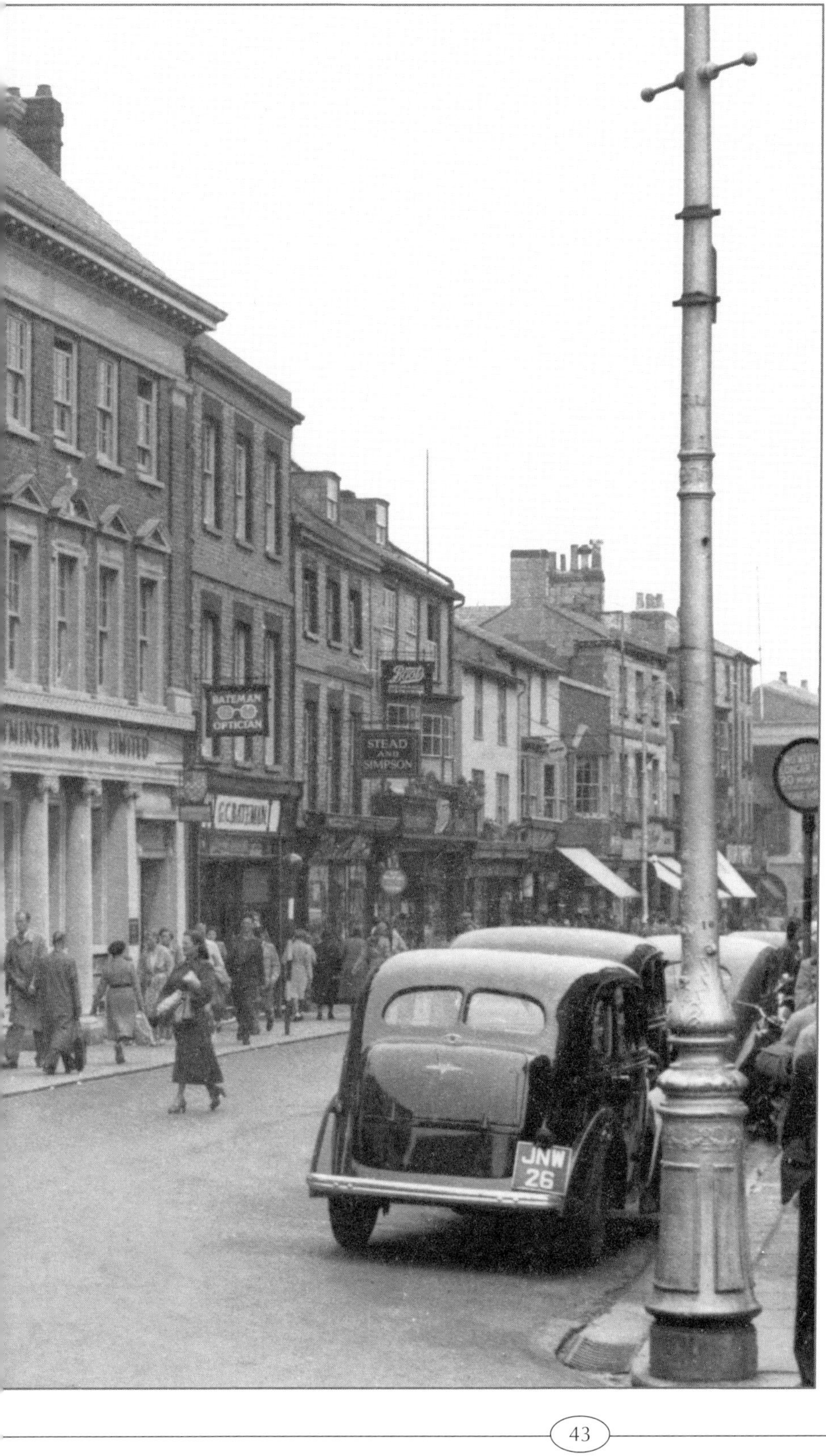


**Newport, High Street c1950** N24005

As the road signs indicate, these were the days before the ring roads of St George's and Medina Way were built to carry the more heavy traffic of the post-railway age. Familiar High Street names like Boots and Burton are here, along with Batemans and Stead and Simpson. The Bugle is a good old-fashioned name for a hotel; at this time it had the kind of interior that would make a theme pub today. The Westminster Bank looks high and mighty, and has yet to merge with the National Provincial.

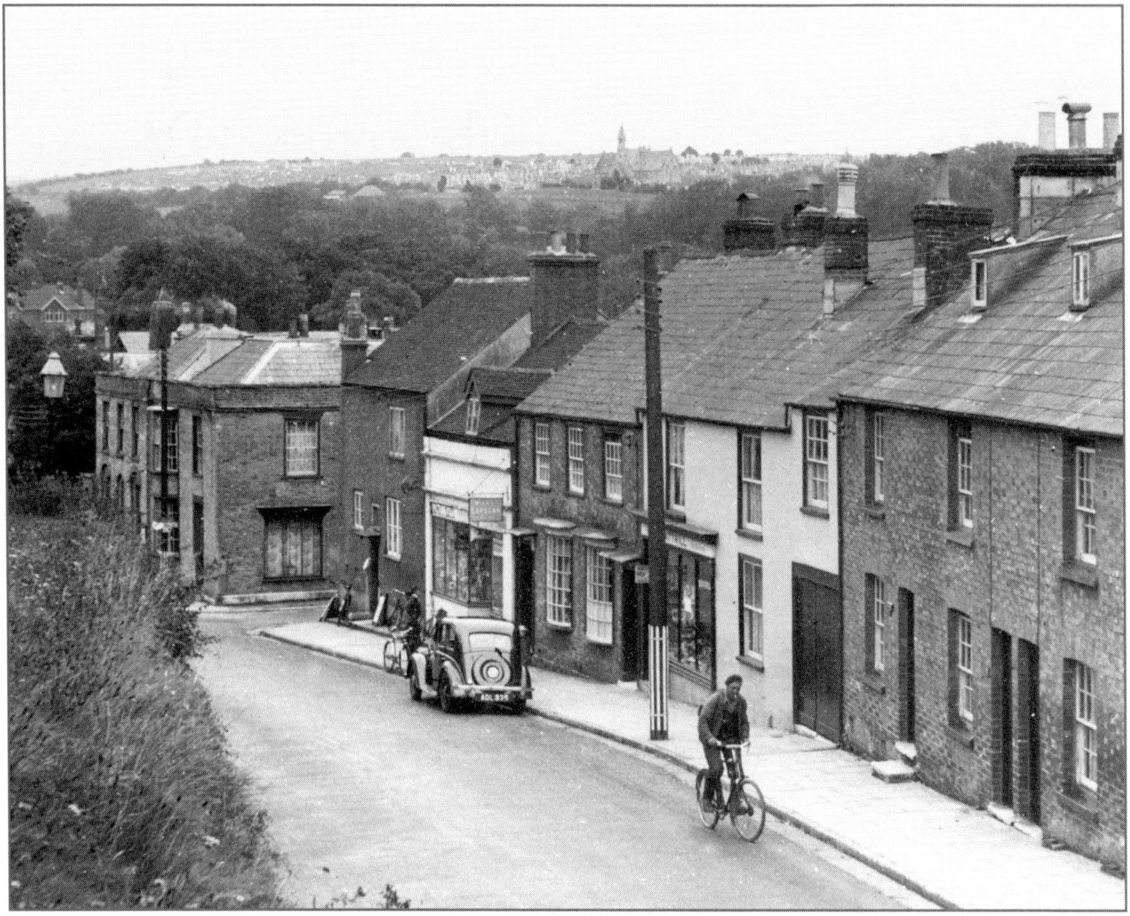

**Carisbrooke**
**High Street c1950** C26002
It needs plenty of puff to bike up this hill, so let's hope the cyclist hasn't stopped off for some Capstan Full Strength from the little shop; he'd have more energy with Bovril, advertised in the shop next door. Lukely Brook flows through the valley below from Bowcombe to join the Medina.

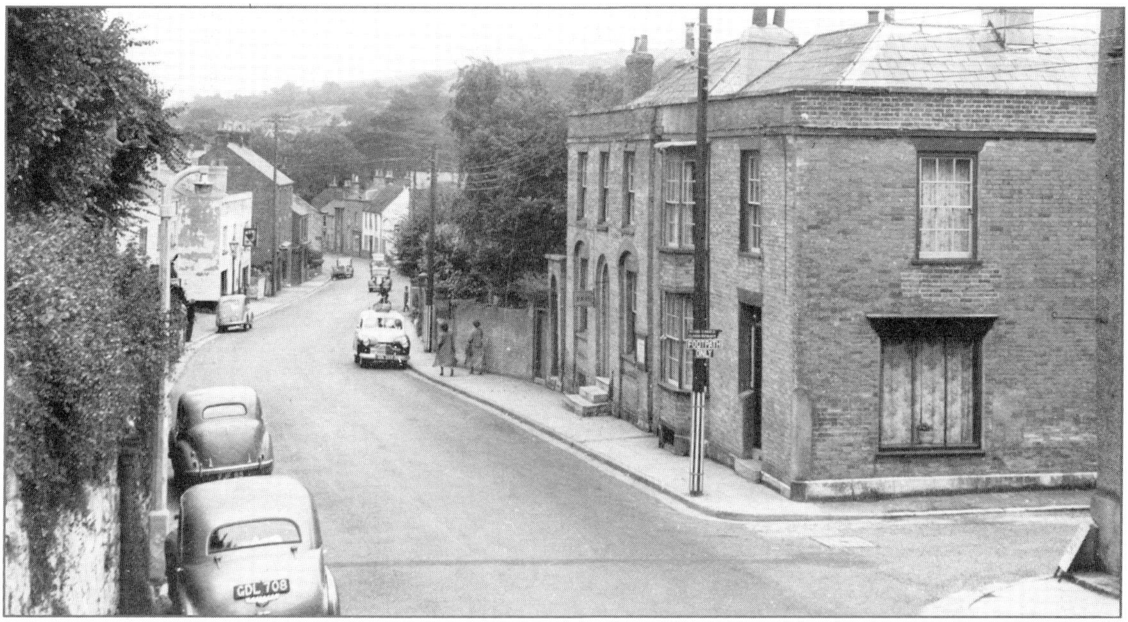


**Carisbrooke, High Street c1955** C26003

This view from further down the High Street shows a range of early 1950s motor vehicles. The poet John Keats lodged in this village with his landlady Mrs Cook. The footpath sign points the way to a footpath to the castle, right, advising that it is closed on Sundays. A little further down, above the steps, a local taxi service is advertised; the two jaunty young ladies appear to be approaching a local taxi, a Standard Vanguard.

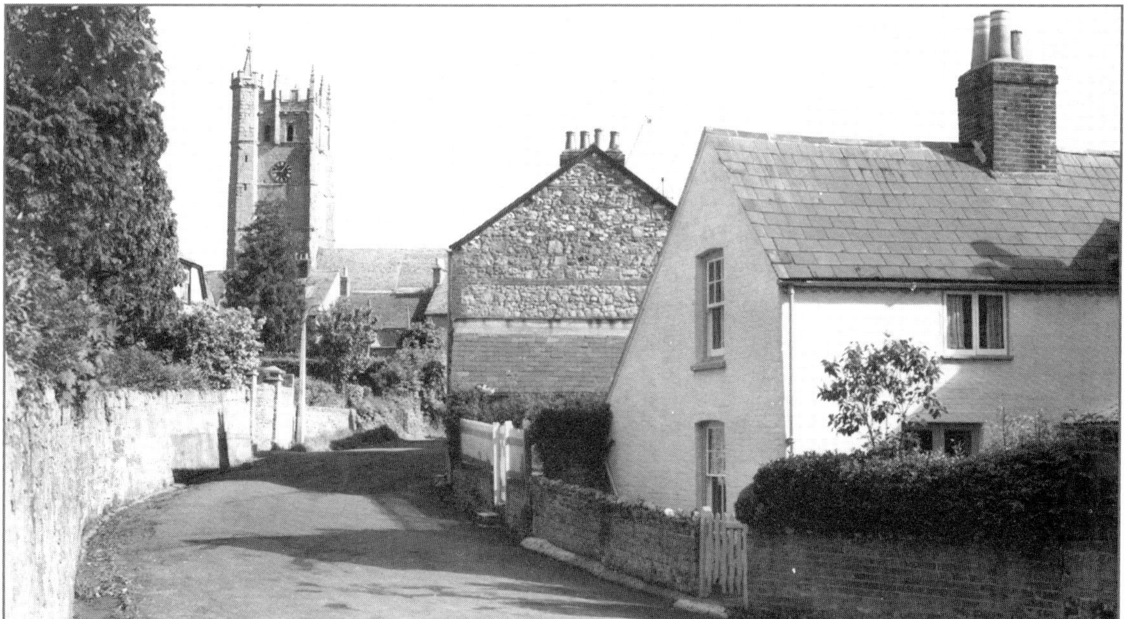

**Carisbrooke, Castle Street c1955** C26031

Sunshine falls on old stone walls draped with ferns, and the light shows all the fine detail on the large 15th-century tower of the church of St Mary. This was the church of a Benedictine priory, which was dissolved by Henry V in 1415. The Lord of the Manor, Sir Francis Walsingham, later demolished the chancel.

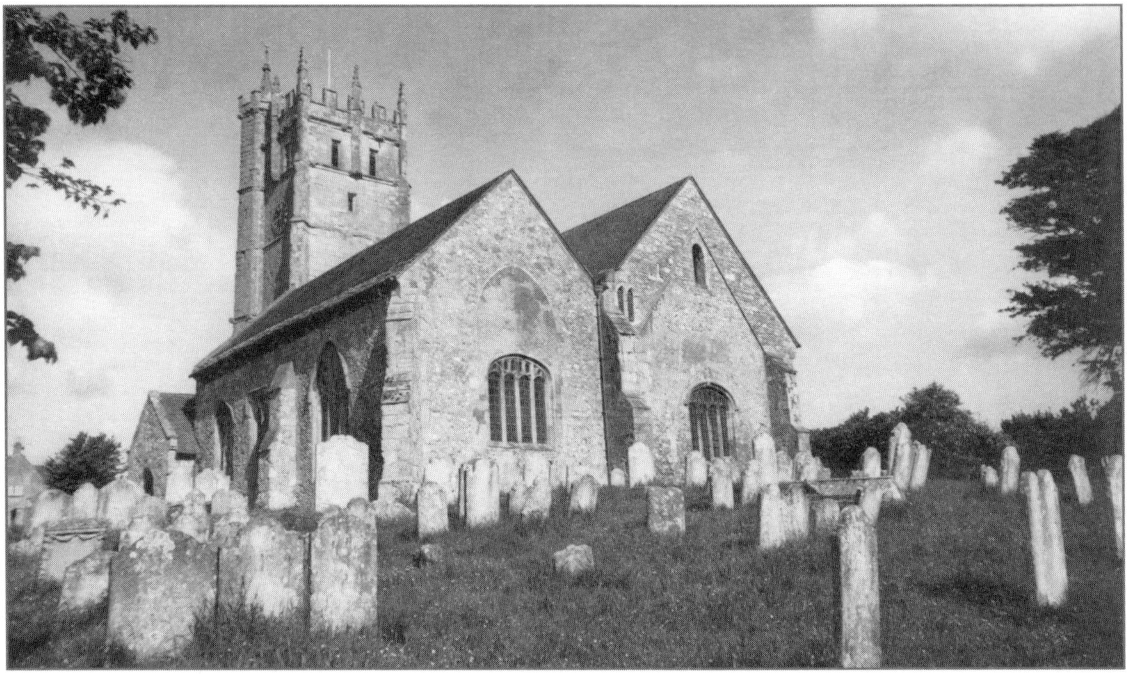

**Carisbrooke, The Church c1955** C26026
Here we face the bulk of St Mary's Church and a regimented array of old gravestones, a sad reminder that all things are subject to change and time, even the church; we can see the alterations to its mighty walls and windows.

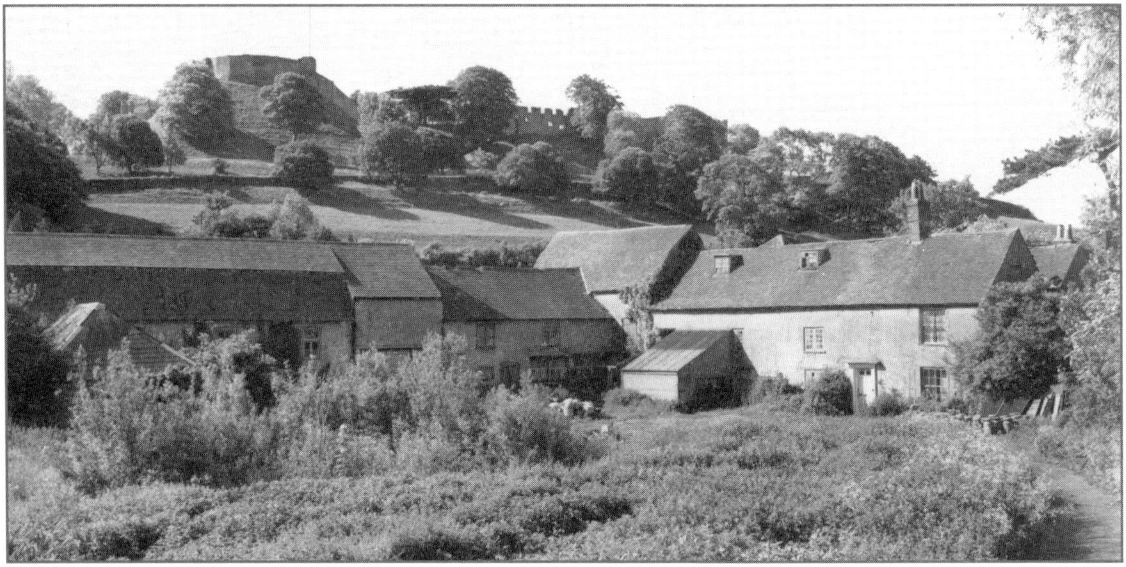

**Carisbrooke, The Castle and the Old Mill c1955** C26035
Carisbrooke Castle stands a mile from Newport. The Romans fortified this hill before the Norman de Redvers family arrived. Keats boasted how his lodgings gave a good view of the castle, and in his poem 'Endymion' he observed that 'a thing of beauty is a joy for ever'. Charles I, imprisoned here from November 1647 to September 1648, held a less sanguine view. His attempted escape through a window in the north curtain wall failed. Here among wild flowers, trees and green pasture, the castle and old mill are a picture of peace. Milk churns betoken a less complicated and pressured farming life.

# Venture to Ventnor

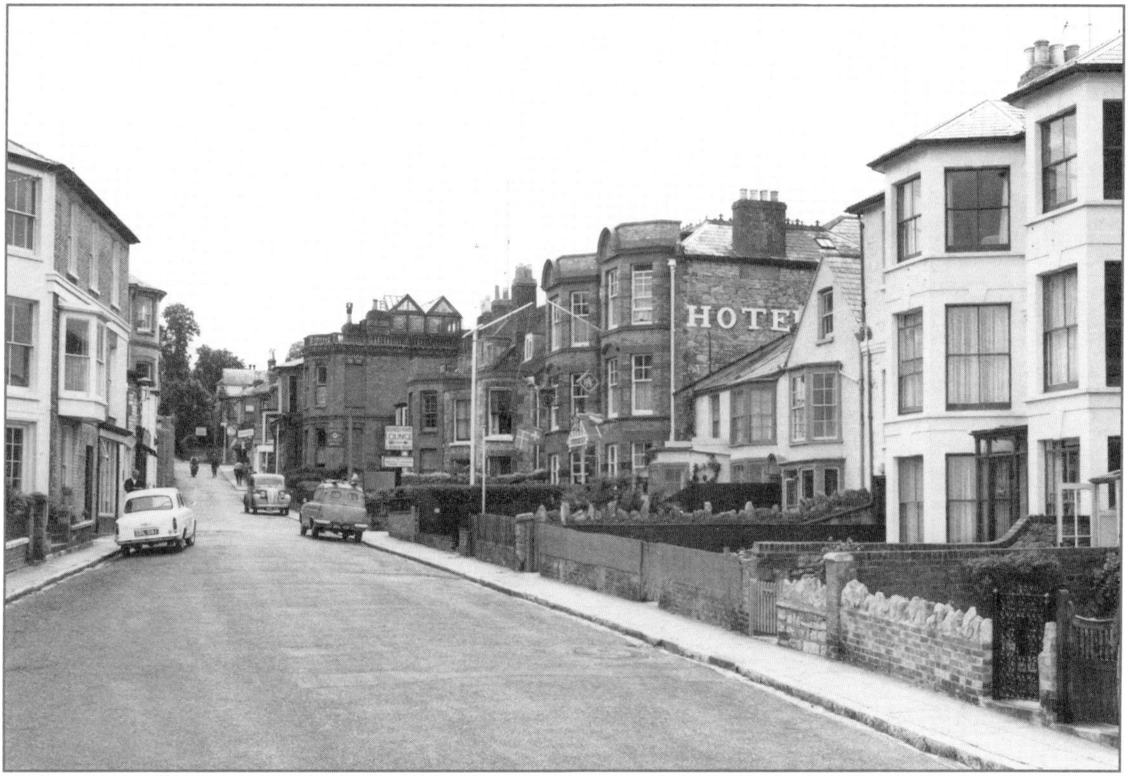

**Seaview**
**High Street c1955** S87049
Some fine old Victorian villas have been converted to hotels here. The sign for the Sunshine Lounge revives memories of those days of hope and simple pleasures. Motor vehicles are scarce, but the Ford Popular parked to the left reminds us that the age of mass motoring is upon us. Lloyds Bank is up the road, one part of old England that is still going strong.

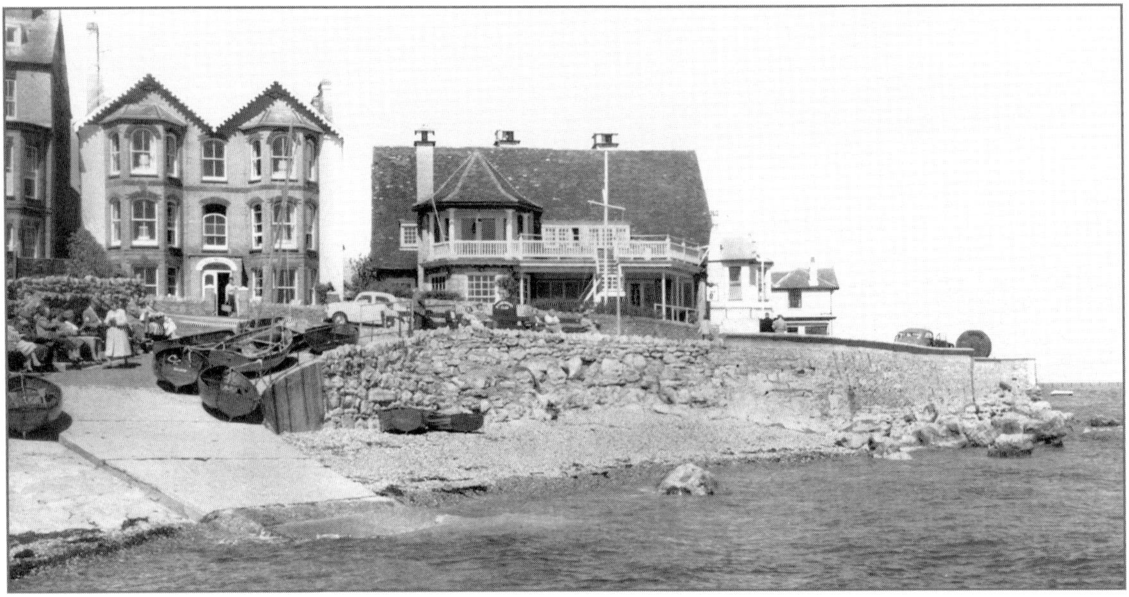

**Seaview, The Starboard Club c1955** S87065
Seaview is a place of narrow streets and alleyways, with gradients running down to the Solent. There is a rope walk where new rope used to be laid out and stretched. Here we can look back at the old club house and a few of the popular clinker-built dinghies on the slip way. The motorists are out of their vehicles, enjoying the sunshine and admiring the view. Here the children of long ago enjoyed the rock pools where they could find lots of crabs and shrimps.

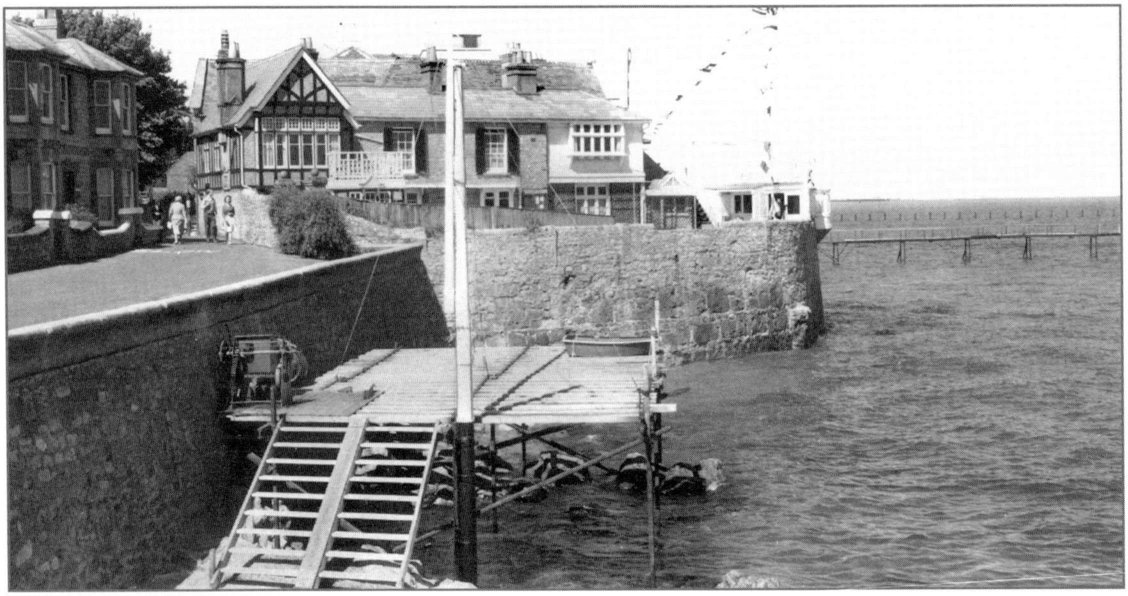

**Seaview, The Yacht Club c1955** S87063
Seaview was considered more select than Ryde, two miles away, and a chain pier was built for steamers during the holiday boom. The pier was lost in a storm in 1951. Here the yacht club appears redolent of all the exclusivity for which that sport and leisure pursuit was famed - nowadays it is more accessible. The popularity of the area added new housing to Victorian and Edwardian stock, but the salterns and the saltern cottages remind us of former salt workings when ponds were made by banks across the harbour mouth.

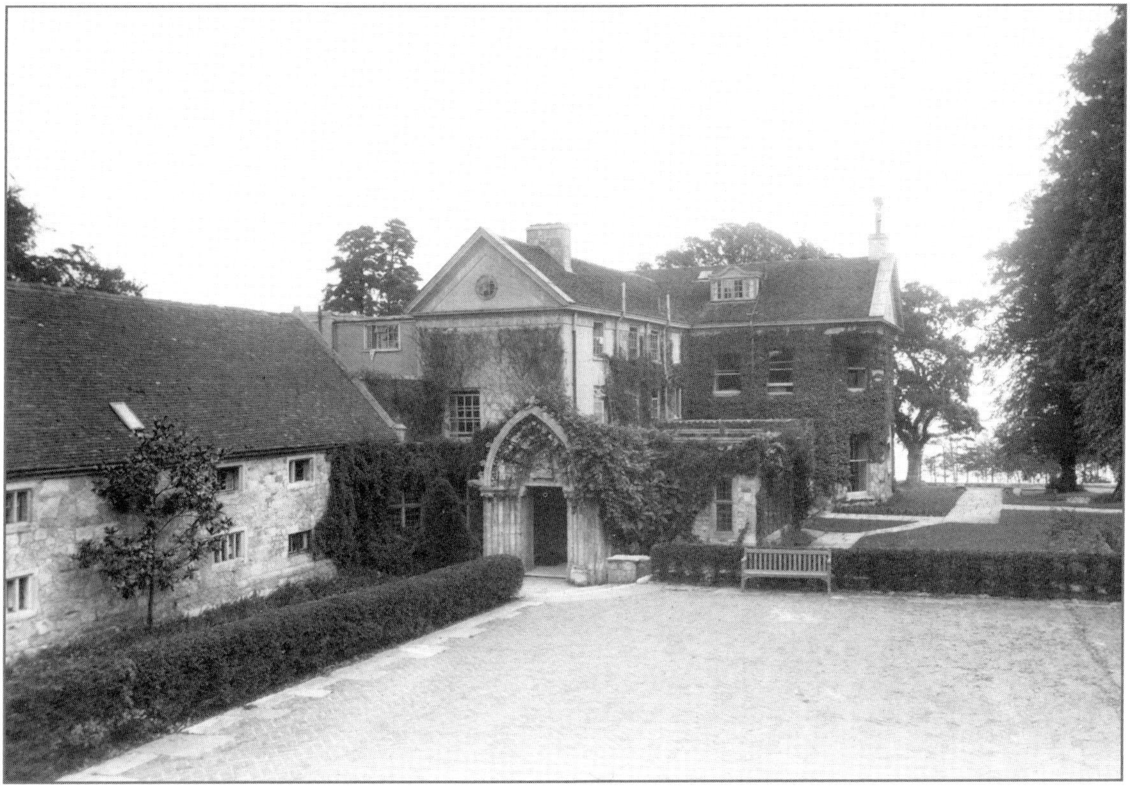

**Seaview**
**The Priory c1955** S87016

This was formerly the site of a Cluniac monastery. Monks toiled on the monastery farm long before the Domesday Book; an 11th-century barn from the original priory farm survives. Later, Queen Victoria reposed under the magnolias enjoying the view across the Solent and Spithead. The priory is now a high-class hotel; facilities include a private beach, swimming pools and a nine-hole golf course, and it is surrounded by woodland, lawns and terraced gardens said to have been designed by Gertrude Jekyll. A beautifully-decorated 15th-century portal, seen here, makes an impressive hotel entrance.

**St Helens, The Green c1955** S514016

Named after Roman emperor Constantine's wife, Helena, this was a significant port used by the fleet at Spithead. The mainly 18th-century cottages cluster around a rectangular 9-acre green, which we can see here. A plaque on one of the houses commemorates Sophie Dawes, a smuggler's daughter, who fled to London to be the Duke of Bourbon's mistress. Wild flowers and wild life flourish here and on the neighbouring grassy dunes, which are known as the Duver.

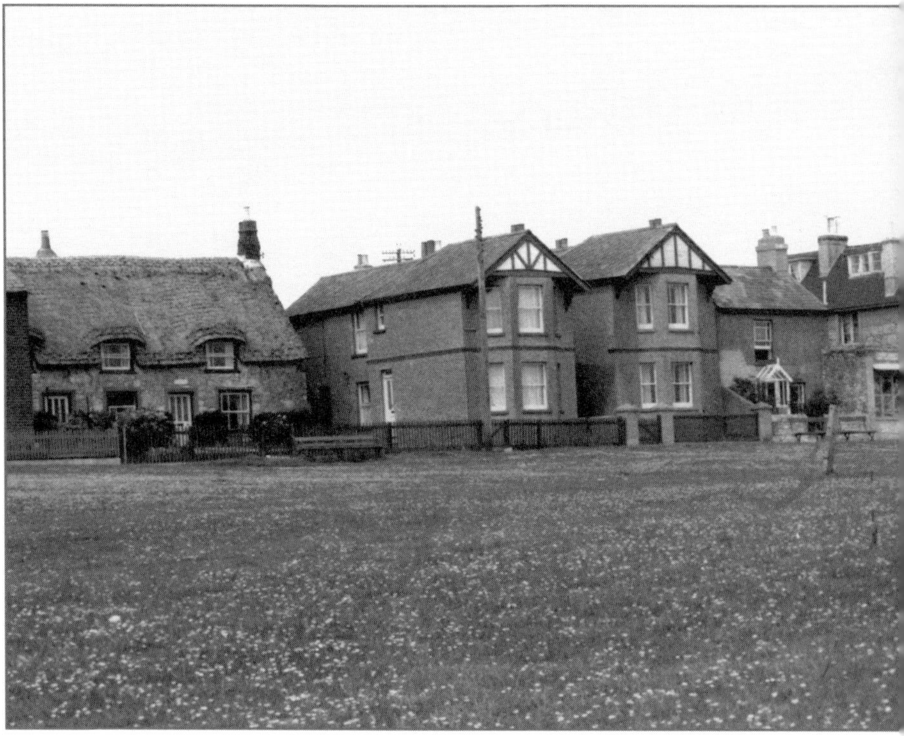

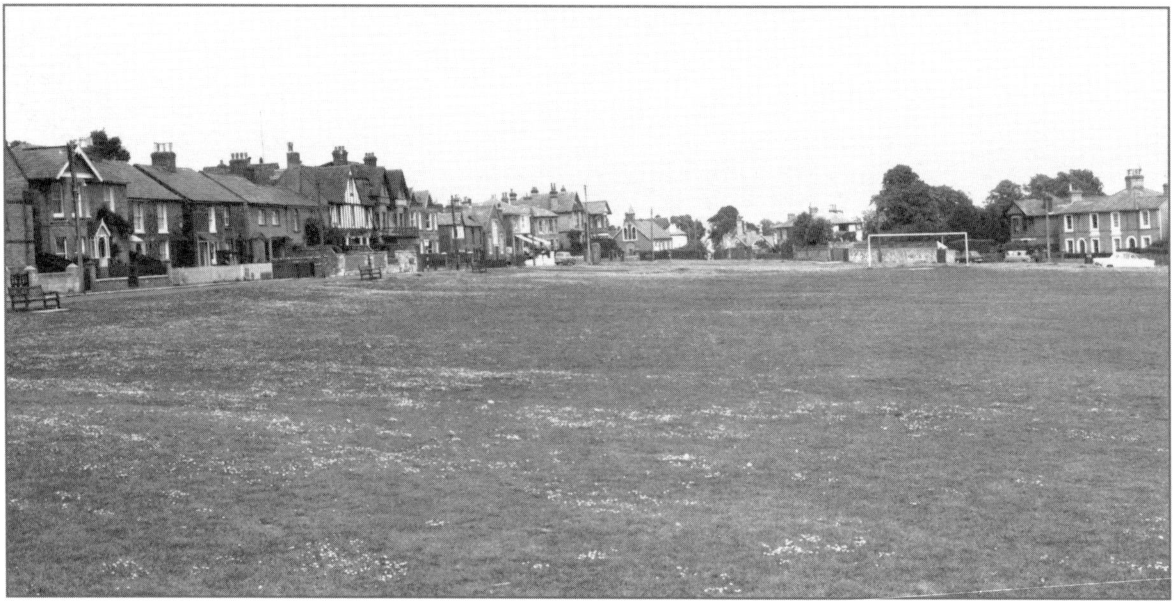

**St Helens, Church Street and the Green c1965** S514005

Here we see the same tranquillity as in picture No S514016, with only different cars to suggest movement in time. This is not the most picturesque part of the island, but there is a lot of history here, and interesting Victorian houses with fake Tudor gables and Norman turrets. A relic of the old Saxon church stands on the shore: the Norman priory was suppressed, and along with its church fell into the sea. A storm in 1703 washed the ruins away, leaving only the tower as a landmark for sailors.

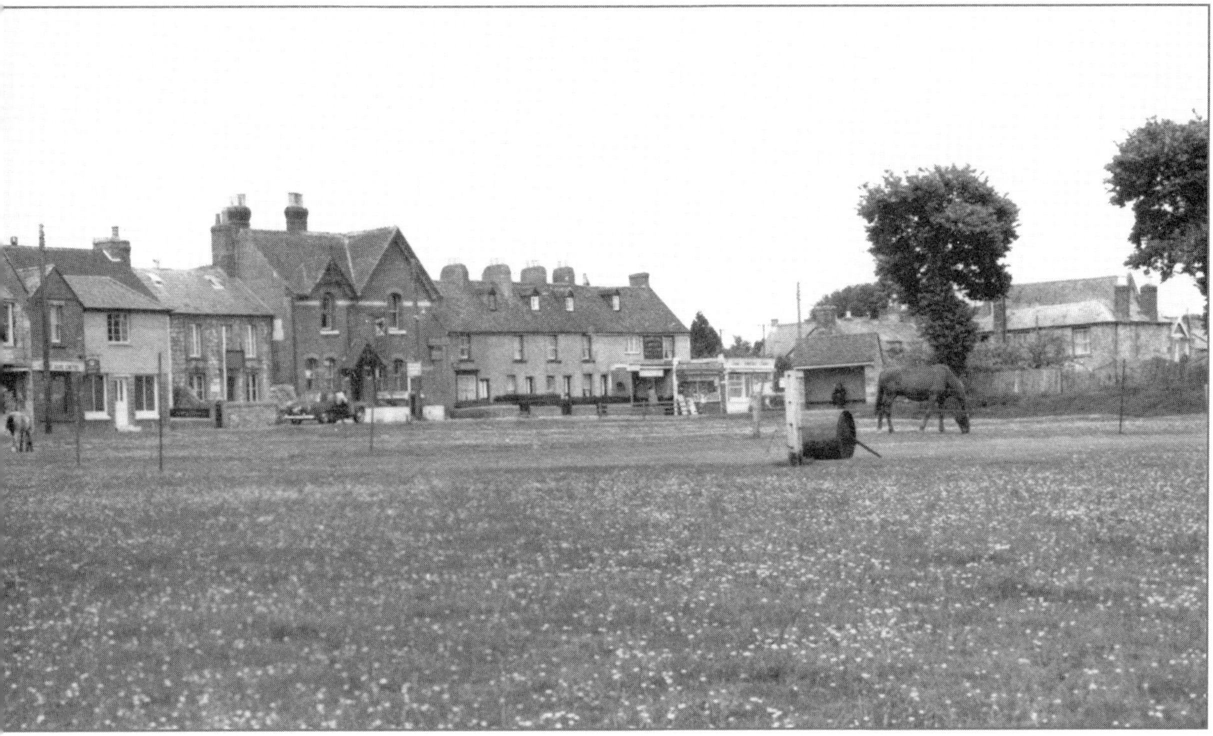

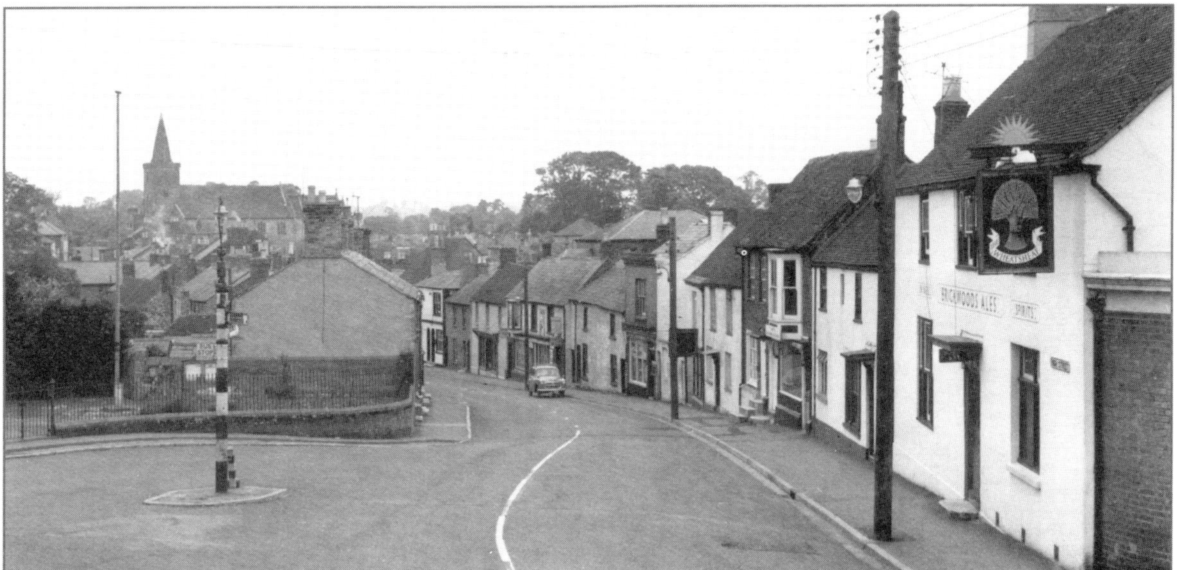


**Brading, High Street c1955** B175021
Henry VIII visited Brading, and Charles I stayed here. It is also known as the King's town, and received its charter in 1547. This delightful view shows St Mary's 13th-century tower, left, and the Wheatsheaf, right. The port and quay were thriving until the eastern Yar was dammed at St Helens in 1878-80 and the estuary was reclaimed; the tidal silt and sand was used for grazing, and provided a breeding ground for herons, warblers and coots. The Wheatsheaf opened in 1768; it is thriving under its current management, providing a hearty welcome and good food.

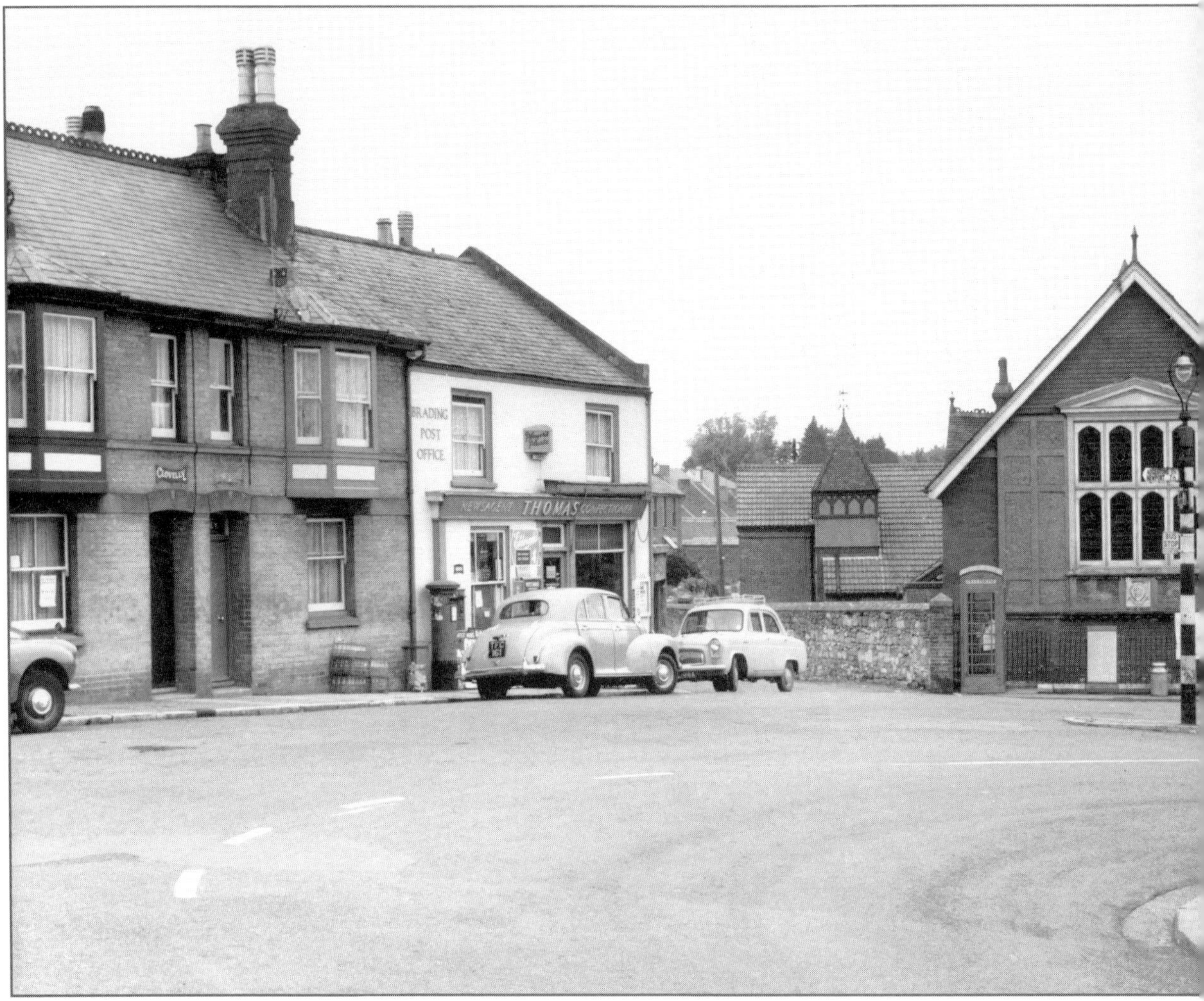


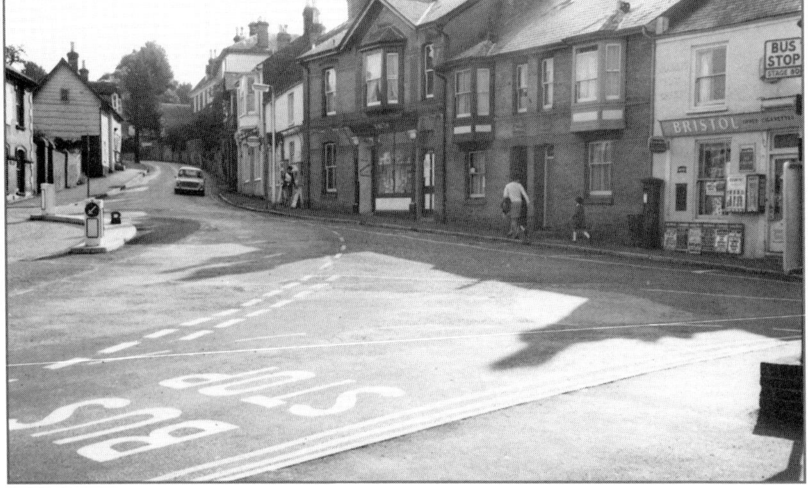


◄ **Brading, The Bull Ring c1960**

B175036

We are facing in the opposite direction to photograph No B175022, with the post office on our left. Bristol cigarettes are advertised in bold letters; to smoke them was to enjoy 'a flavour you'll never forget'. If the shop was shut, you could get your fix from the machine. Smith's are open to develop your snaps. A young, fashionably-dressed mother strides up the hill, her daughter racing along behind her. A BMC 1100 approaches, offering the latest in modern motoring and British optimism.

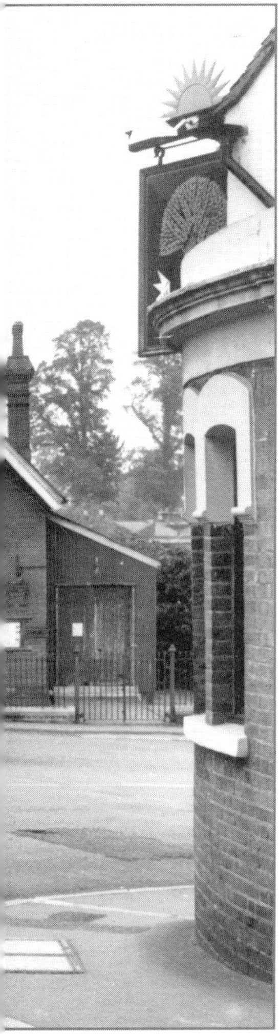

**◄ Brading, The Bull Ring c1955** B175022
This view takes us a few steps back up the hill and round the corner past the Wheatsheaf. There is not much activity around the village post office, and cars are still relatively scarce. The village has many fine buildings and curiosities, including a bull-baiting ring and a church tower built on pillars to allow processions without them leaving consecrated ground.

**▼ Brading, Little Jane's Cottage c1955** B175025
Here we have a contrast in old architecture. Little Jane's Cottage, dated AD 1547, and resplendent in old stone and thatch, contrasts with the corrugated structure next door. Motorcycles were more commonplace in the fifties, particularly for working men. The cottage, the home of Jane the young cottager, is the oldest house on the Isle of Wight, and stands opposite the ancient church; it is a place of narrow galleries and twisting stairs, used now as a museum. Leigh Richmond, a popular curate at the turn of the 18th century, wrote some moral tales published as 'The Annals of the Poor', including one called 'Jane the Young Cottager', based on a pupil at his bible class. Delicate in constitution, she died aged 15 and is buried behind the chancel, where her epitaph reads: 'A child reposes underneath this sod, A child to memory dear, and dear to God; Rejoice; yet shed a sympathetic tear; Jane the young cottager is buried here'.

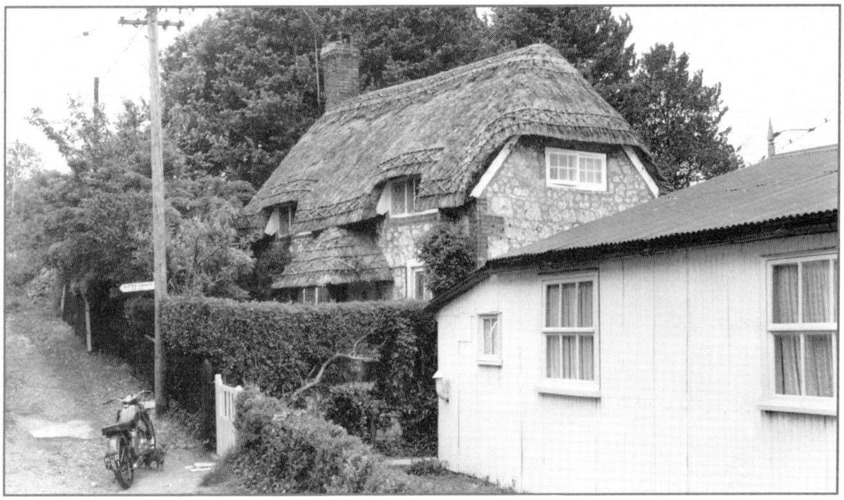

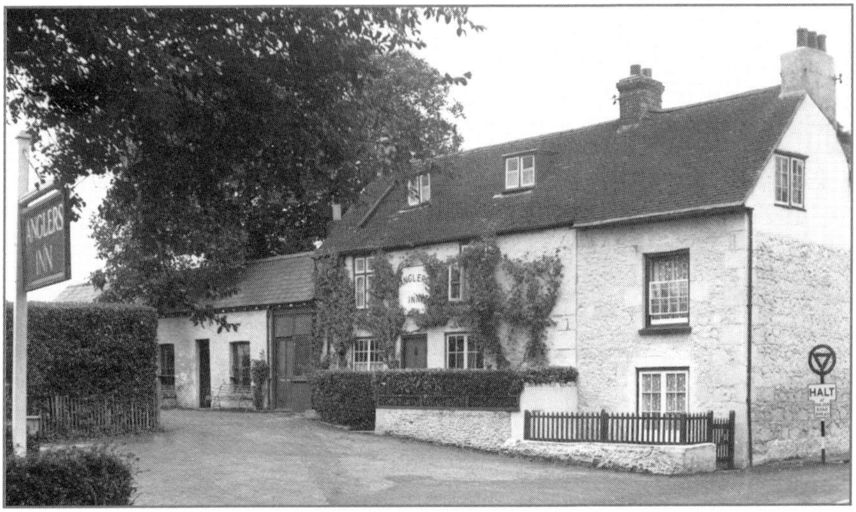


**◄ Brading, The Anglers Inn c1955** B175012
One can imagine the conversations after coming in from a sojourn on the riverbank. Life was different on the 1950s. Much of the old might be preserved or conserved now, but the pace of life and the general outlook is all much too hurried for the old anglers who gave this inn the name. Who would obey the Halt at Major Road ahead sign now, if they could spot the chance to nip in front of the oncoming traffic?

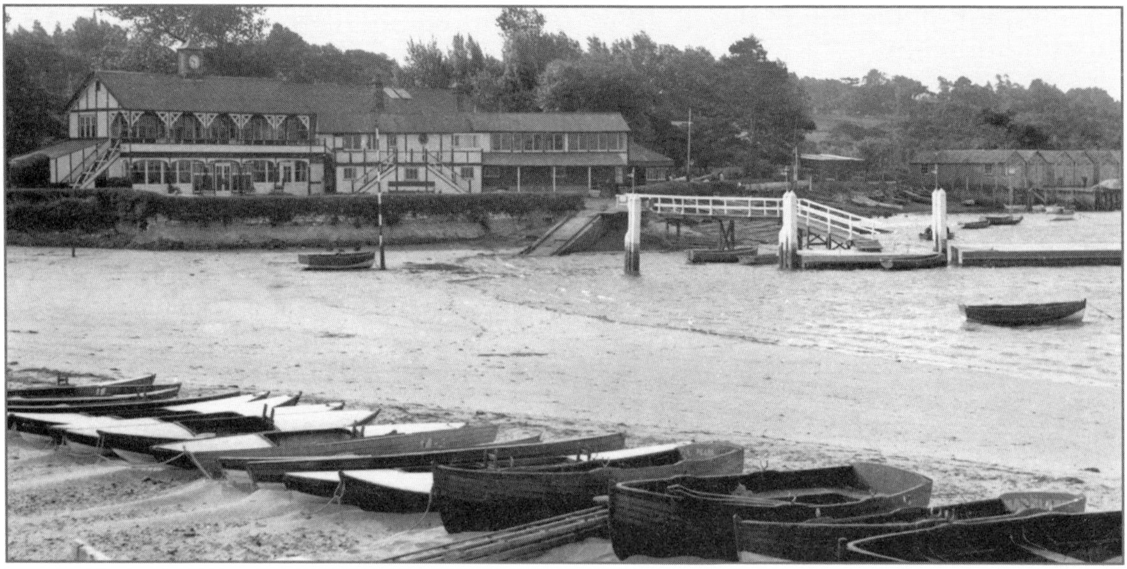

**Bembridge, The Harbour c1955** B64009
Bembridge was an island itself until the inland harbour of Brading haven was reclaimed. This is the most easterly point on the Isle of Wight. In the 1950s the population was about 2000, mainly residential; with its excellent sands, it has been a popular resort. This scene has all the charm of vanishing England - note the architecture and the clock tower. Clinker-built dinghies and canoes make a tidy row on the sand, and all is quiet. This natural harbour , with lifeboat pier, is a yachting centre. The mainland ferry service lasted only from 1882 to 1888 owing to harbour silting.

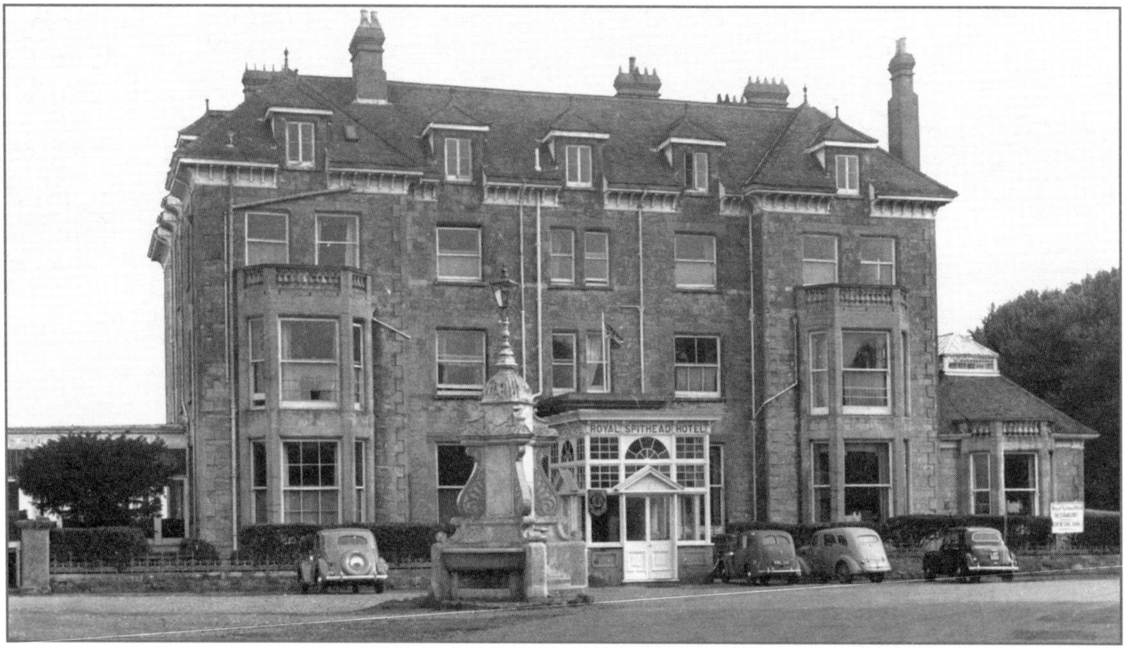


**Bembridge, The Royal Spithead Hotel c1955** B64012
They don't make cars like these any more - or hotels like this, for that matter. One wonders about the lives and business of all those who came to stay here during the austere 1950s, when Britain still had something of an empire and popular culture was yet to emerge in all its colourful diversity.

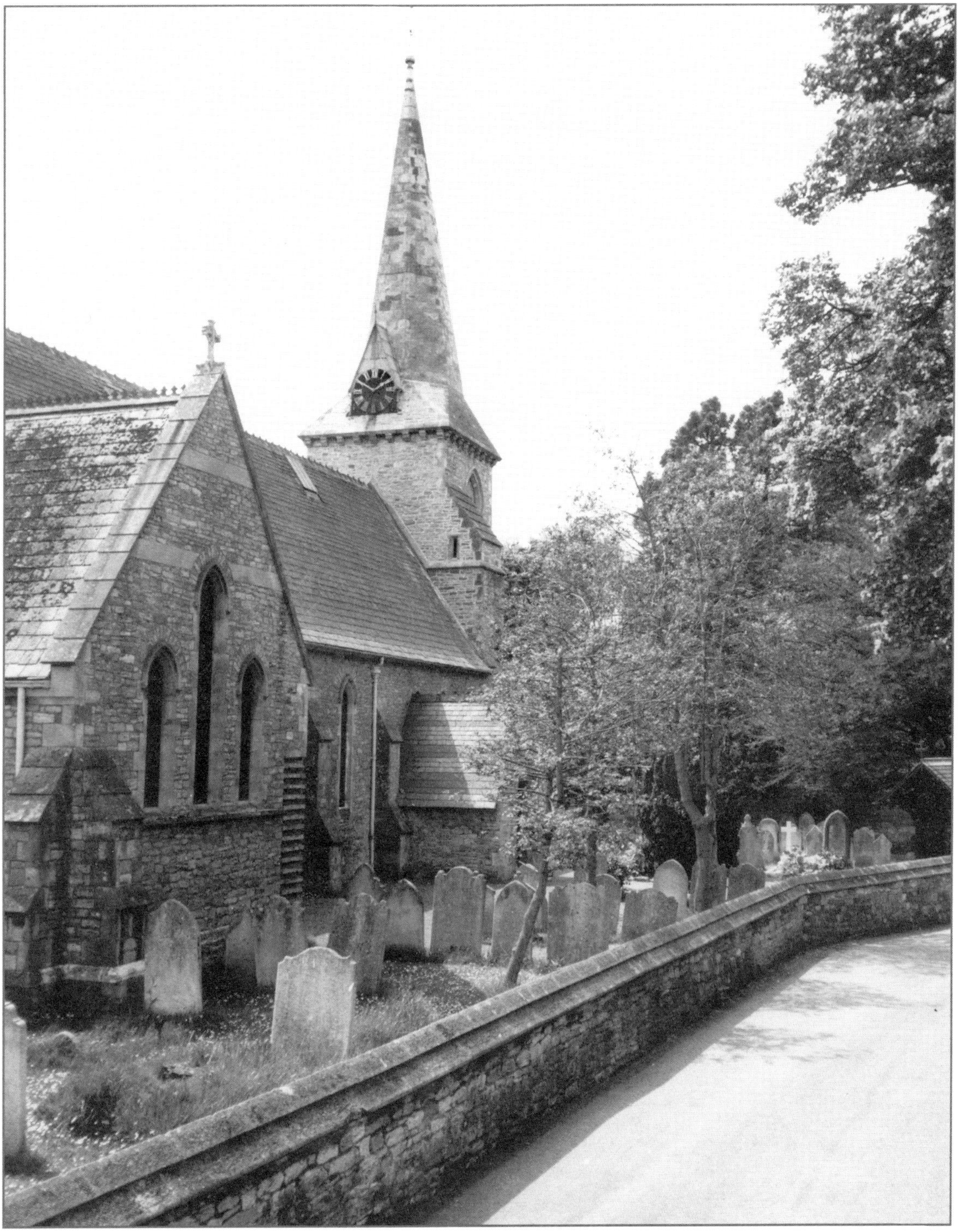

**Bembridge, The Church c1955** B64041
The village sprawls from the wooded harbour to the downs; Druids are said to have performed rites near here, and smugglers were once active. The village, quiet and preoccupied with fishing, is a place of history; it has fine old buildings, like this church ,and a preserved 17th-century windmill.

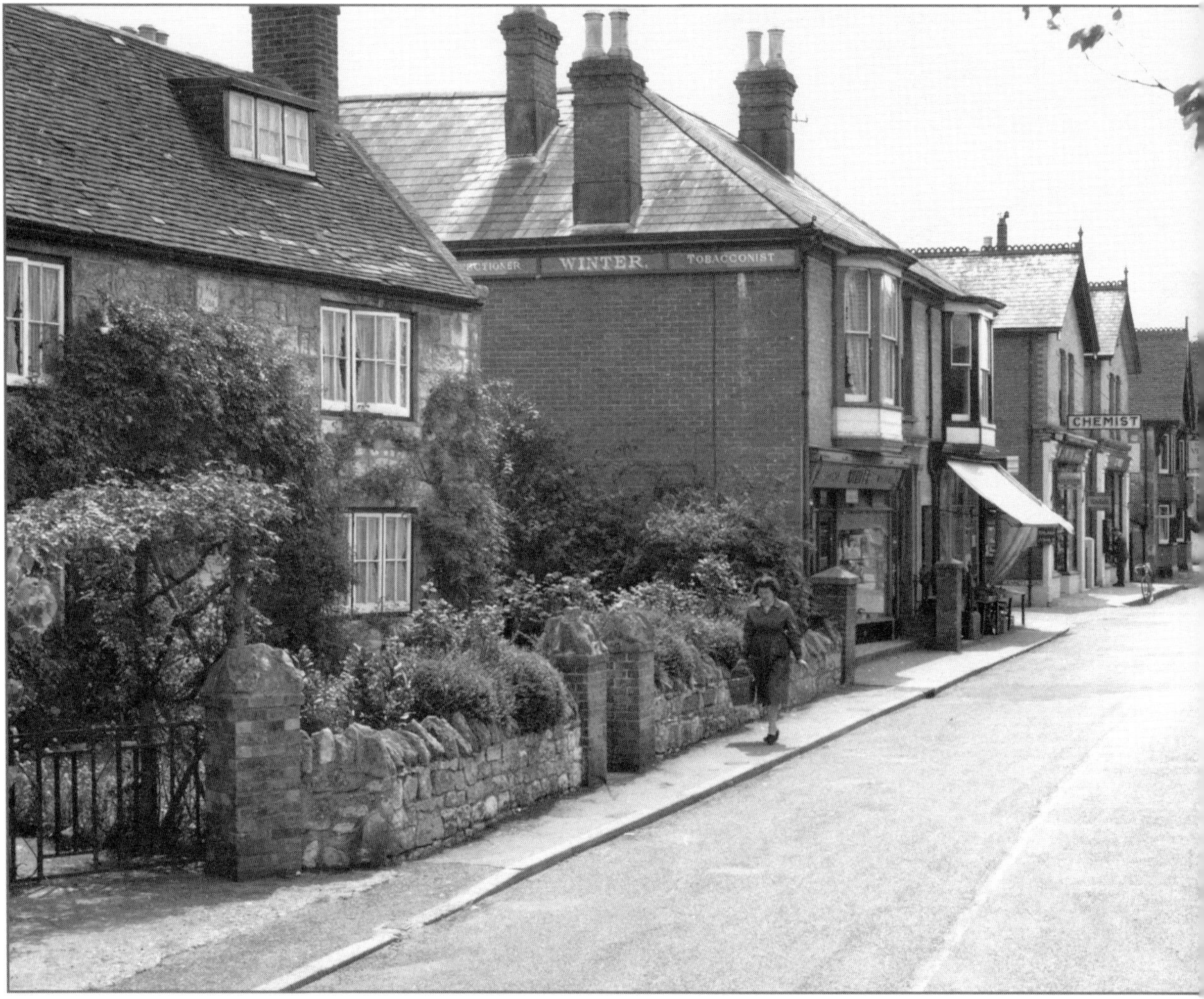


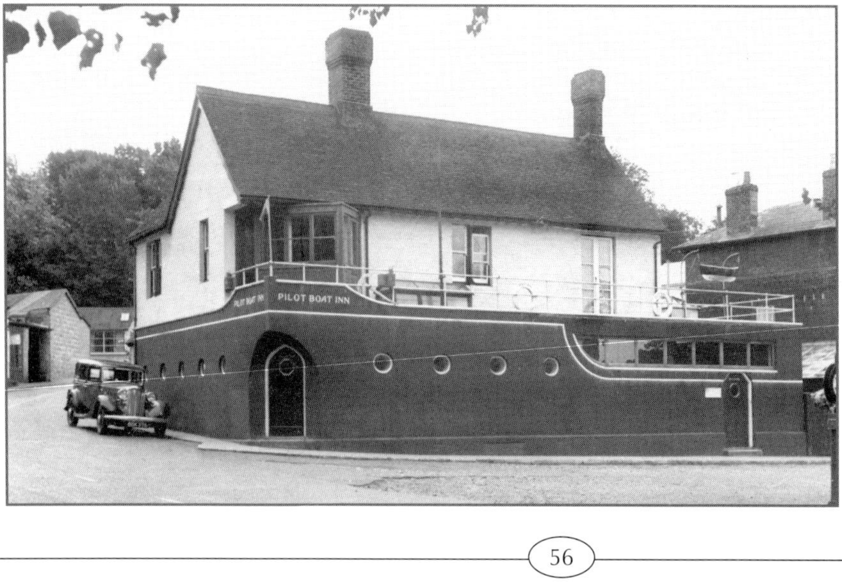


**Bembridge**
**The Pilot Boat Inn**
**c1950** B64014

Built in the shape of a boat near the old railway station site, the inn represents not just Bembridge but the whole island image. The lifeboat model above the railings reminds us of the heroic rescuers on the waves.

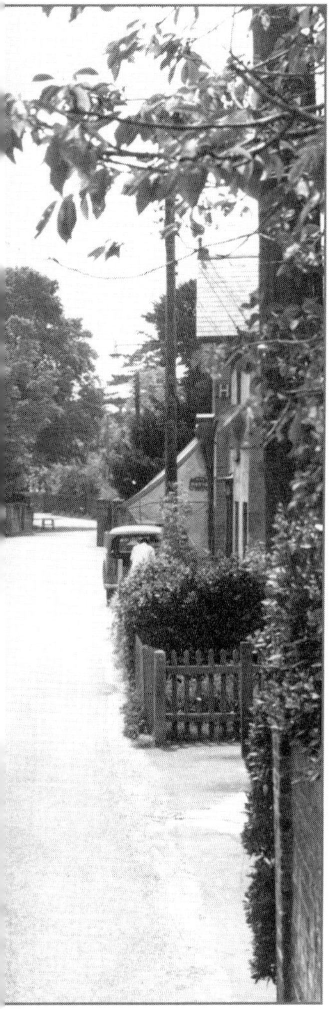

**Bembridge High Street c1955**

B64036

This is village life at its romantic best. Here all the shops have very simple signs, including 'Ye Olde Village Inn AD 1787'. A trader is sorting the load on his van, while a woman trips on home with her little bit of shopping. The scene is made complete with all those well-tended and abundant gardens.

**White Cliff Bay View from the Downs c1960** W86006

A path along the cliff top affords an excellent view of the bay. This is the age of the caravan holiday, and farmers had a nice little sideline with these campsites. This is an area popular with school field trippers.

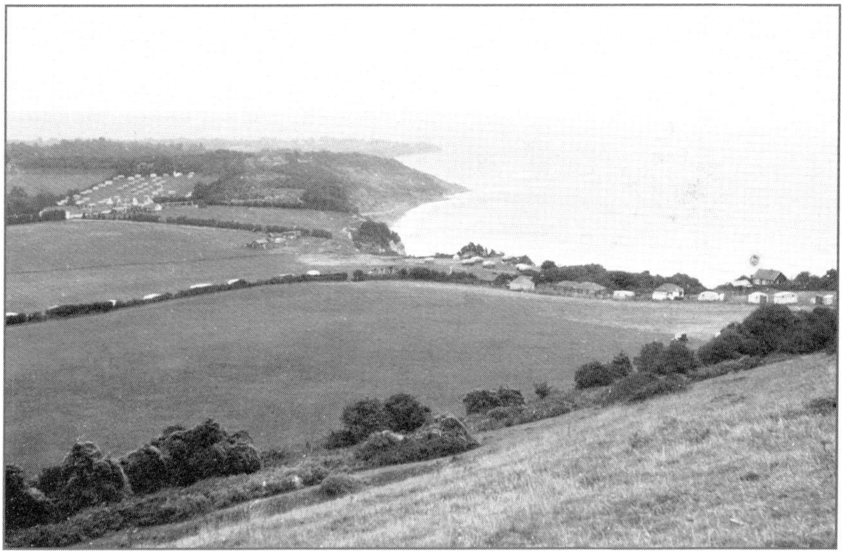

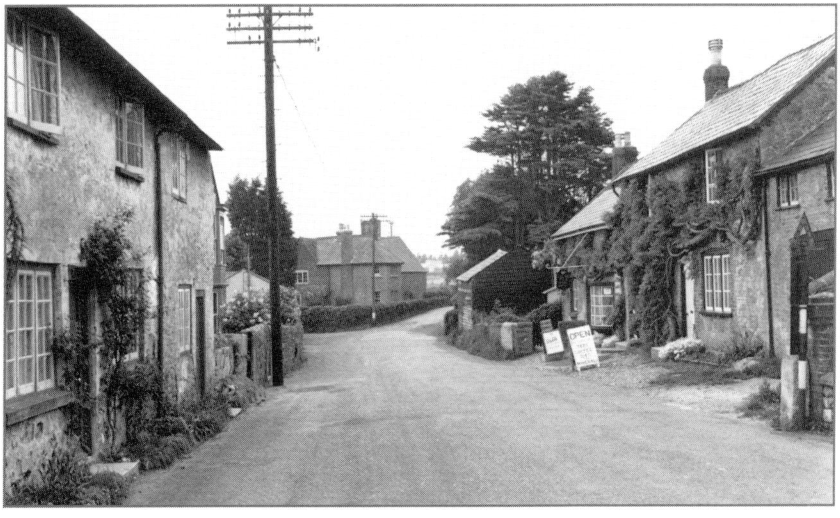


**Newchurch The Village c1955** N113006

Newchurch, once the island's largest parish, is situated above the Yar valley. Telegraph poles are in evidence, so these are modern times, for all the olde worldeness on view. This photograph of the centre shows pretty cottages bowered in wisteria. There was a large house here called Knighton, which was demolished so that a hated nephew would not inherit. It was owned by the Morvilles; Hugh Morville was one of Beckett's murderers.

▼ **Newchurch, The Village c1960** N113001
Here the eye is drawn to the white weatherboarded church. This has a 14th-century rose window. The farmer's David Brown tractor is hauling a hay cart, and passing one of the new wide windscreen Morris 1000 vans. The roadside warns of a steep hill behind. It is not clear whether the tractor is going to stop at the inn - I know I would have if I had been toiling in the hot fields.

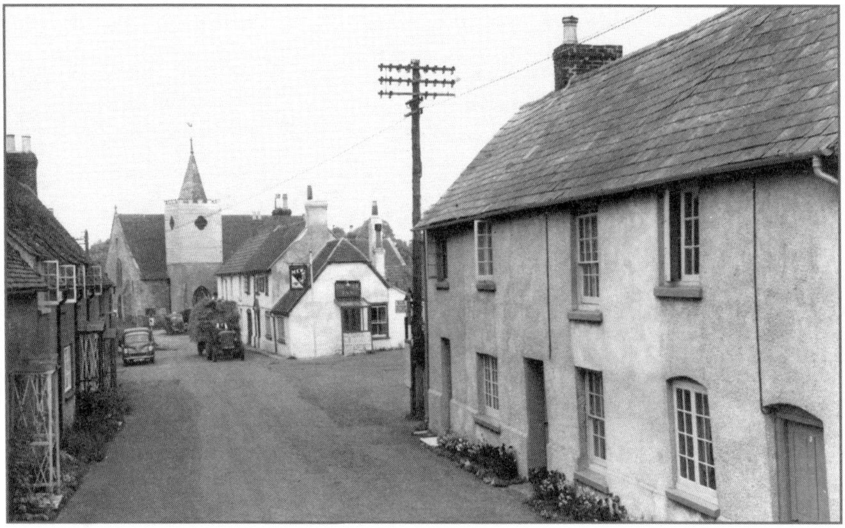

▼ **Newchurch, The Post Office c1960** N113008
Here we have a closer view of the church and the Pointer Inn, and here's that tractor again. The inn's history links it to Squire Thatcher, a hunting enthusiast who imported cubs to breed for hunting and cocks for fighting. There is not much sport going on here, though; it is just a quiet and pretty idyll under a summer sky.

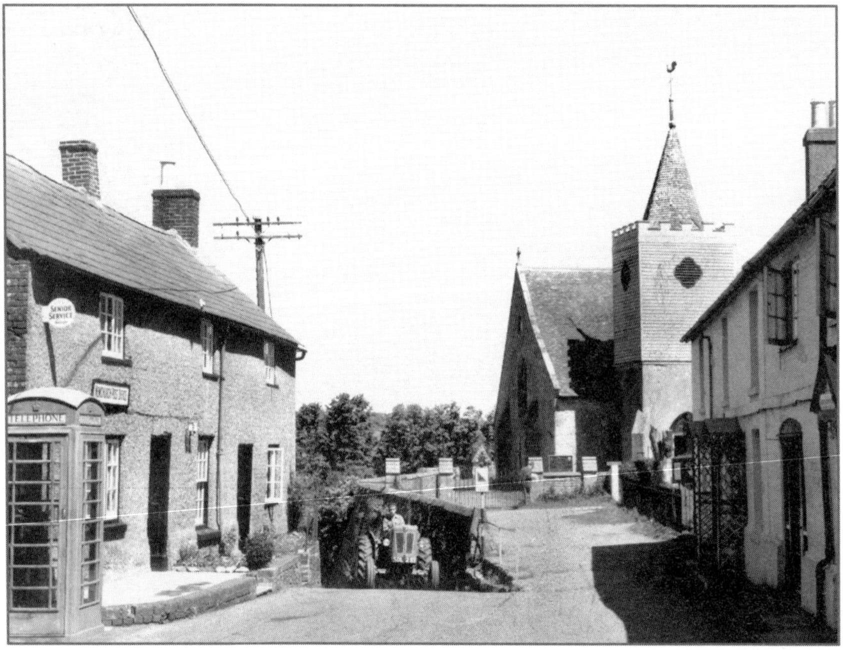


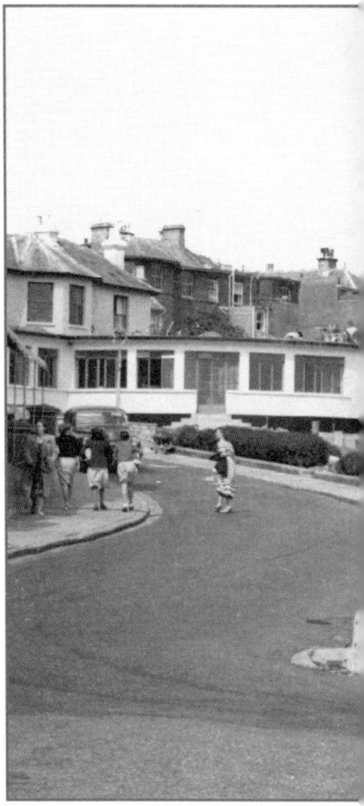

▲ **Sandown**
**The Promenade c1955**
S57008
Perhaps Sandown was more in tune with popular taste even when this picture was taken, compared to neighbouring Shanklin and Ventnor - the Rivoli Art Deco cinema came here as early as 1934. Sandown has associations with famous figures from the past. Lewis Carroll enjoyed his holidays here, and John Wilkes built his house, Villakin, on a site marked by a plaque on the corner of the High Street. The bay is best viewed from the cliffs. The fancy entrance to the pier, leading to a sort of cabin structure, advertises dancing to the Jack Smith Quintette. In those good old days cycles could be left propped against the kerb, not padlocked to the street furniture.

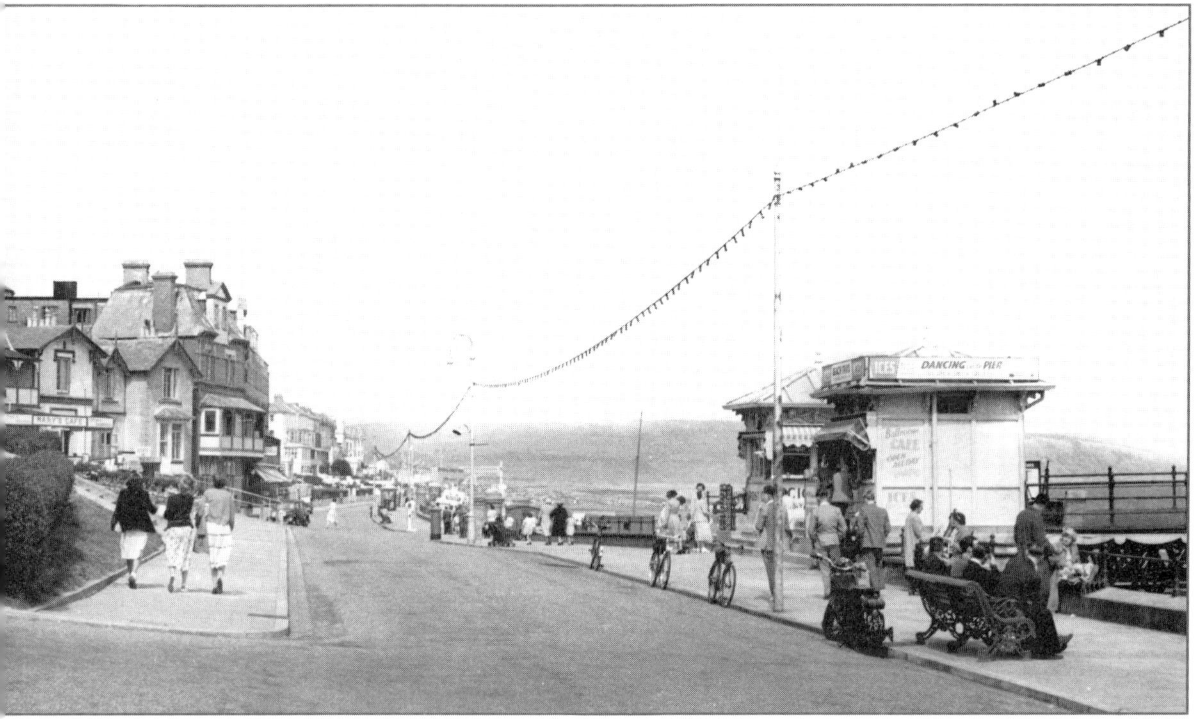

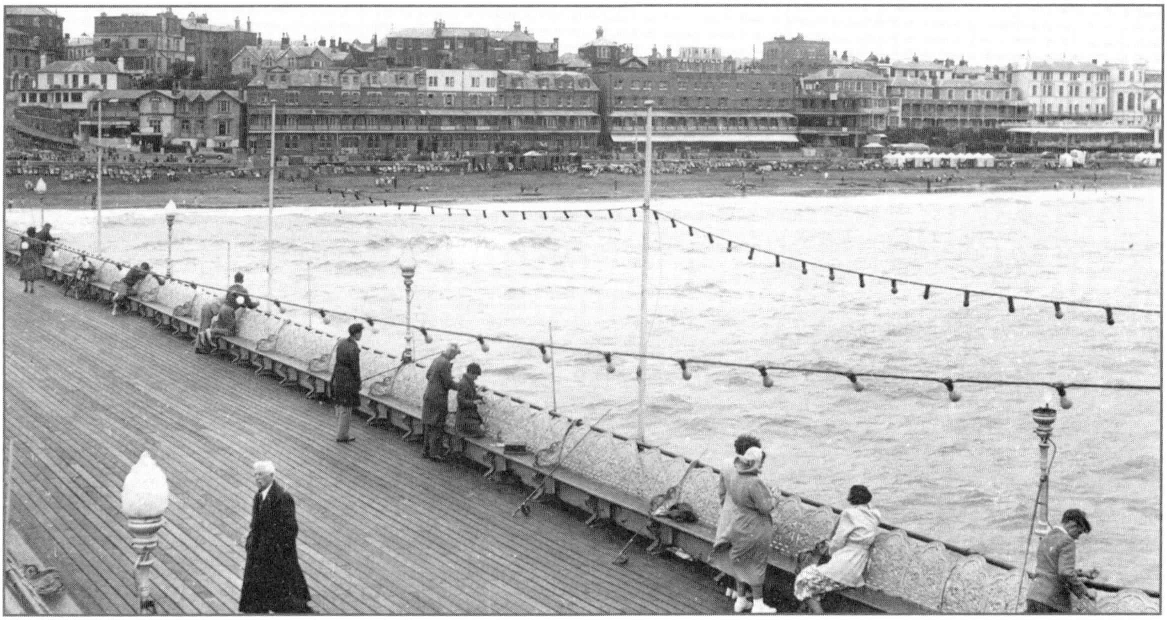

**Sandown, View from the Pier c1955** S57025
The pier was built in 1878. The English always seem to think that a bit of French adds class, hence the Trouville (a hotel?)in the centre. As we can see, there is quite a steep descent to the sea front. A coach parked behind the beach tents suggests that this is the season for day trippers, but judging by the coats and mackintoshes, it is a bit draughty on the pier. Still, the British are always optimists, and perhaps it will clear up. Meanwhile the fishermen are chancing their rods in the choppy sea.

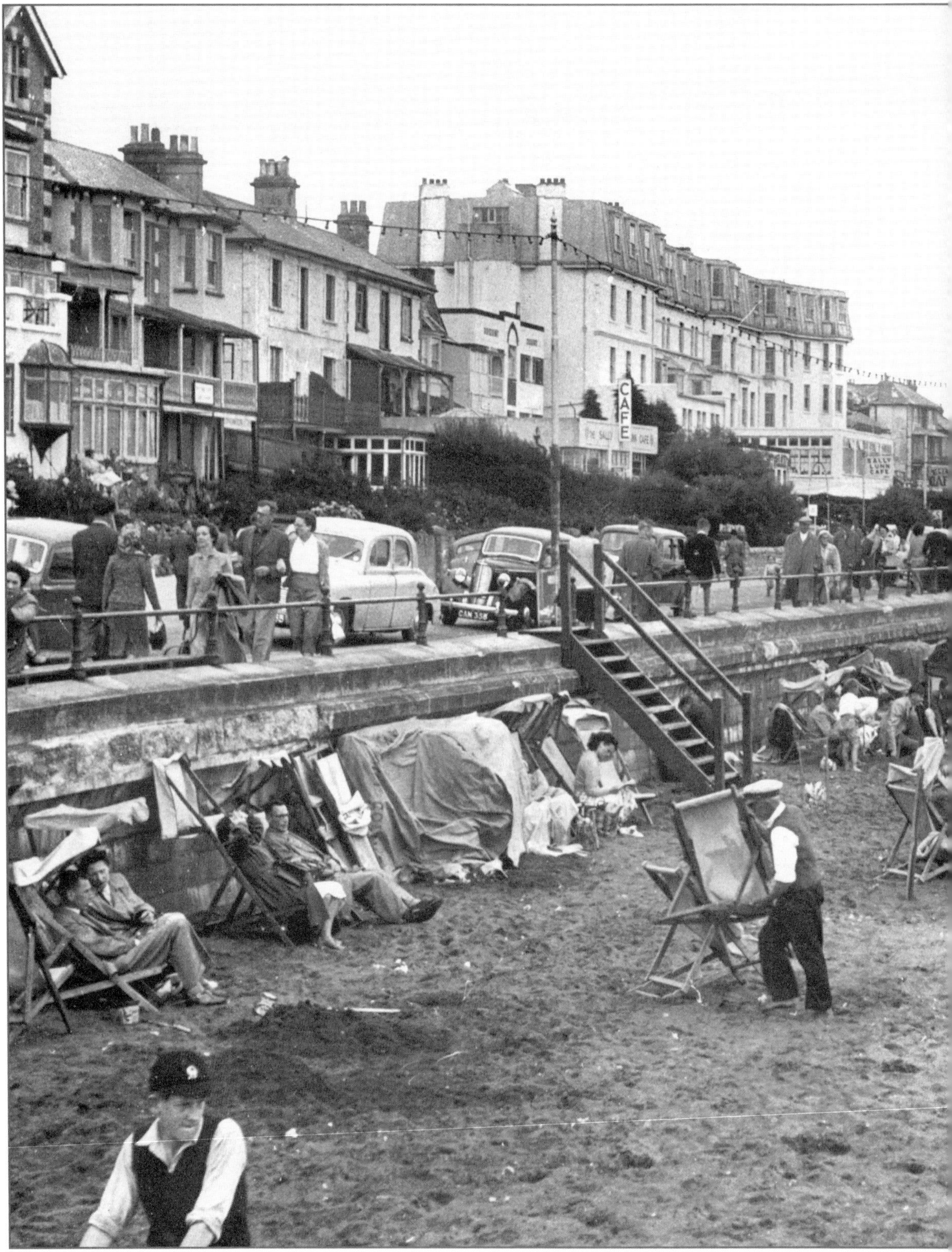
CAFE

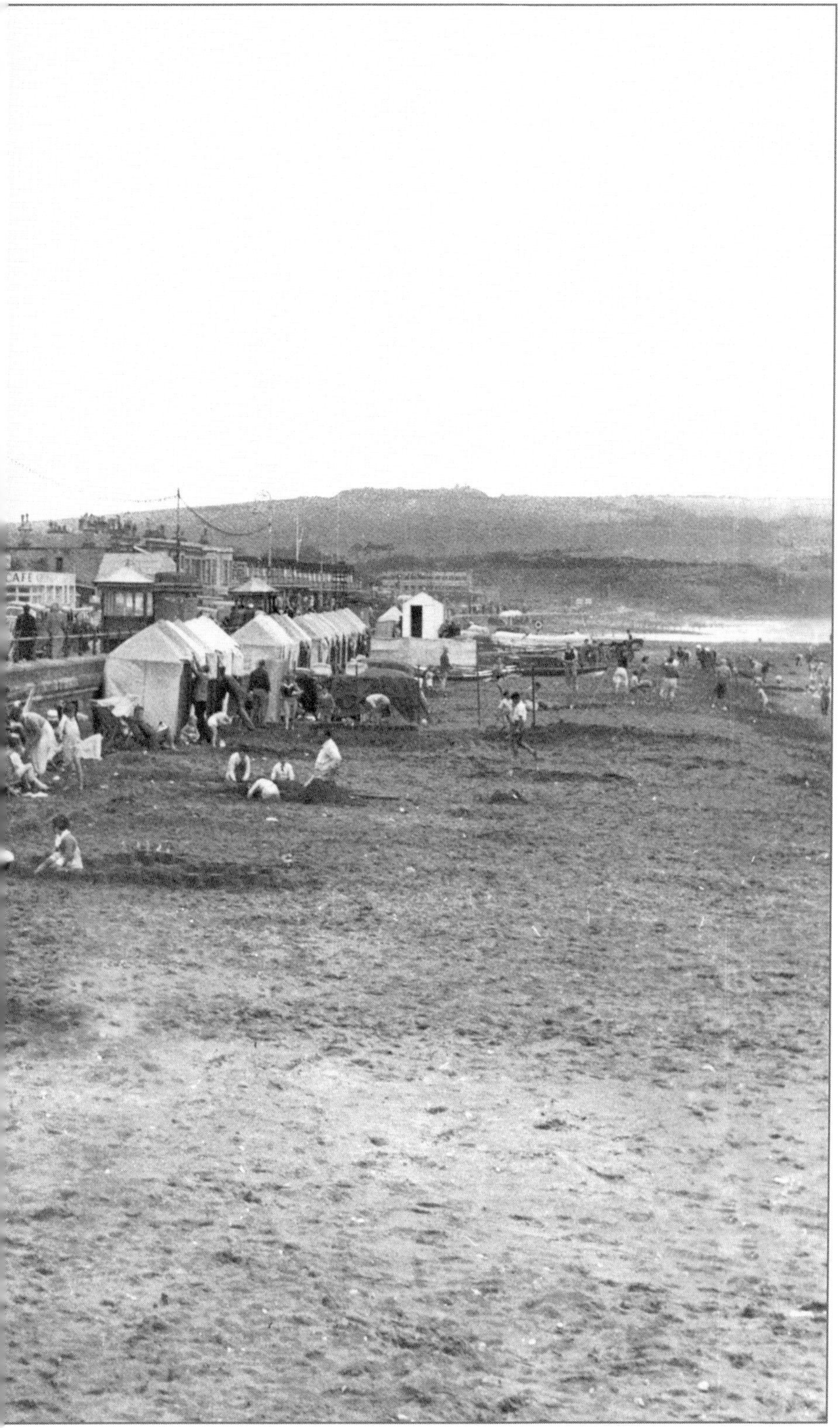


**Sandown, The Beach c1950** S57019

Here we have a closer view of the beach and its modestly-dressed sun seekers. The wearing of pullovers suggests it might be breezy, though it is shirt-sleeves for those who have decided to dig and bury themselves in the sand - or are they on the way to Australia? There is no old church here; John Wilkes had to go to Shanklin to pay his respects. The Victorians put Sandown on the map; earlier, Henry VIII and Charles I had coastal defences here.

▼ **Shanklin, The Old Village c1950** S104026
John Keats lodged here, and wished he had had a penny for every visitor passing his lodgings en route to the chine. The chine, not far along this road, is a ravine about 60 yards wide by 100 yards deep. The stream cutting through cascades sweetly into the pools below. All is very green and slimy, with ferns hanging onto the valley sides. There is so much to inspire the poet here; even Darwin thought there was no place like it.

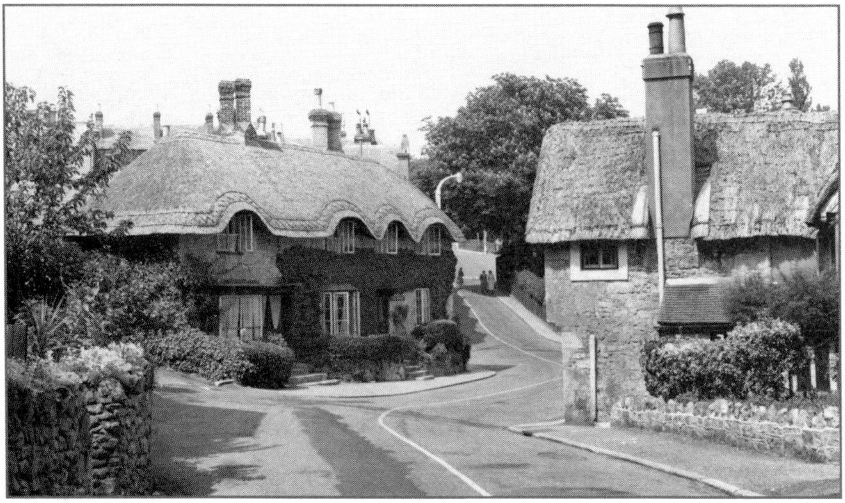

▼ **Shanklin, The Old Village c1950** S104028
Two lady strollers look keenly at the scenery as they pass the delightful Crab Hotel. No wonder Keats came here in search of health. Longfellow's verse is cut into a brick pillar of the inn on Shanklin Chine: 'O traveller, stay thy weary feet; Drink of this fountain pure and sweet; It flows for rich and poor the same. Then go thy way remembering still The wayside well beneath the hill, The cup of water in His name'.

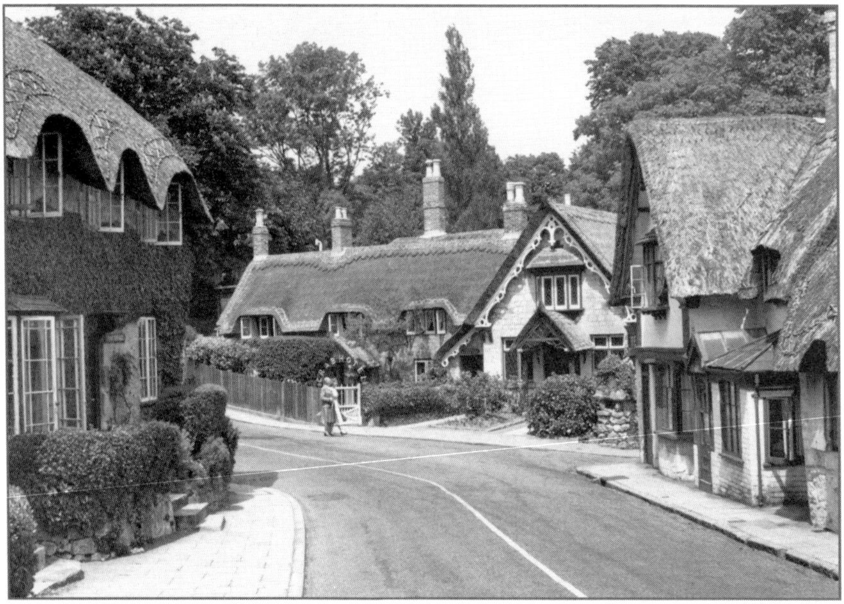

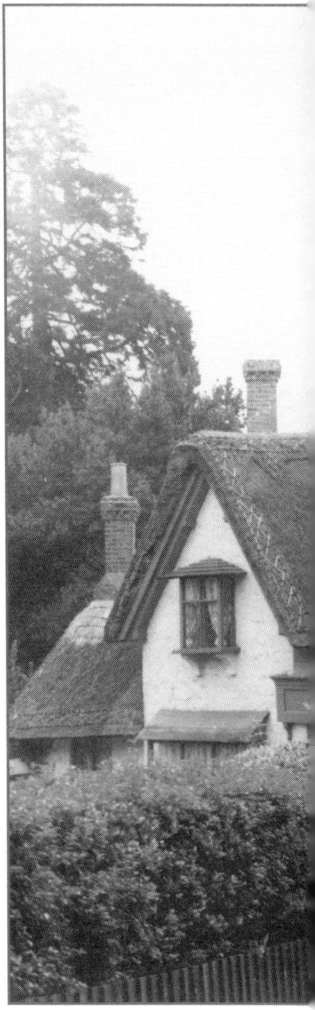

▲ **Shanklin**
**The Old Village c1955**
S104066
This scene is so idyllic it is almost unreal; The Thatch and Pencil Cottage Tea Room evoke images of an idealised past. Everyone looks animated amongst these old houses and ancient trees. The 'Ye Olde Sweet Shop' sign catches the eye. Let us hope that the gentleman is not so enamoured with his lady friend that he has not heard the car just peeping out around the corner!

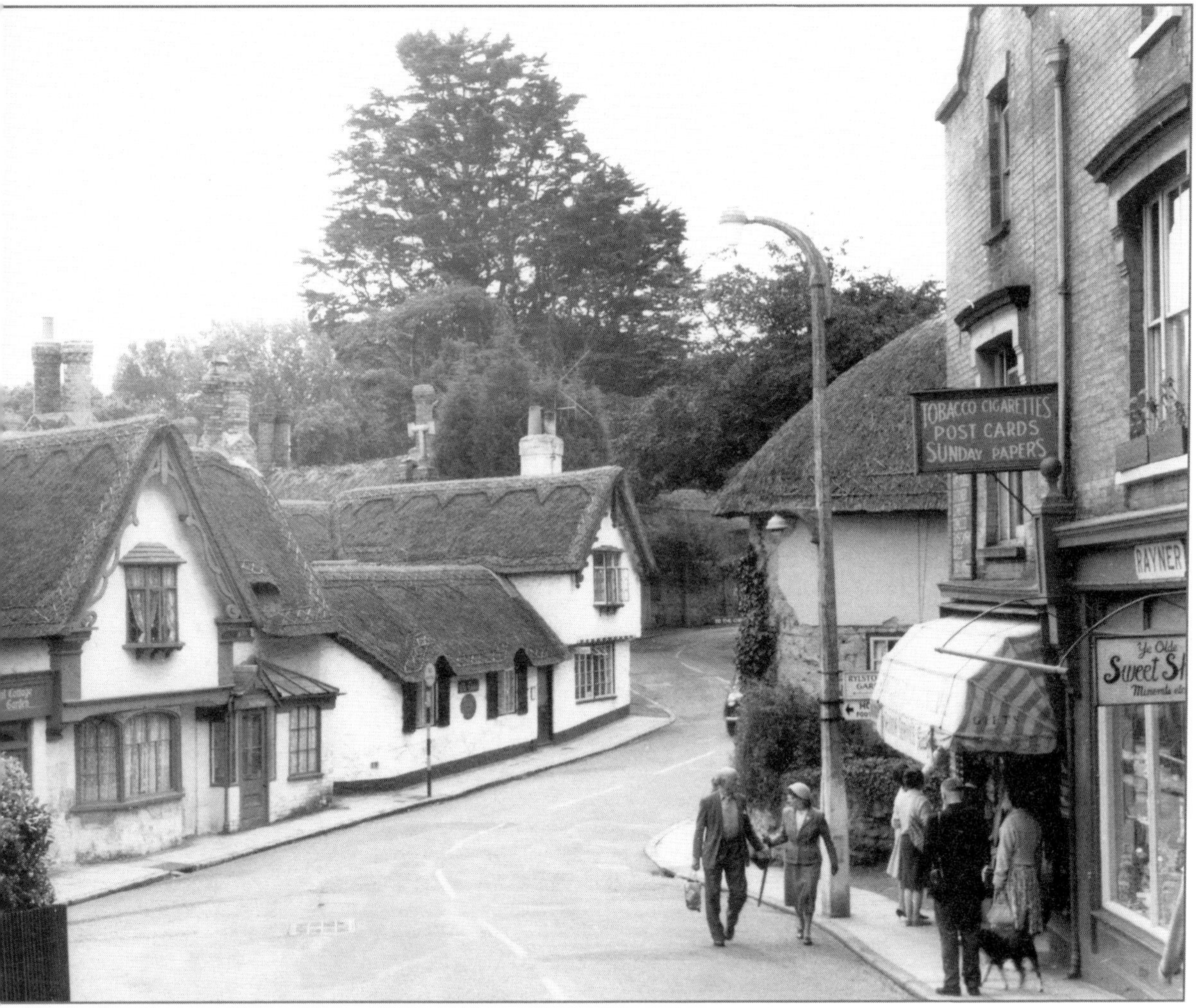


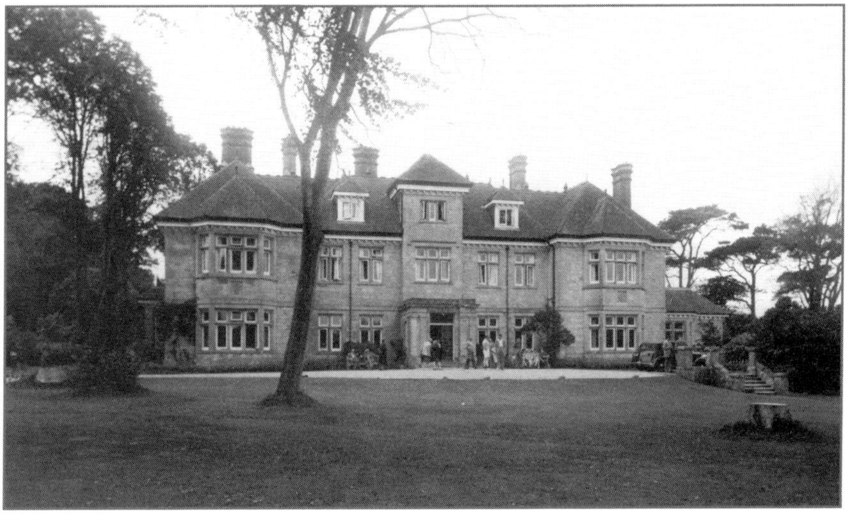

**Shanklin, The Manor House c1950** S104006
This is one of over 20 manor houses on the island, evidence of prosperity in the 16th and 17th centuries. The manor is now a very good hotel with excellent food and wine. Surrounding heights reach 800 feet. The old church stands under ash trees on its mound at the manor gateway. A plaque on the wall outside honours the memory of all Shanklin men who served and died in the Great War 1914-18.

▼ **Shanklin, Keats Green c1950** S104039
Keats Green, along the cliff walk, is very pleasant by lamplight and popular with tourists staying in the overlooking villas and the Keats Green Hotel. The hydrangeas and well-kept turf are a picture, as these walkers are aware. Undoubtedly they remembered their holiday walks for many years after. The walk leads steeply down to the sea front.

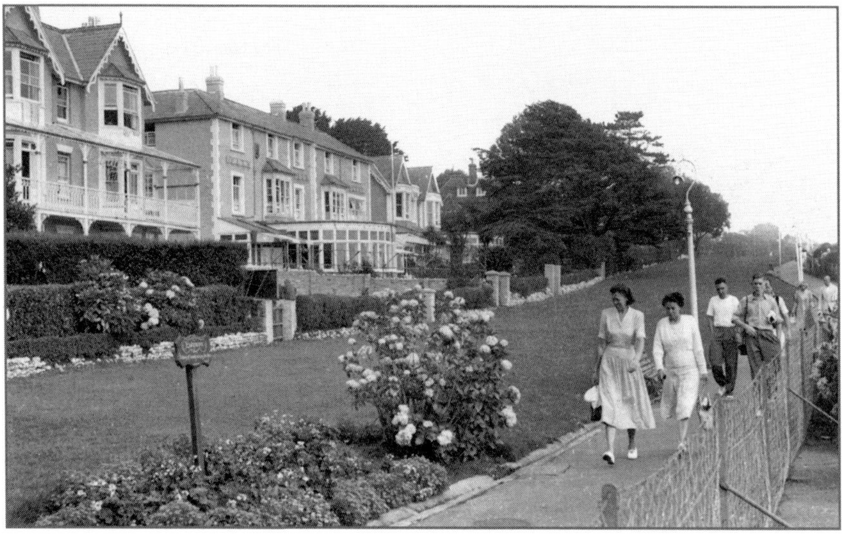

▼ **Shanklin, The Sea Front c1950** S104047
A Triumph Mayflower heads a stately line of parked cars; they are mostly black, and many are pre-war - exports still came first for a car industry struggling to get Britain on its feet again. Still, there are many Britons on their feet in this scene, playing pitch and put or tennis in the foreground or pursuing more traditional pastimes on the shore. Of particular interest to vehicle buffs is the Council drain-cleaning lorry.

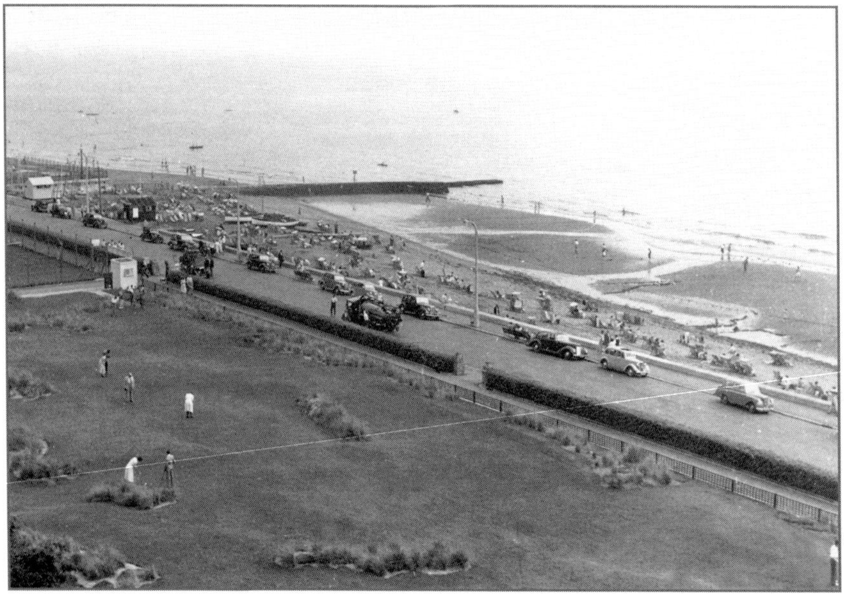

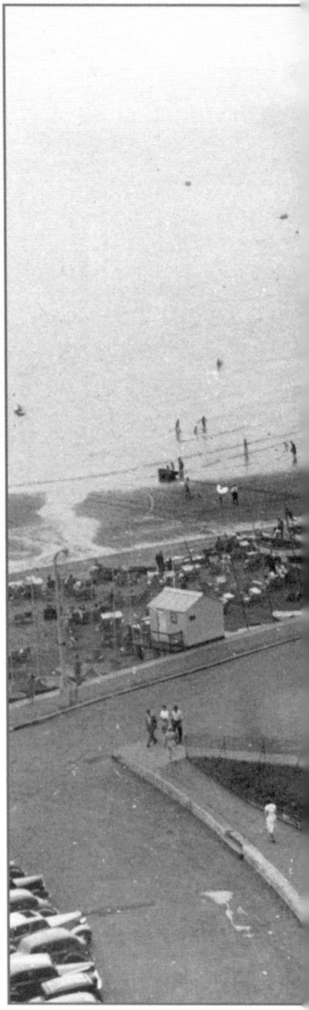

▲ **Shanklin, The Beach and Pier c1950** S104048
Nearing the point where K
Green joins the pathway d
to the beach, we see that t
drain-cleaning lorry is still
Little has changed here sin
young Muriel King, a regul
holiday-maker here, now i
her 80s and living in Winsl
enjoyed seaside holidays
before the war, taking phot
and counting to 6 before
closing the shutter. From th
distance the pier looks like
giant insect out for a paddl

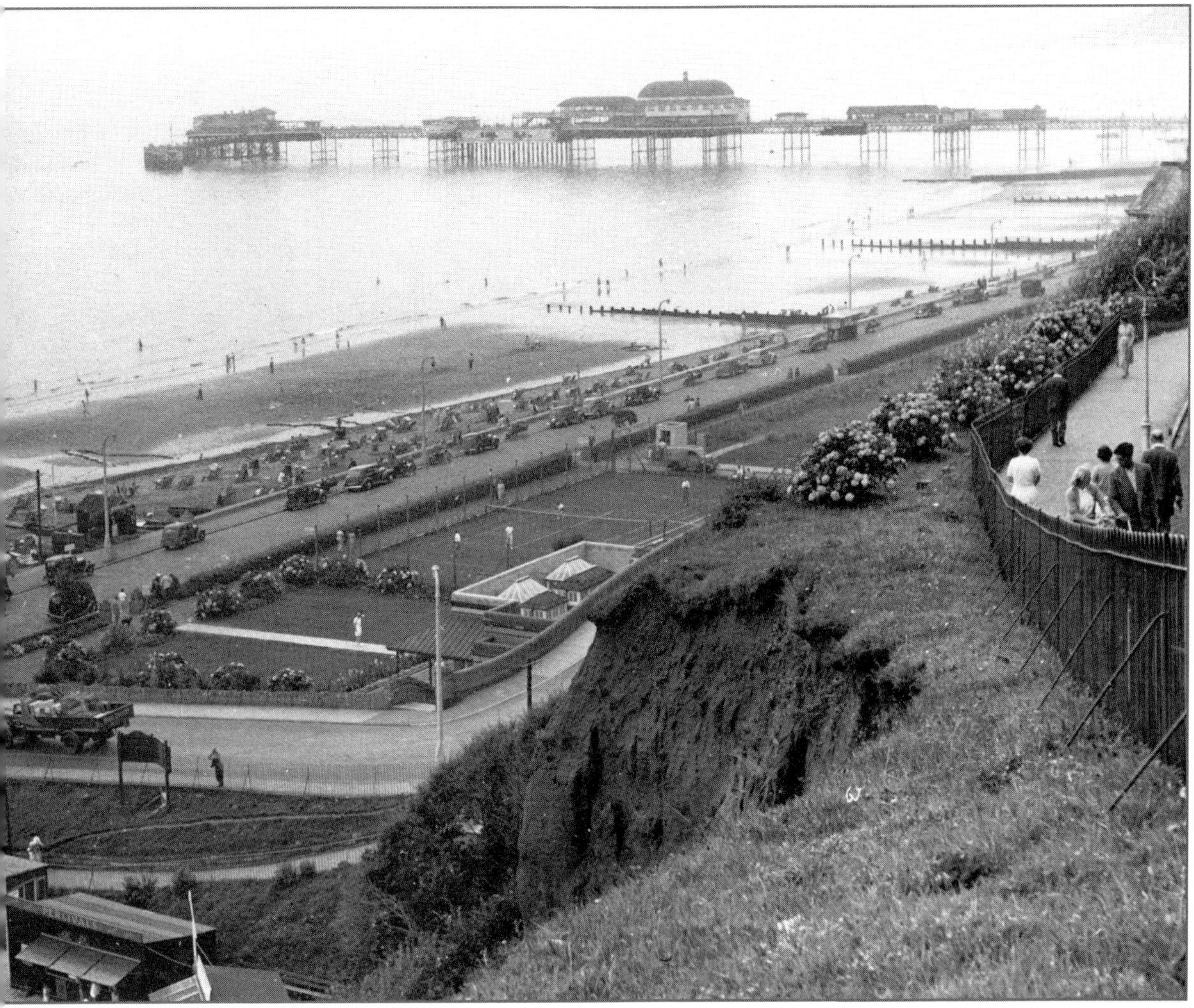

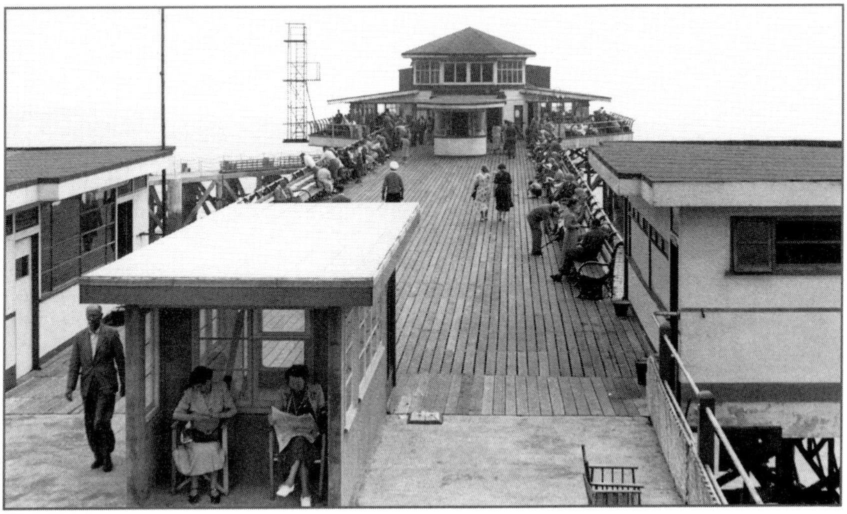

**Shanklin, The Pier c1955**

S104062

This is not a particularly attractive piece of architecture - it looks rather like portakabins on stilts - but piers are about people and atmosphere. The atmosphere here appears restrained and chilly. Two ladies in the foreground shelter are lost in a world of their own. I wonder what was the top news story that day. Further along the planking, people find other things to absorb them, but very few are looking at the sea.

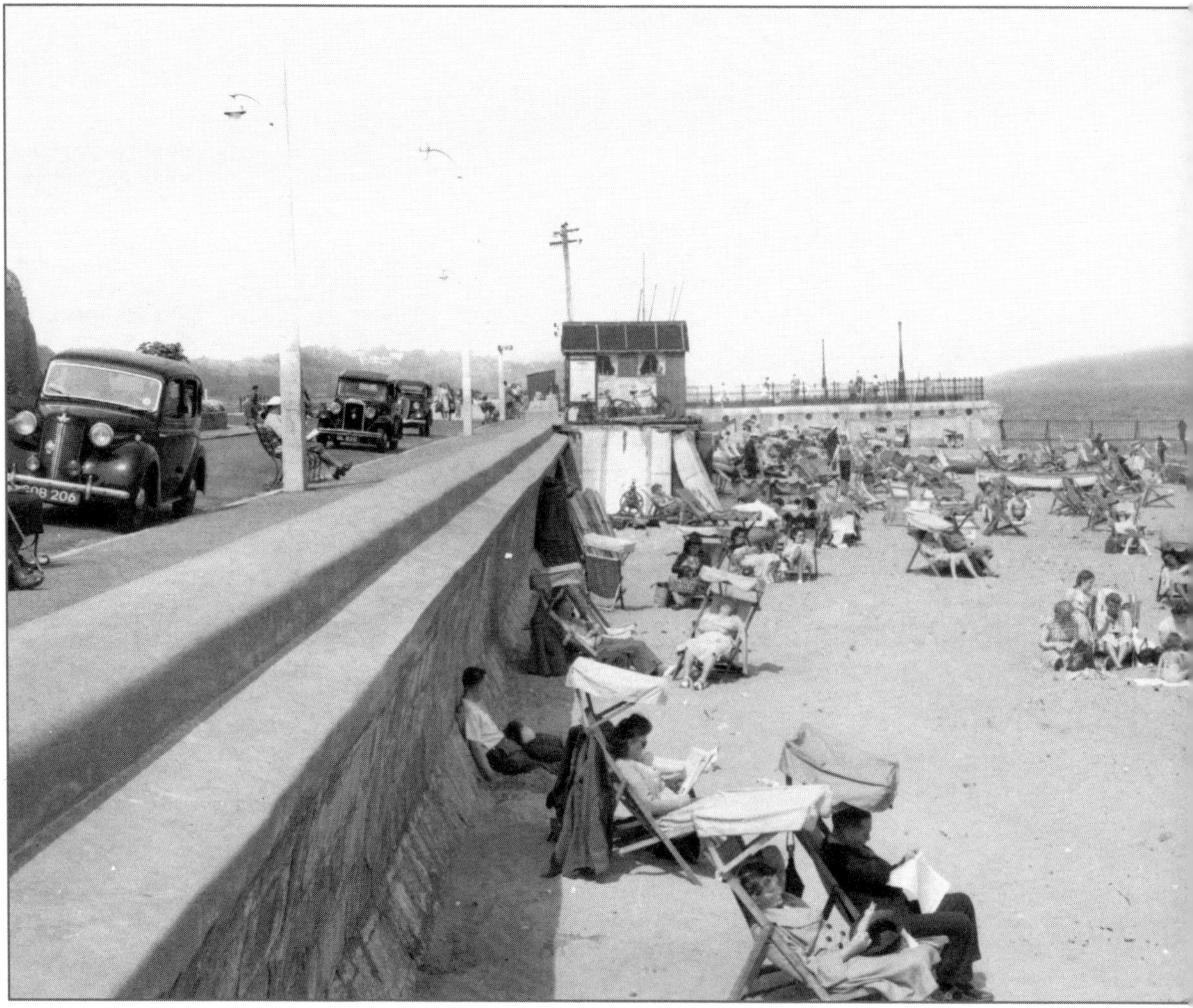

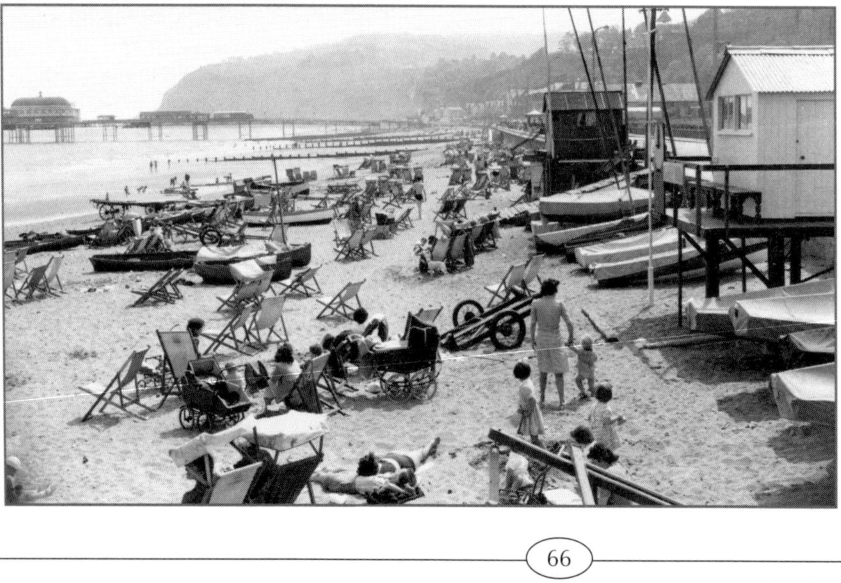

◀ **Shanklin**
**The Beach c1950**
S104035
We are looking south toward the pier, and empty deck chairs take up most of the beach space. Boats and trailers are also much in evidence. The pier was built in 1891; it was badly damaged in a storm in 1987.

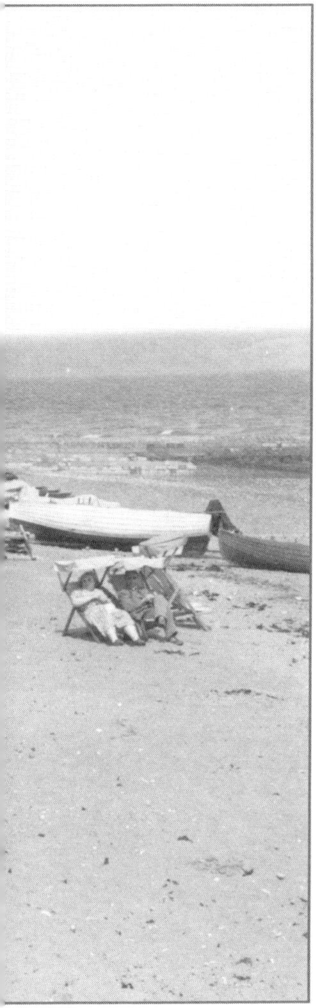

◄ **Shanklin, The Beach c1950** S104031
Down on the beach we can feel the heat. The affluent owners of a motor car could easily park it on the road behind them. Sunglasses, or shades as we call them now, were worn here for a purpose, not just to be fashionable; there is no posing here, just relaxing.

▼ **Shanklin, Small Hope Beach c1955** S104053
Under the steep cliff face, it's time for a spot of cricket, with spades coming in handy as makeshift wickets. Beach huts and tents are in abundance, giving the scene a medieval tournament look.

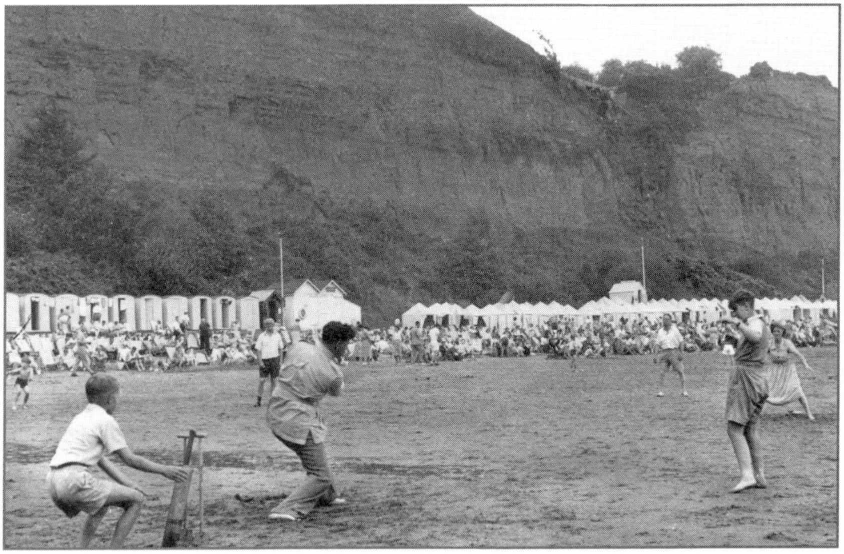

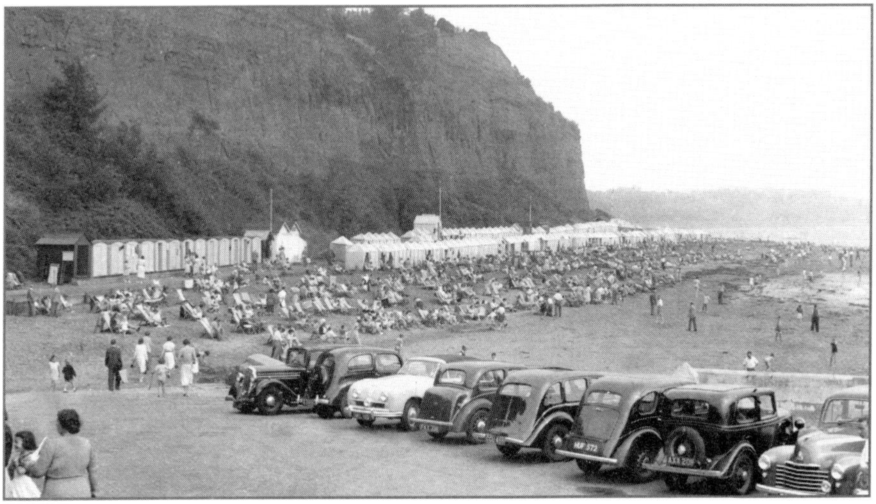

◄ **Shanklin, Small Hope Beach c1950** S104043
This wider-angle view of the beach reveals the sober dress of beach folk, who are all behaving in a very orderly way. An array of mainly pre-war cars is equally well-ordered. Only the Austin Atlantic soft top, third from left, cuts a dash - it was designed for the US market.

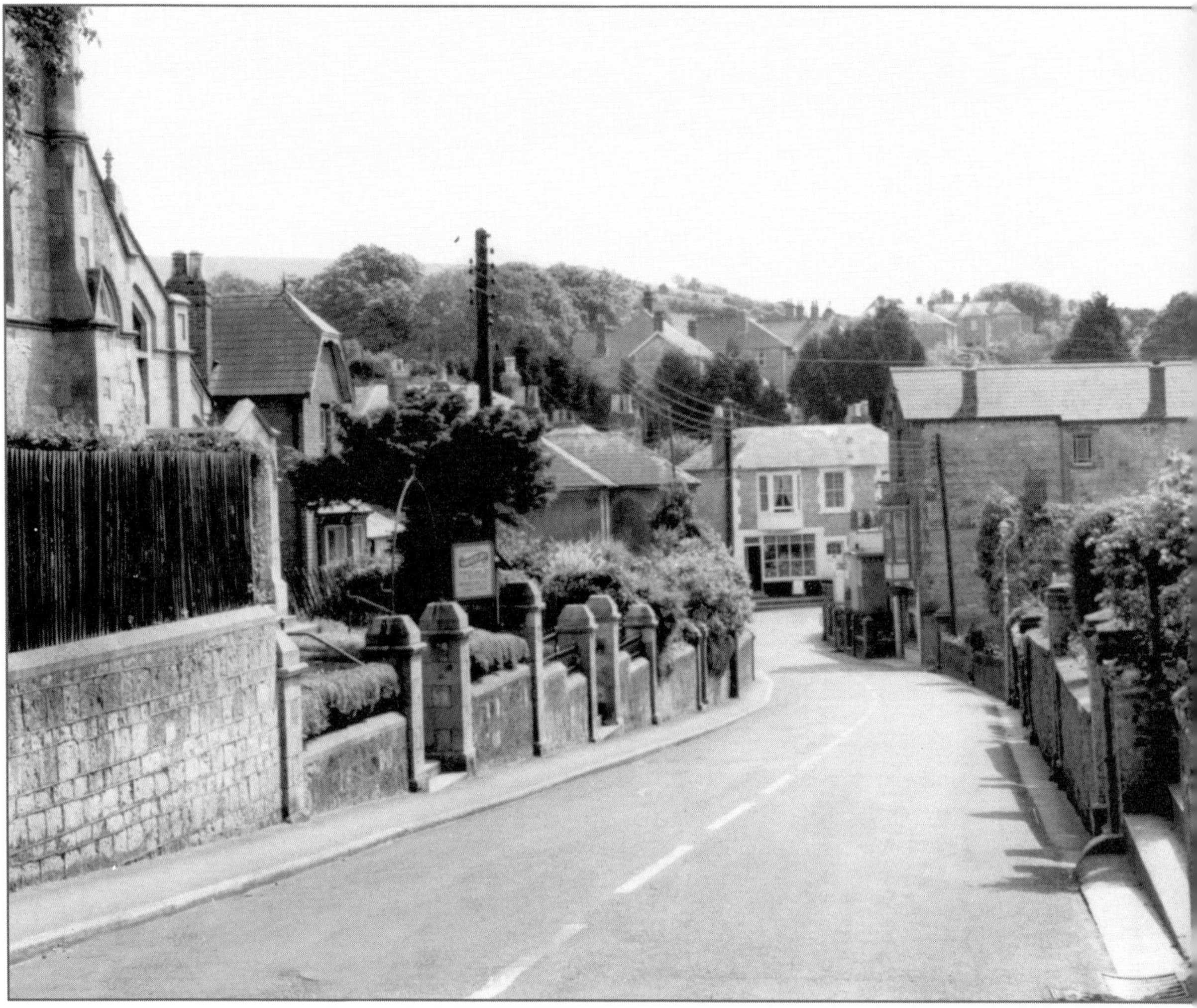

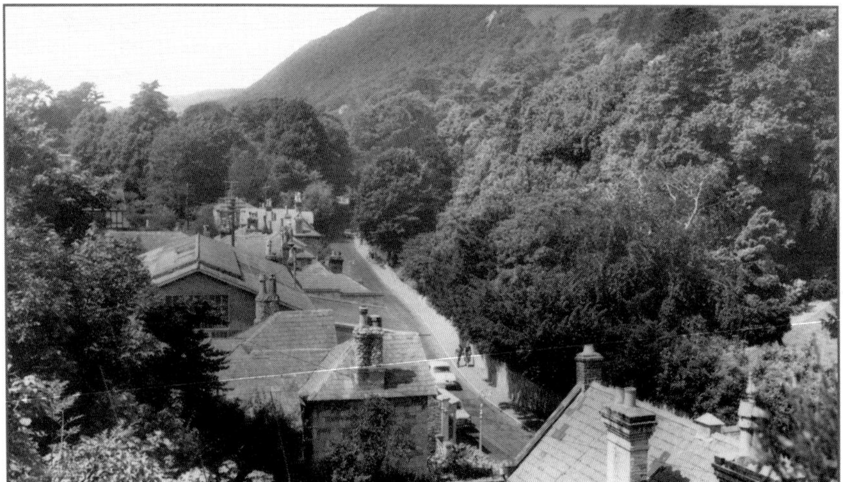

**Bonchurch From the Cliffs c1960**

B139111

Bonchurch faces the sea from the heights of St Boniface down, which reaches 787 feet; down and village are named after a Saxon saint. Rooftops and chimneys break through the verdant cover which has kept this place so popular since Victorian literary folk came here.

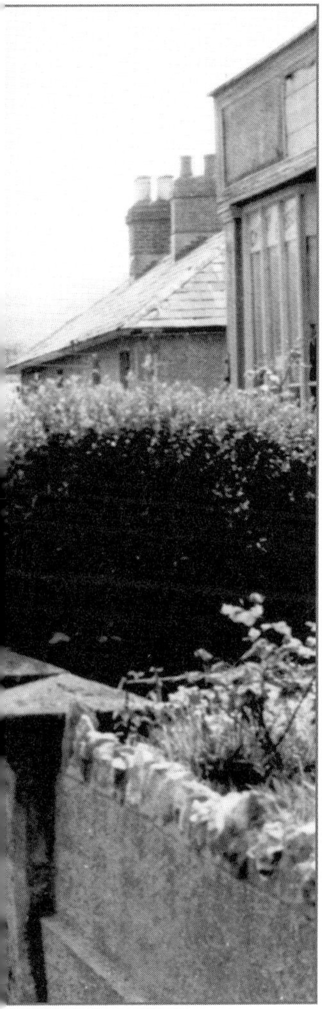

**Wroxhall, High Street c1955** W546006

This village is just a few miles south-west from Shanklin, in excellent walking country and near the high point of St Martin's Down. The church is to the left of a very quiet High Street. Appuldercombe House, with gardens by Capability Brown, home of the Worsleys for 300 years, is close by. It was rebuilt in the 18th century in classic style with a room for every week of the year and enough windows for all the days. It was later used as a school, and then stood empty; it was bombed in 1943.

**Bonchurch, The Village c1955** B139011

A couple contemplate the rippling water. This was part of the novelist H de Vere Stacpoole's garden, where there is an inscription and memorial to his wife Margaret. Large houses help Bonchurch retain its Victorian ambience. Macaulay lived here awhile at Madeira Hall, and Tennyson included it on his rambles; he was once accosted by ladies who cut his hat to pieces for souvenirs.

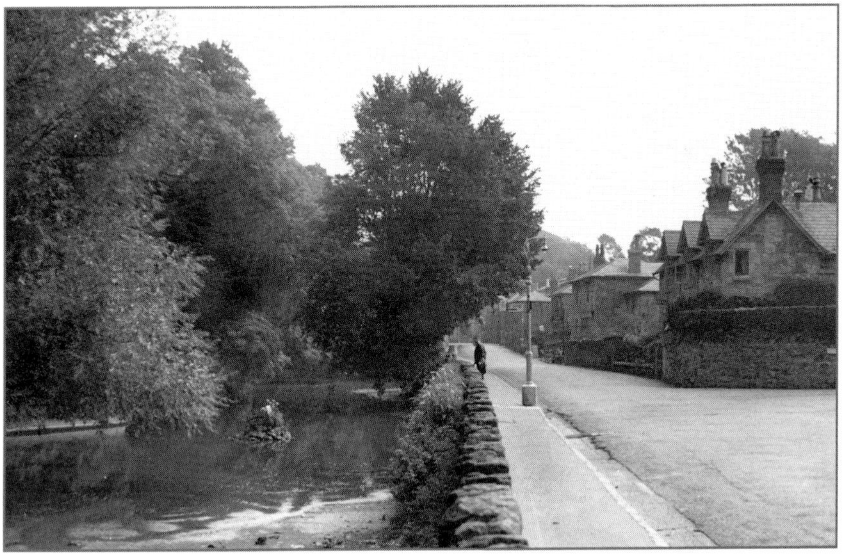

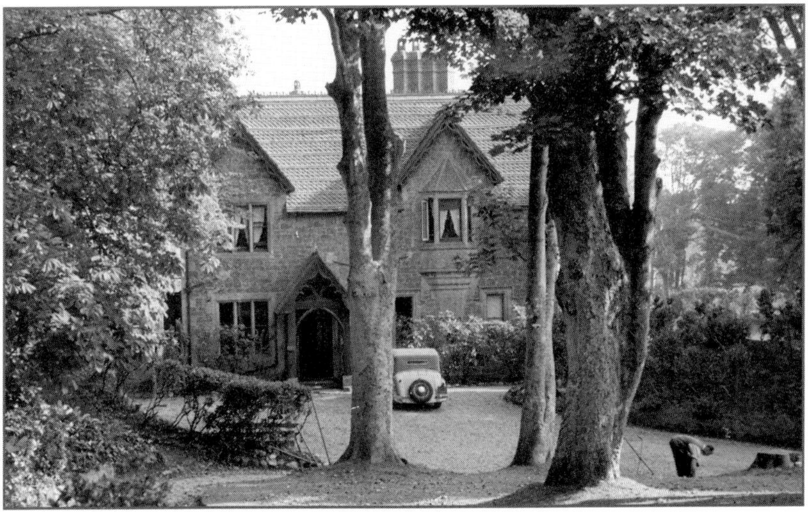

**Bonchurch, The Grange Private Hotel c1955** B139068

Here is a grand house nestling among the trees, with a grand touring car parked outside. One can imagine young people unloading expensive luggage and tennis rackets, their blazers flapping open, the graceful blonde young ladies with their beaux. All would be a far cry from when Dickens rented Winterbourne in the village for the summer of 1849, spending his mornings writing 'David Copperfield' and his afternoons wending his way up and down St Boniface Down.

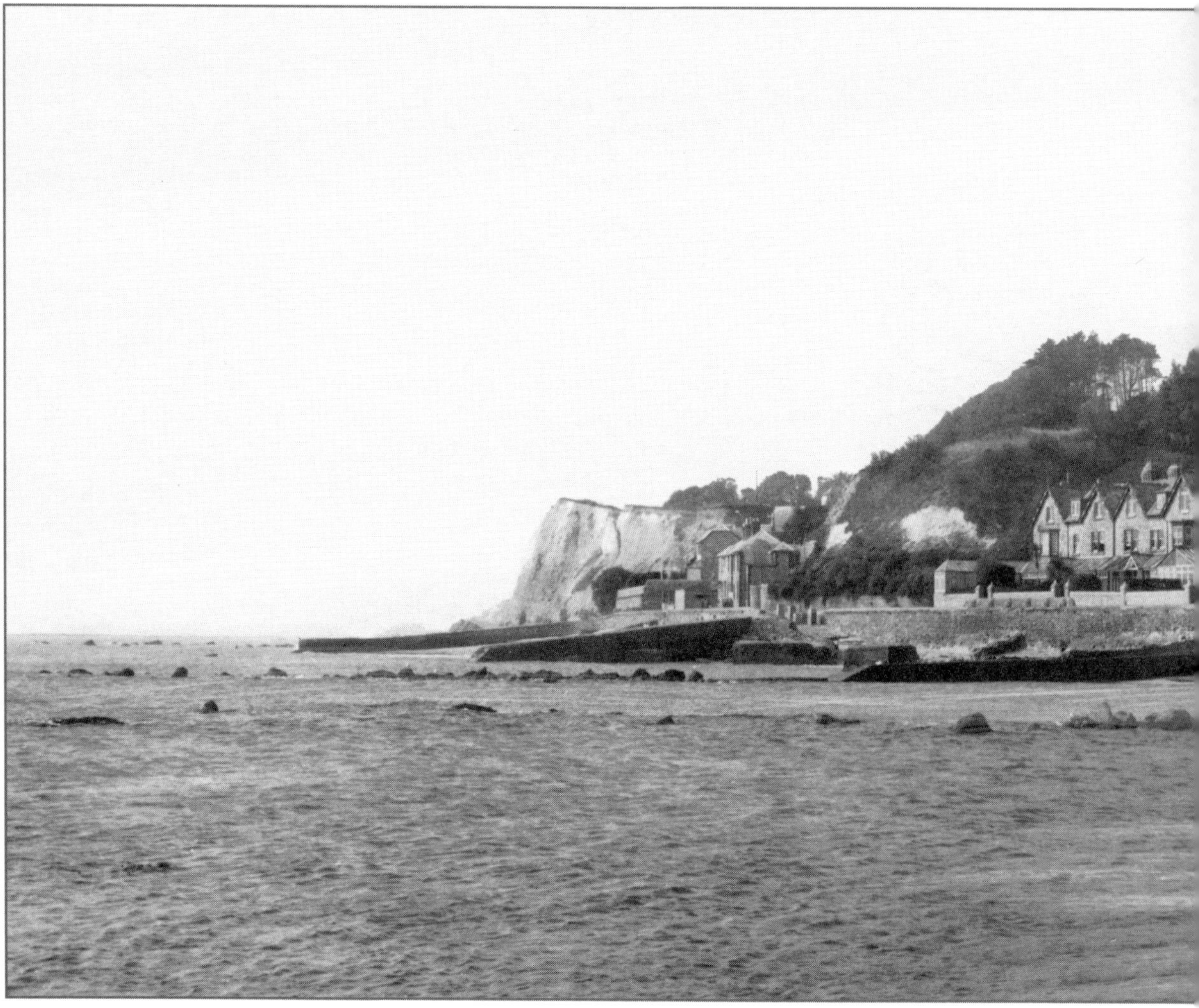

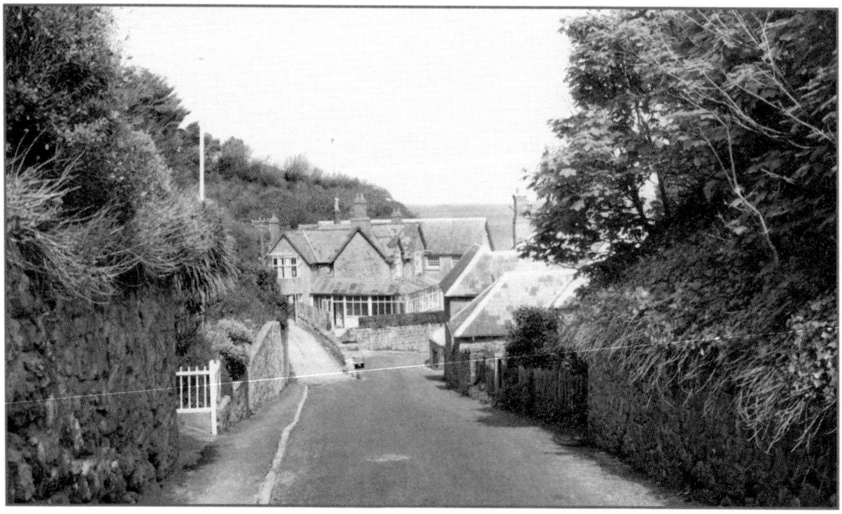

◄ **Bonchurch, The Road to the Beach c1960**
B139109
In 700 AD, a Devon boy called Boniface entered a Hampshire monastery. Coming to the island, he visited the Undercliff and established his church. For all the years and changes, one can still imagine those wild and early days, but now it is tourists and children who make their way eagerly down to the beach.

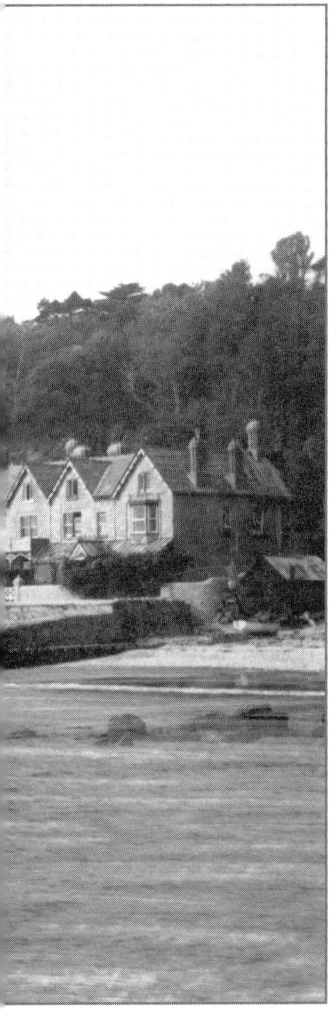

◀ **Bonchurch, The Shore and the Cliffs c1955** B139007
Gentle waves lap the shore line, along which stretches a fine terrace of houses. No wonder so many famous men came here and chose to stay forever. The preacher and writer William Adams, the author of 'The Shadow of the Cross', lived at Winterbourne and is buried in the old churchyard, but perhaps Swinburne is the most famous person to be buried here. The old church, built near the sea, has a simple 13th-century nave and chancel. A new church was built higher up in 1847.

▼ **Bonchurch, The Beach c1960** B139115
We are looking to the north-east, close to where the 19th-century training ship 'Eurydice' met its doom. Tourists, dressed for the part, have motored down in their new Ford Consul. Parked in behind is an Italian Farina-styled Austin A40, one of the first true hatchbacks. The times when you could have any colour car so long as it was black are long gone, and the swinging sixties age of merchandising is almost here! Tables, chairs and umbrellas beckon towards the delights of the Crab and Lobster Tea Garden.

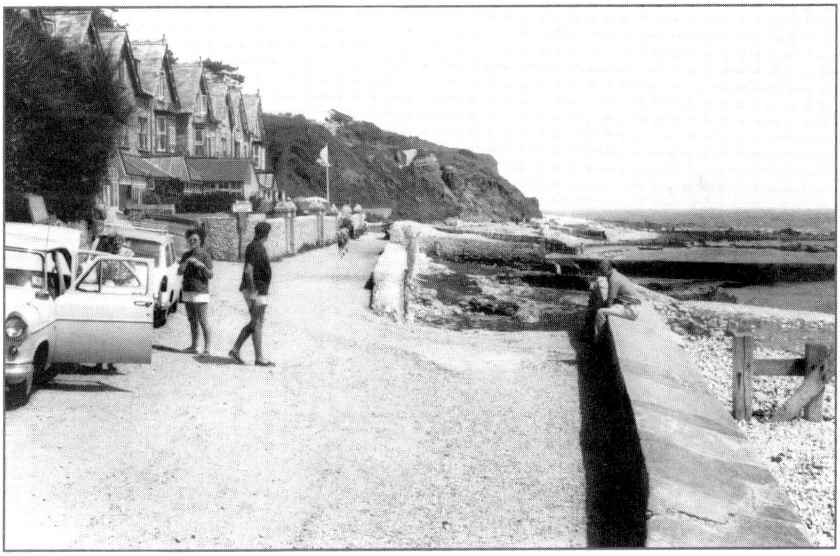

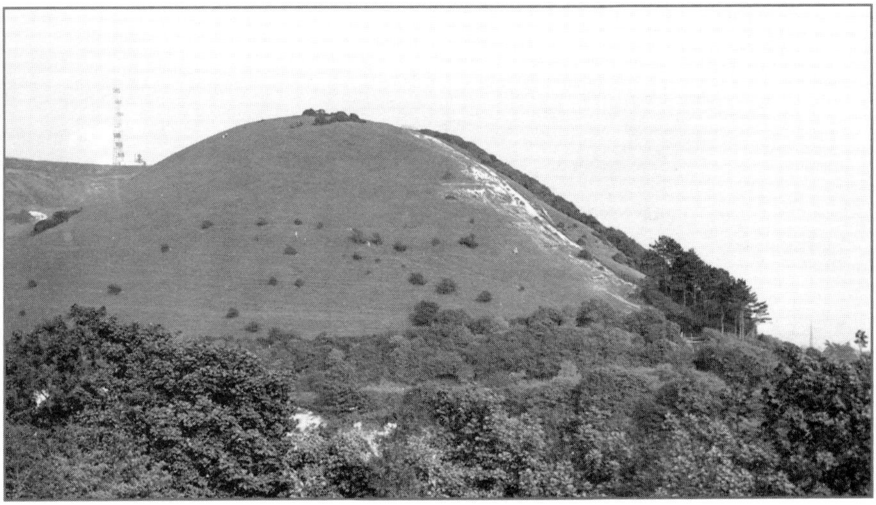

◀ **Ventnor, St Boniface Down c1955** V1023
The highest point, at 787 feet (240 metres) offers views over the southern cliffs. The mast is evidence of the area's importance in early radar research; it monitored the D-Day landings and is now a Civil Aviation Authority radar station. The downland is very accessible to walkers; the grass is often interwoven with wild plants and orchids.

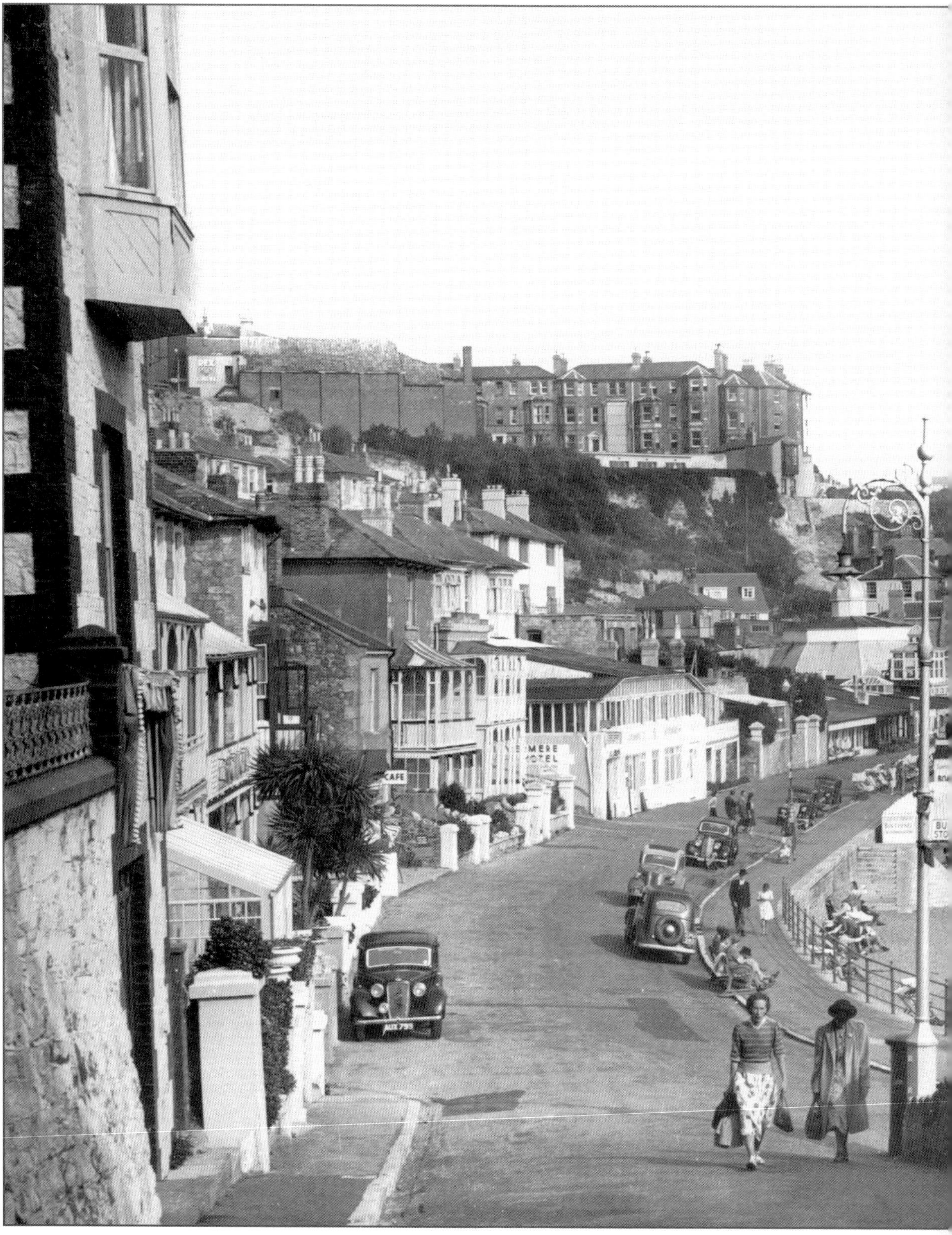
CAFE
HOTEL
BATHING

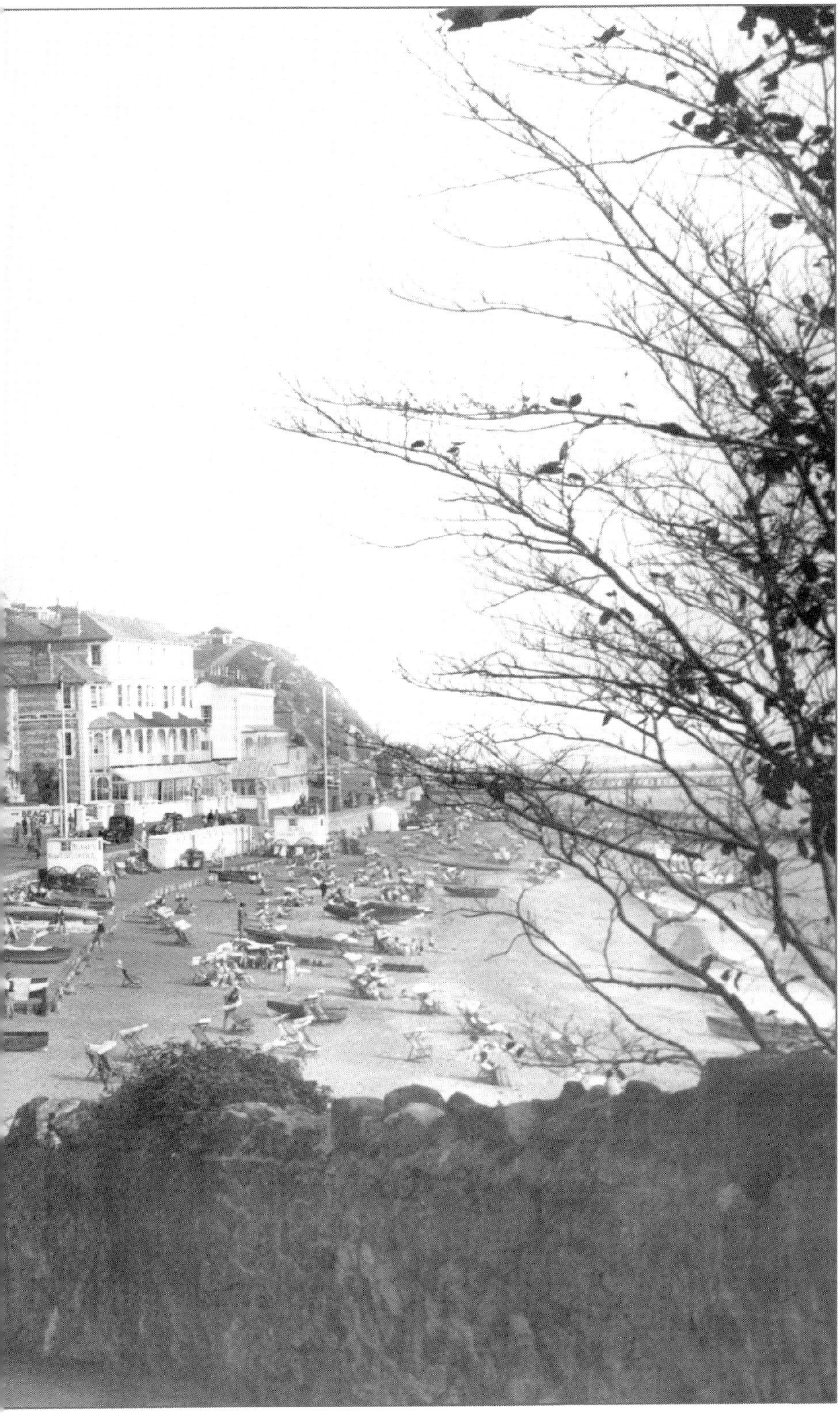

**Ventnor**
**From the West c1950**
V1020
Ventnor shelters under Boniface Down; this view shows houses rising in steep terraces. From a cluster of fishermen's cottages, the town expanded as a health resort. Sir James Clarke promoted Ventnor through his treatise 'The Influence of Climate in the Prevention and Cure of Organic Diseases'. The town is sited within a complex of landslide areas, which is a permanent worry for property owners.

▼ **Ventnor, The Beach c1950** V1016

The mighty cliff rises beyond the broken pier. The great undercliff extends for seven miles from Dunose Point to Blackgang Chine, offering all the picturesque scenery of wild vegetation and blocks made to tumble from regular buffeting by sea and storm. The intricacy of Ventnor's building line blends perfectly with this distinguished landscape.

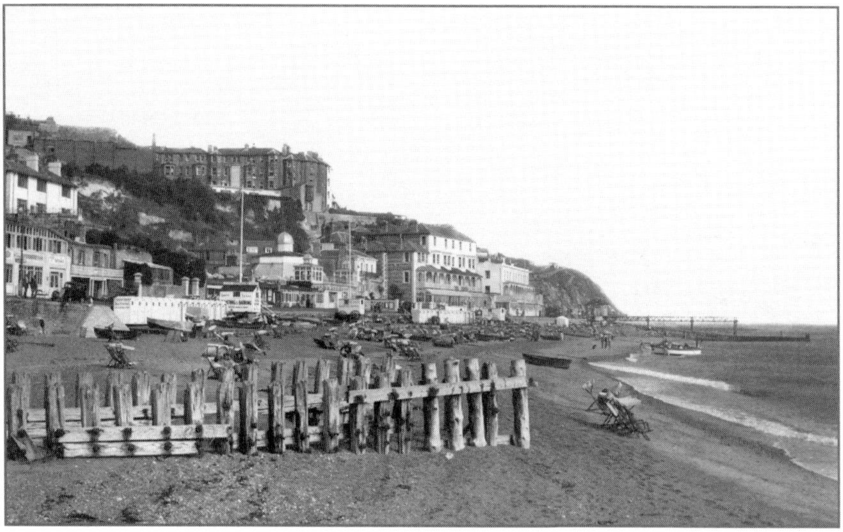

▼ **Ventnor, The Beach c1950** V1054

We are moving closer toward the beach. Could it possibly be more crowded? This is the English seaside at its very best, with crowds of baskers and bathers, and majestic limousines. The Milk Bar is the only sign of imminent youth culture.

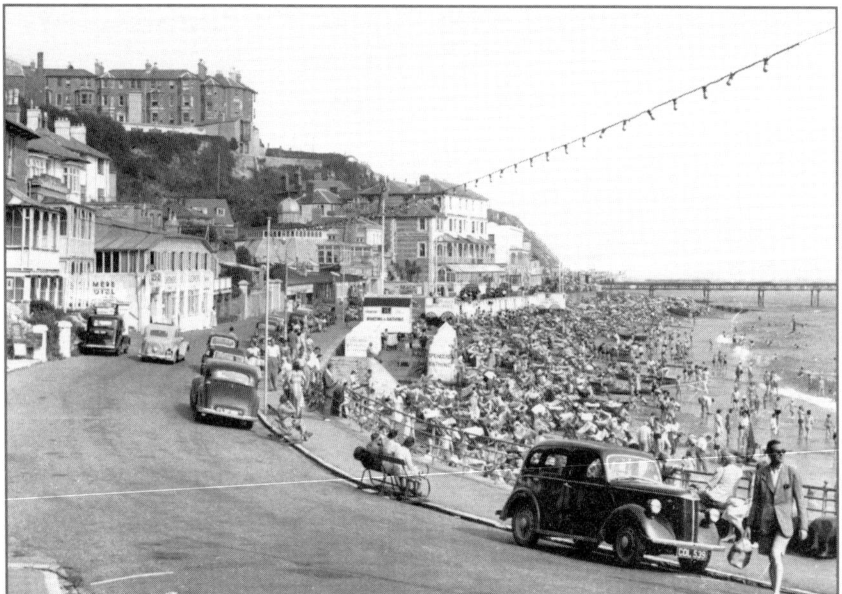

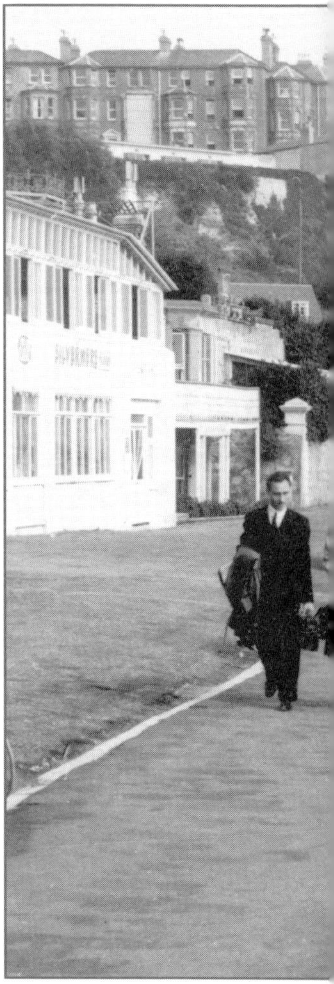

▲ **Ventnor The Promenade c1950**

V1004

The 19th-century pier was built to land visitors directly from the mainland, but here it looks as if it has taken too much battering from the weather. Curious-looking old bathing machines remind us of a time even further in the past, with advertisements for Blake's boating and bathing with ladies' and gents' bathing accommodation. The Hotel Metropole stands ready to welcome a flow of discriminating holidaymakers.

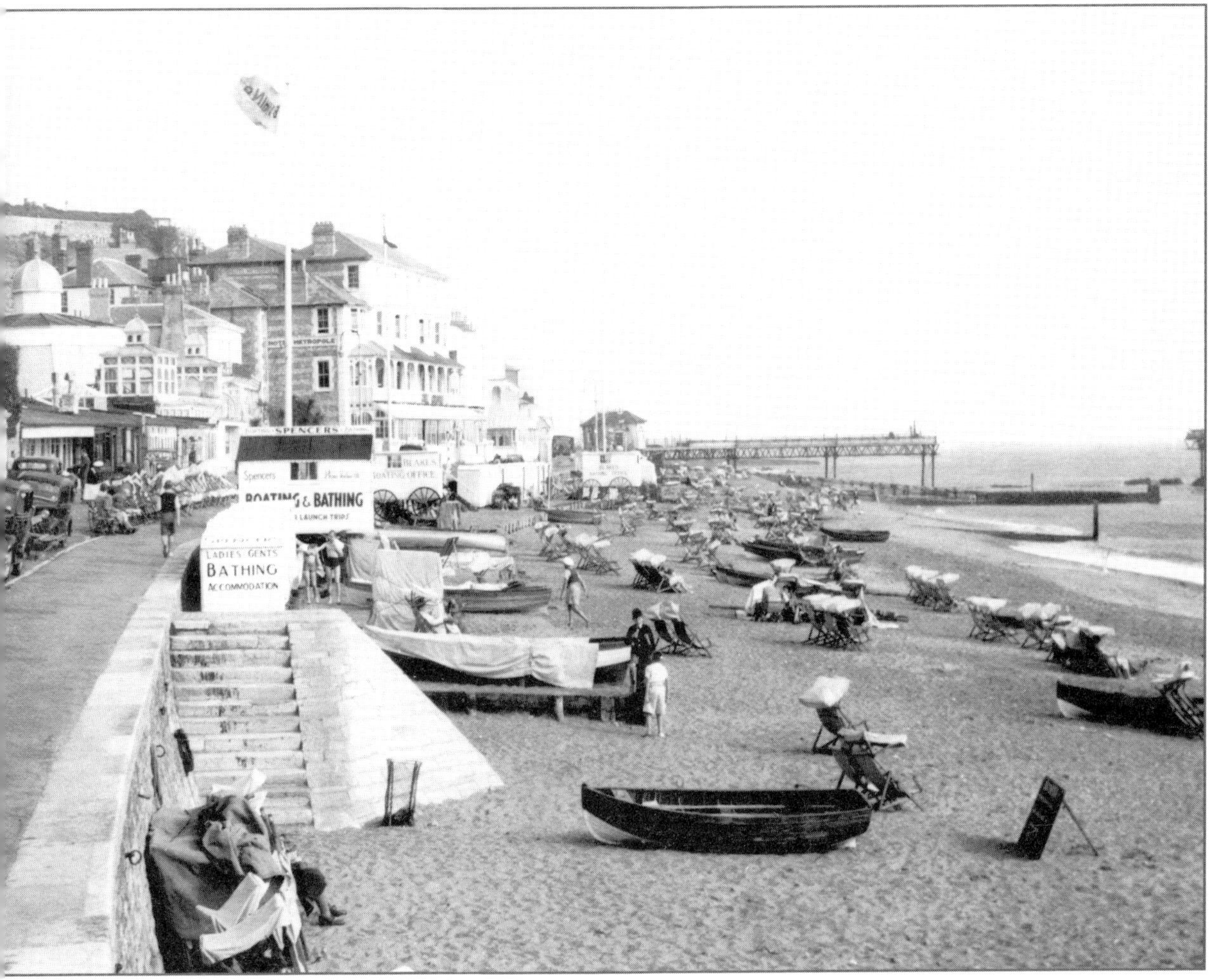


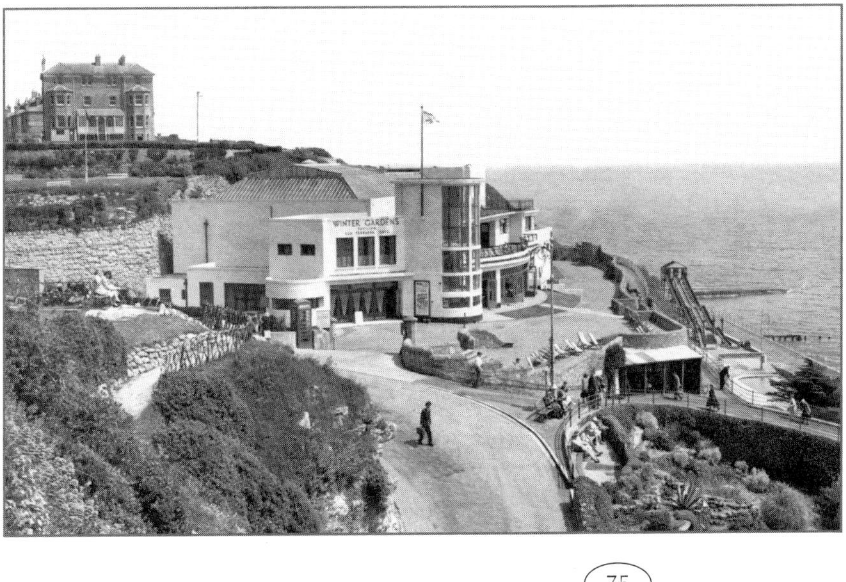


◄ **Ventnor**
**The Winter Gardens**
**c1950** V1027

Flights of stone steps and zig-zagging roads link the town's different levels; here, a hairpin bend leads down past the Winter Gardens, centre of so much evening entertainment. We also glimpse something of the exotic gardens. By the sea, a tall slide offers excitement for the youngsters, but these days they prefer to skateboard down the steeply descending roads and paths.

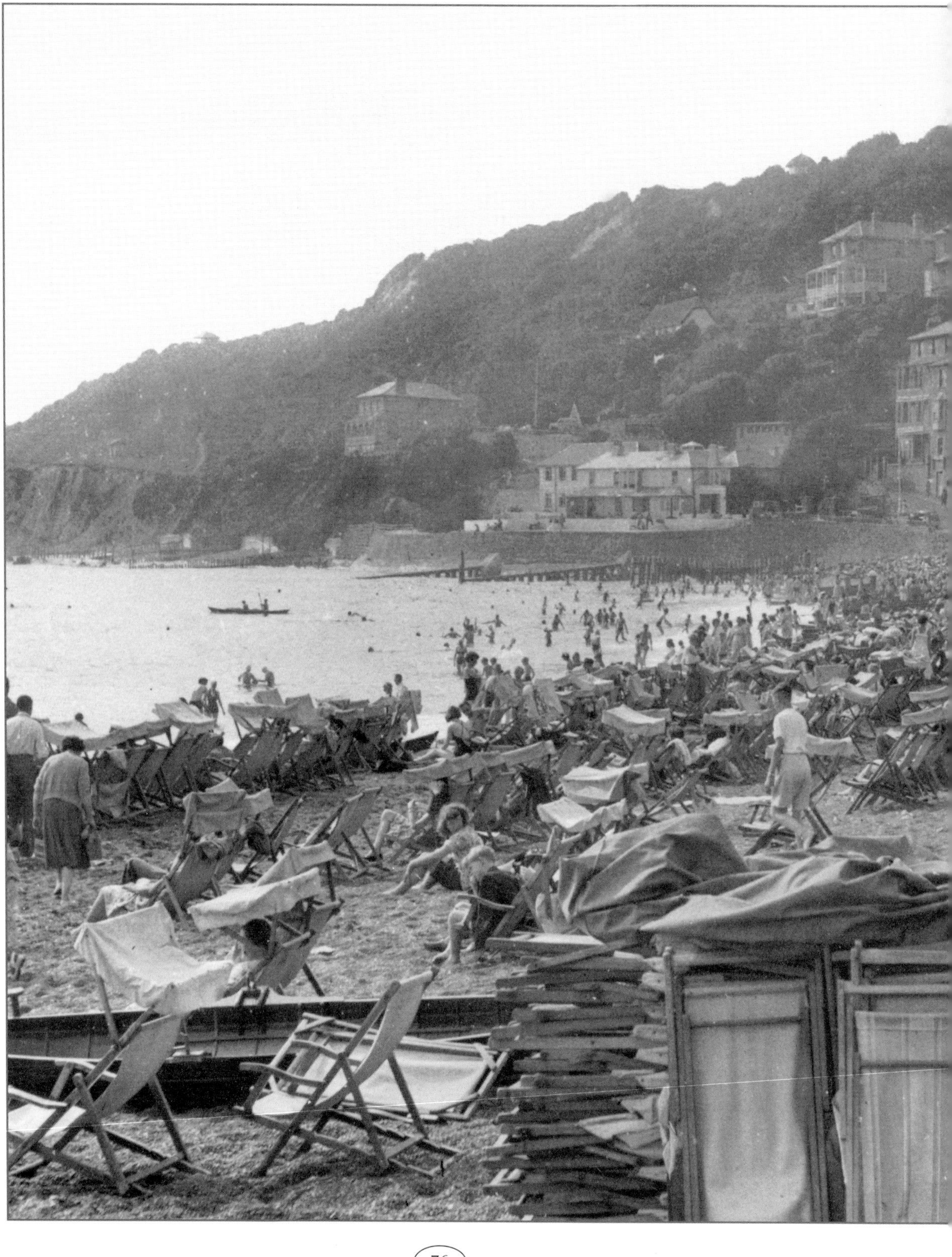

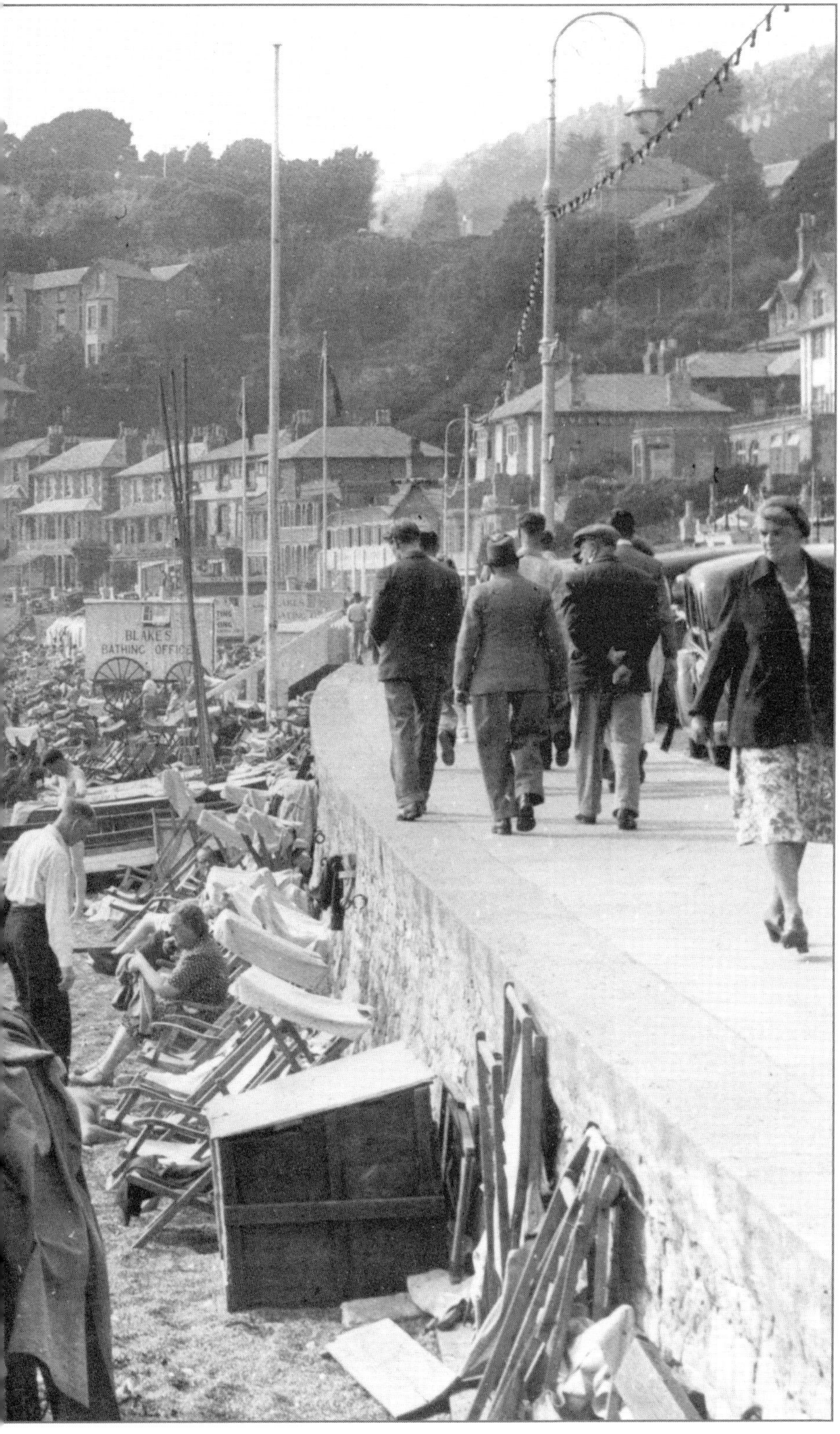


**Ventnor, The Beach c1950** V1044
This view west along the beach had hardly changed since the turn of the century, when long-skirted ladies lounged in deck chairs or boldly popped into bathing machines. Even now, the scene is much the same.

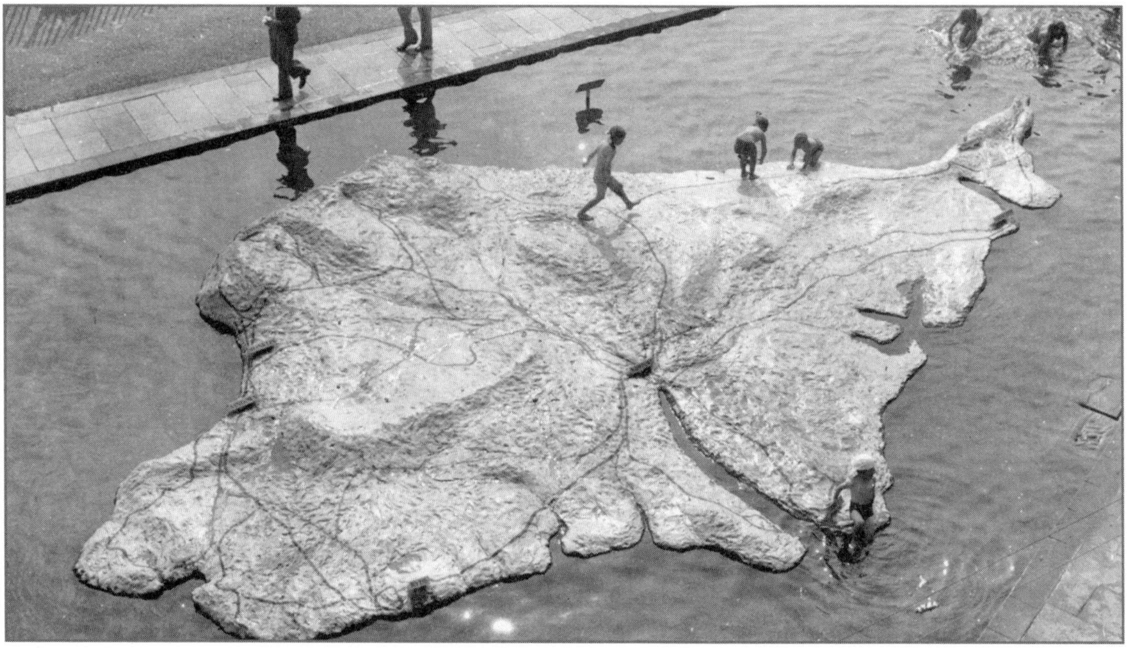

**Ventnor, The Childrens' Pool c1950** V1040
What better way to teach the children local geography than with this large-scale model of the island in a pool. The huge gash, bottom centre, represents the Medina Estuary, leading to Newport. Far right, or west, is Yarmouth and Freshwater. Sandown and Shanklin are in the bay, left, and Ventnor on the Undercliff just beyond.

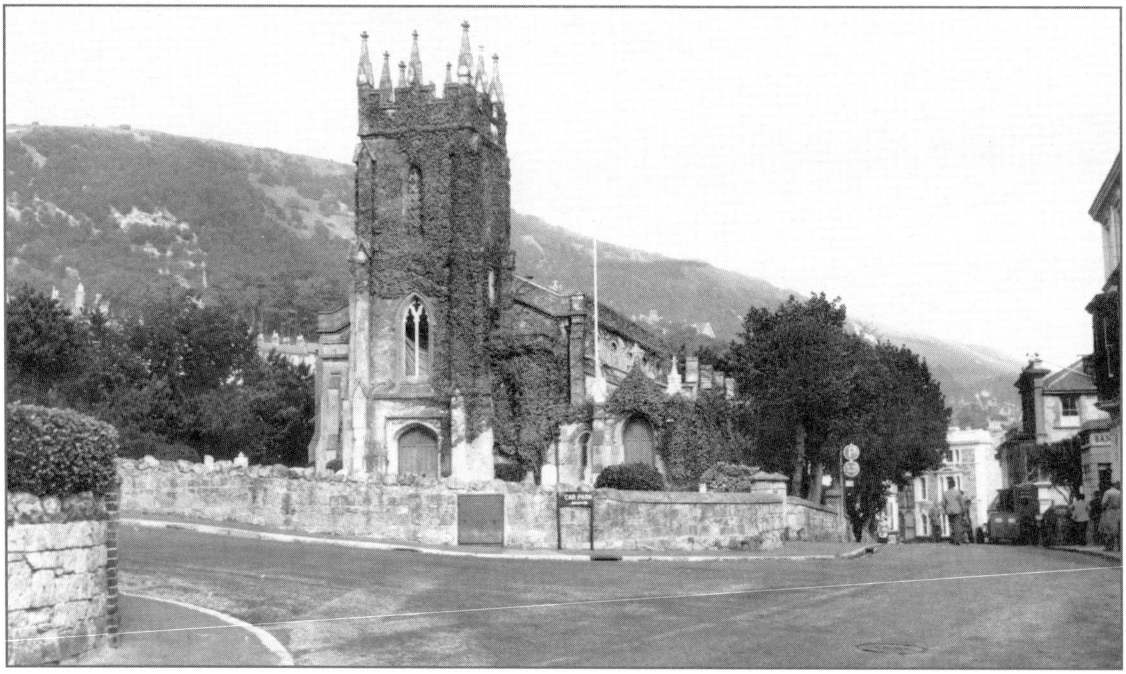

**Ventnor, St Catherine's Church c1950** V1001
The town is well off for churches. This one was the first to be built; it is of local stone with a pinnacled tower in 13th-century style.

# Beyond the Point

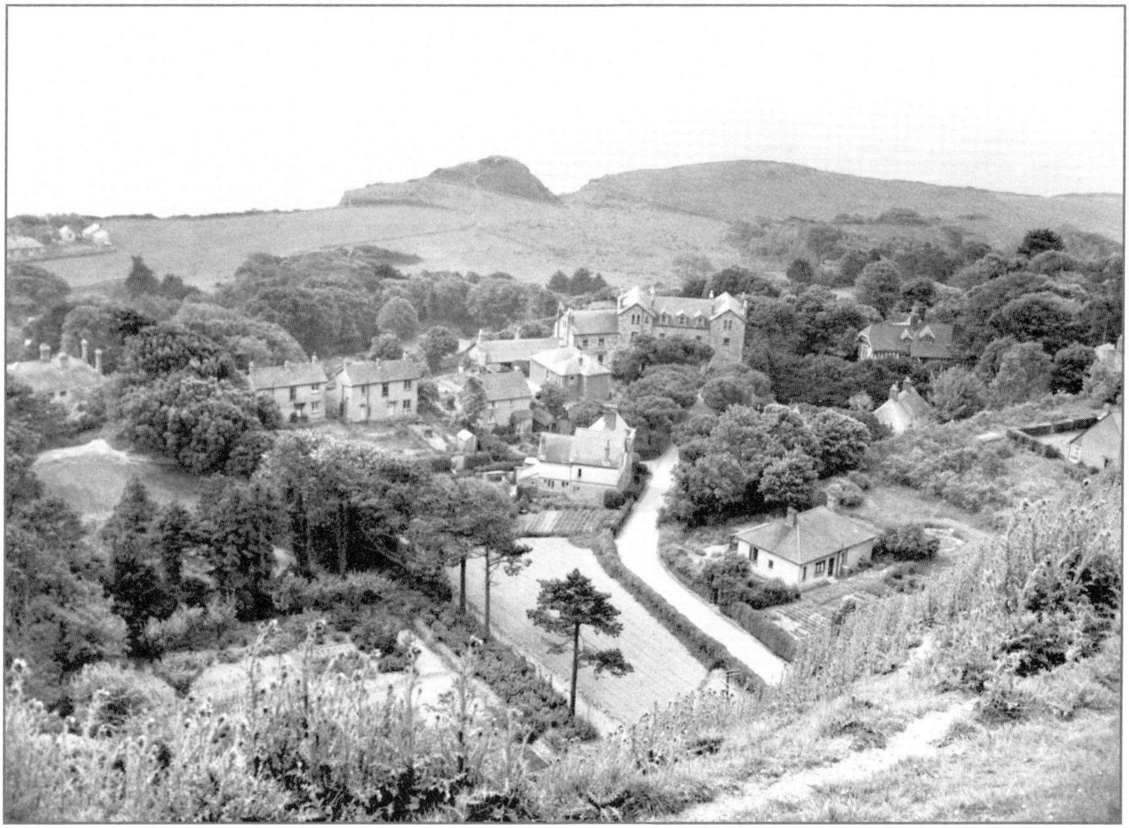

**St Lawrence**
**From the Top Cliff c1955** S573035
Moving towards St Catherine's, the southernmost point, we reach St Lawrence. Though older than Ventnor, with a 13th-century church, the two settlements have joined. A chapel dedicated to St Mary was built in the 13th century, becoming part of the church. This fine view shows grand and small houses nestled between leafy trees and undergrowth.

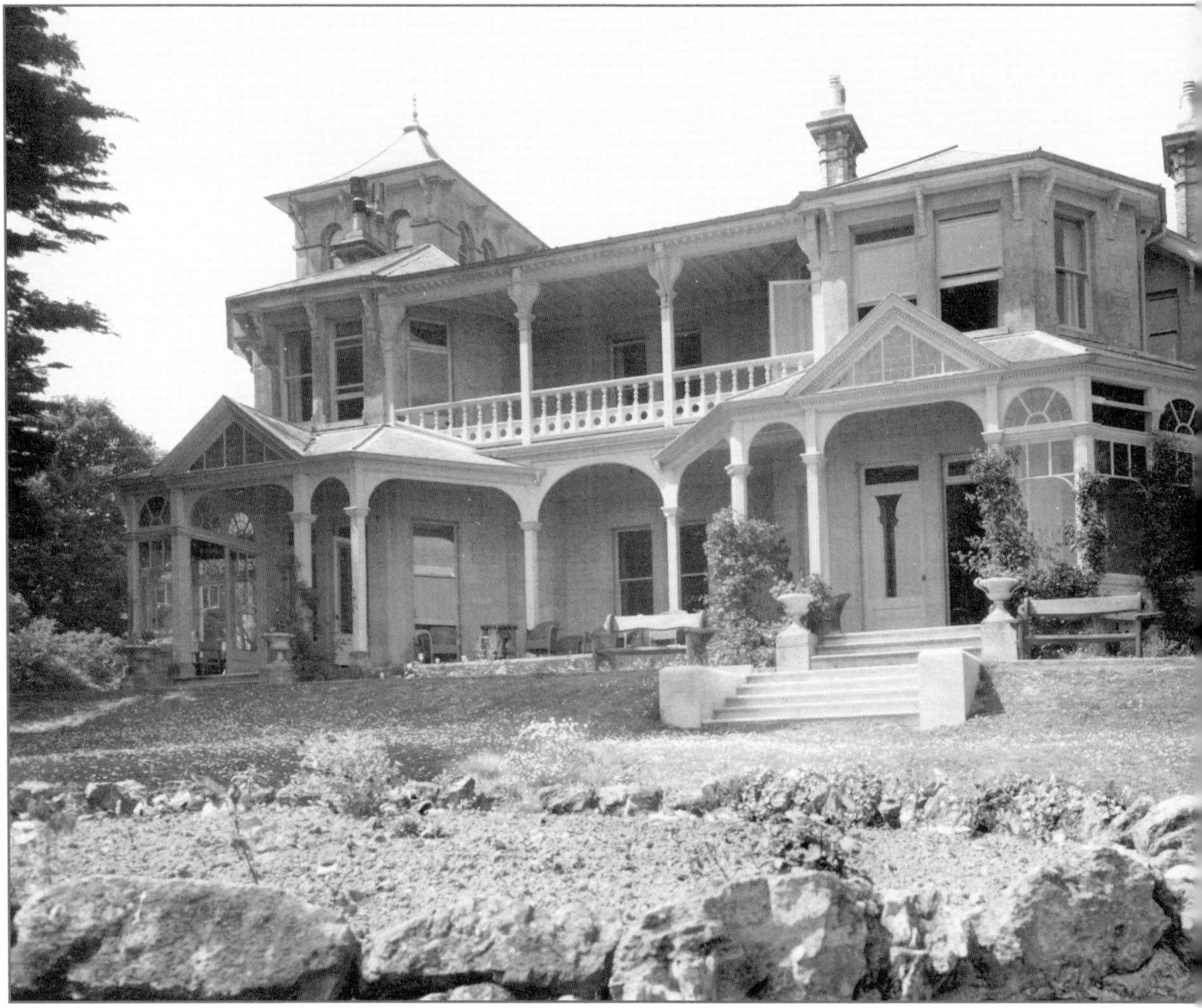

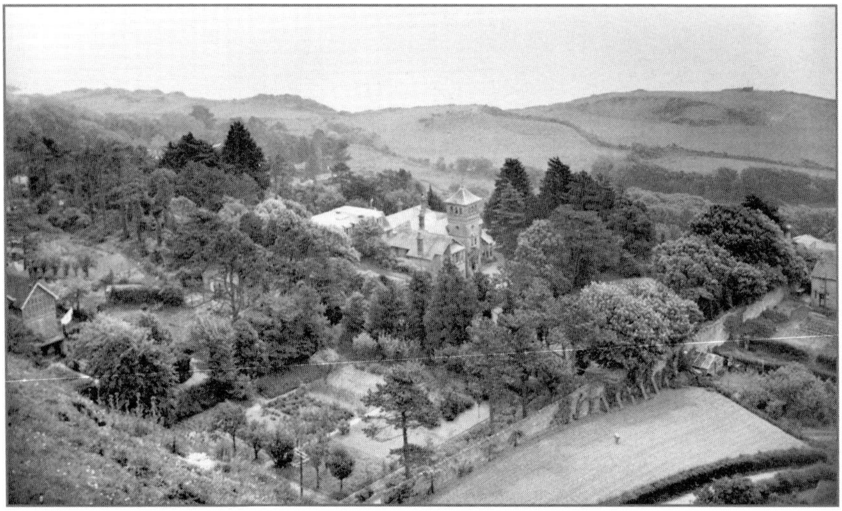

**St Lawrence St Rhadegund's from the Downs c1960**

S573032

The great house just peeping through the trees is seen here from the heights; it seems a little bit of paradise. Medieval pilgrims landed on the south coast at Puckaster Cove, crossing the down to the Holy Well of Our Lady and St Rhadegund at Whitewell, returning by a path known as St Rhadegund's path.

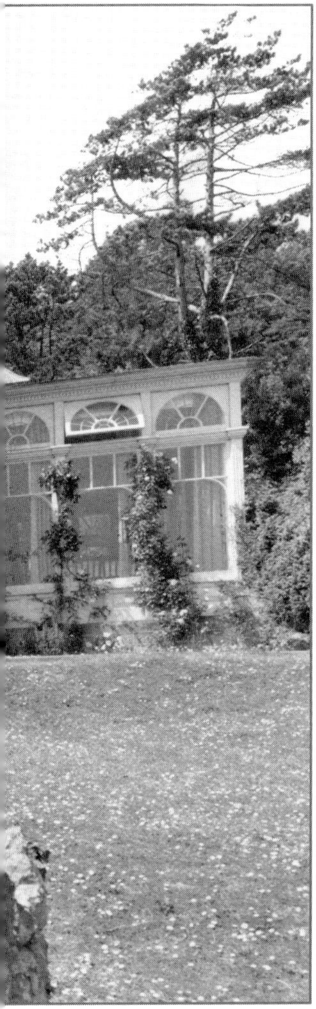

◄ **St Lawrence St Rhadegund's House from the South c1960**

S573001

St Rhadegund, a Germanic princess, was the patron saint of the de Estur family. Captured and taken to France, she founded a convent. This fine residence commemorates the name and local association.

▼ **St Lawrence, Woody Bay c1955** S573029

This is an area of landslip, the famous undercliff; here, too, are ancient hunting parks - Old Park, once island governor Sir Richard Worsley's estate, is one of 3 old hunting parks. This view shows the bay living up to its 'woody' name. It is a fine habitat for over 300 species of exotic bird within the Tropical Bird Park.

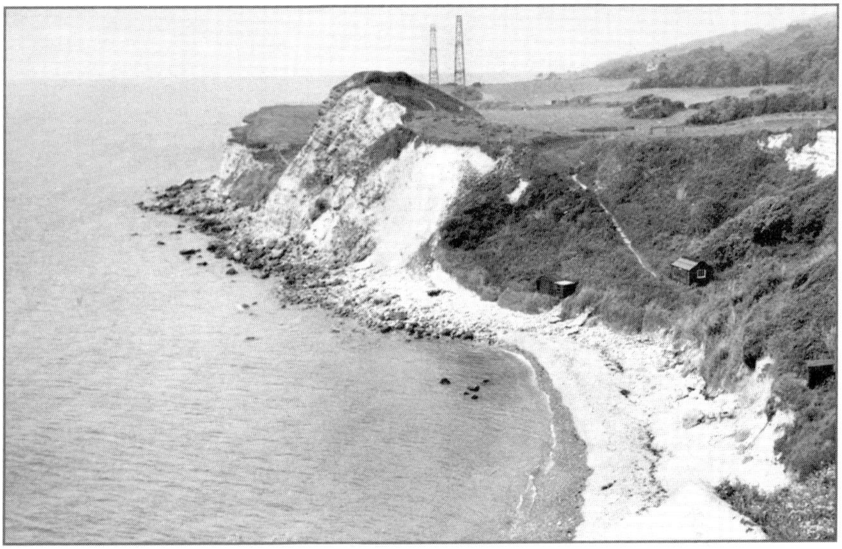

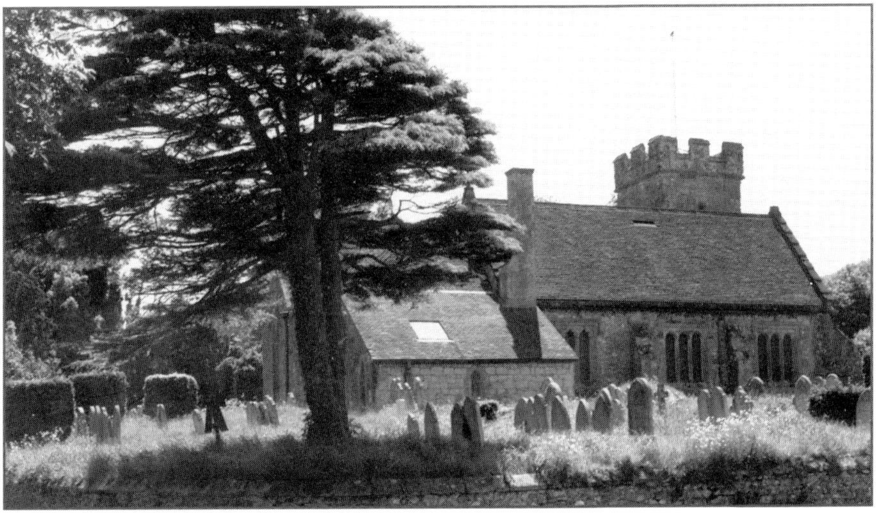

◄ **Whitwell The Church c1955**

W467003

The churchyard looks overgrown, perhaps because relatives are too old or have moved away in this more mobile age. The village is set in rolling downland north of St Lawrence; it was once the site of two chapels, one dedicated to St Rhadegund, the other to the Virgin Mary, now made into one.

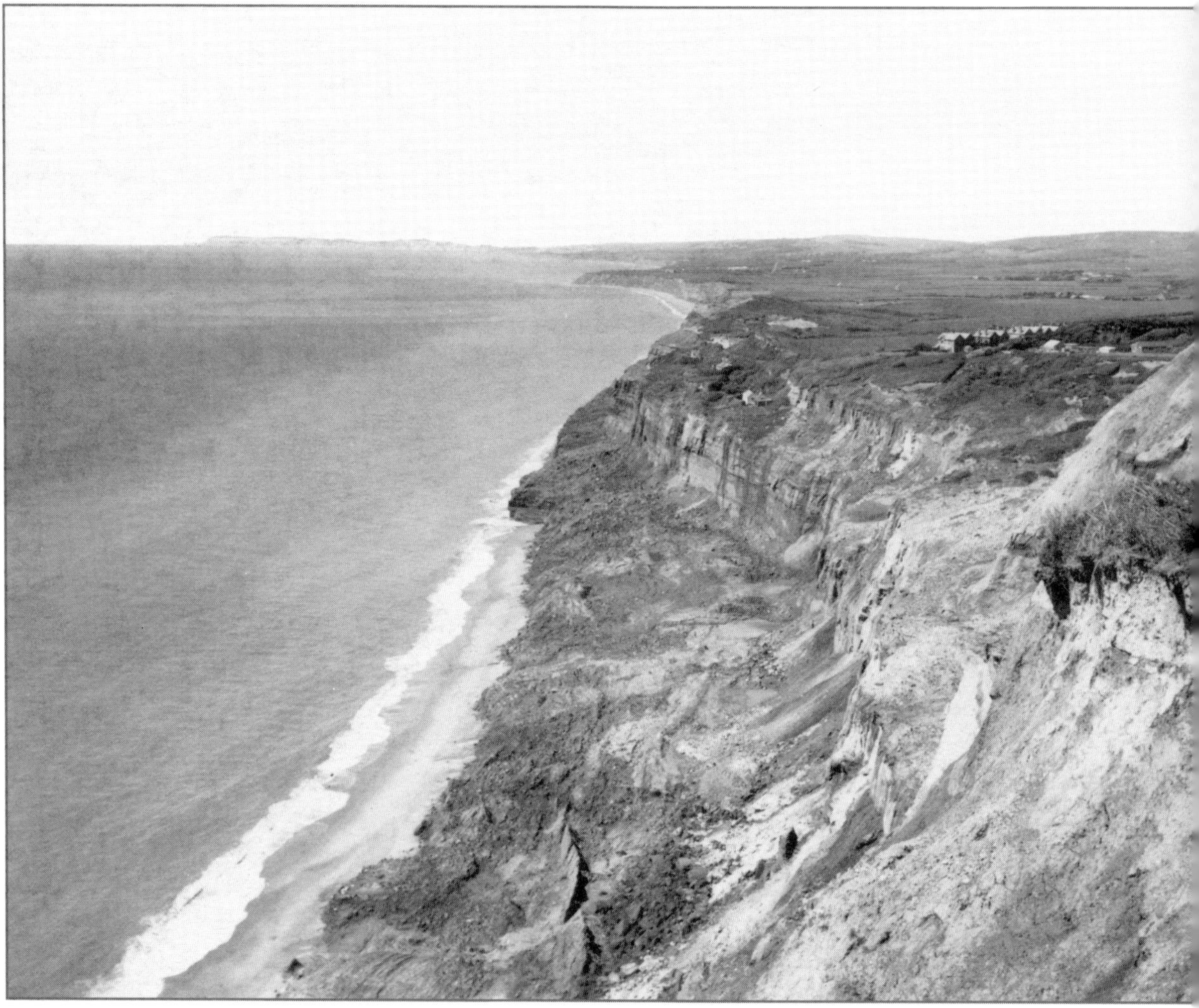

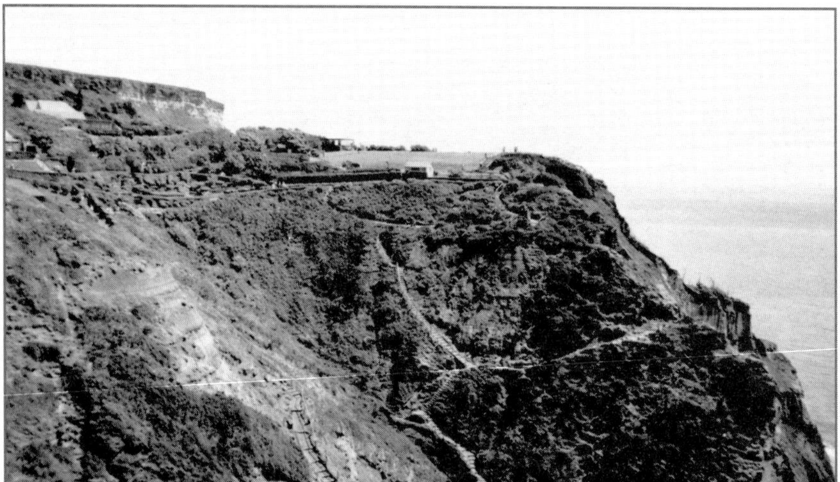

◄ **Blackgang Chine c1960**
B113038
Human intrusion is well evidenced here; the area has become increasingly commercialised, with attractions like Buffalo Creek, and Isle of Wight County mimicking the Wild West and the Grand Canyon. But it would take a lot to diminish the ancient charm of the area. The ruins of a 14th-century lighthouse are out of view here, on the coastline.

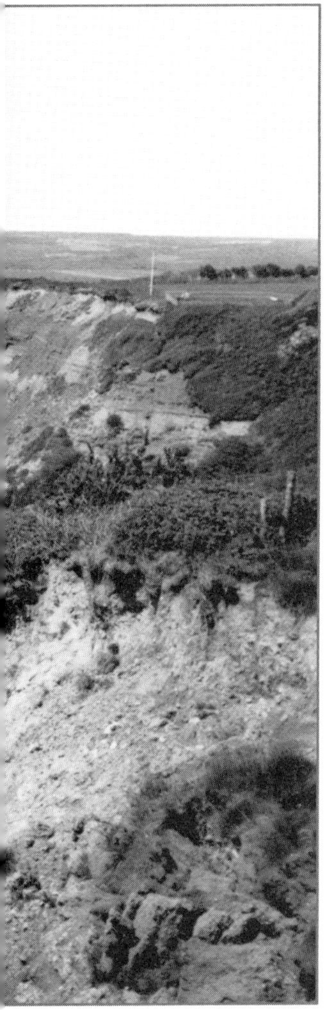

◀ **Blackgang Chine, The Cliffs c1960** B113037

Rounding St Catherine's Point, we reach the dramatic scenery of Blackgang Chine. Through millions of years, soft sands and clays slipped over the underlying gault clay to form the green and abundant world of the Undercliff. It is a haven for wild plant and animal life. The Chine is a great cleft in the bright yellow sandstone and blue clays of the cliff. St Catherine' s Point and Down offers commanding views of the south coast and beyond, the Needles.

▼ **Blackgang Chine The Gardens c1960**

B113040

The Chine plunges 400 feet. Popular with smugglers, it remained savage until tamed by the Victorians. These gardens are testimony to their achievement. For an even better view, someone has set up a telescope, top right.

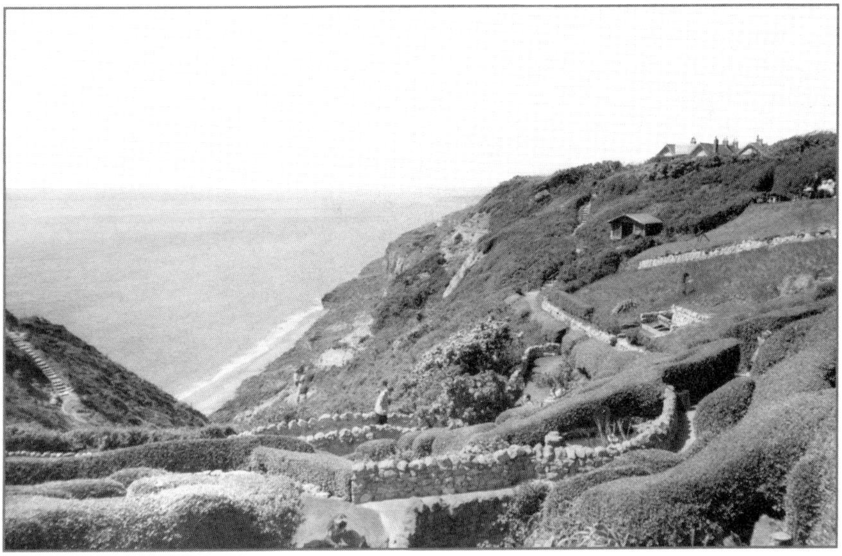

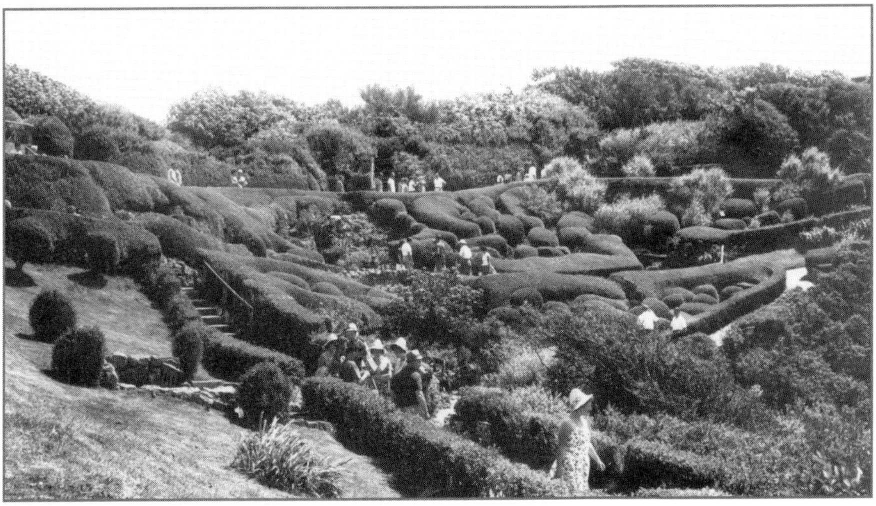

◀ **Blackgang Chine The Gardens c1955**

B113054

What a day this must have been. The heat would have been bringing out all those summer aromas of plants and cut grass, while the blue sky gave these mere mortals the illusion of peace and timelessness. This looks a far better day out than the local Jaws of Death and Mouth of Hell that appeared in the Blackgang of the 1970s.

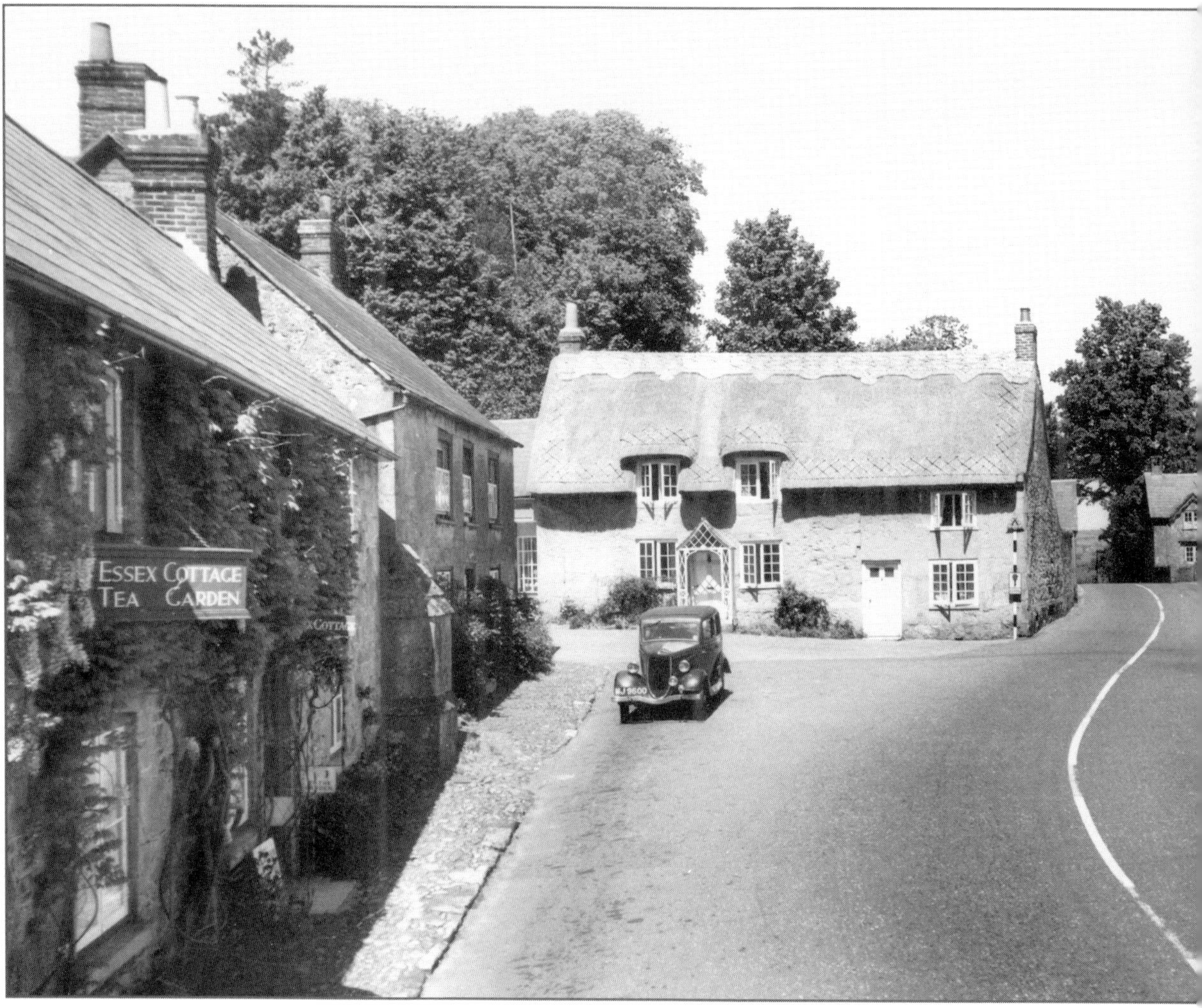


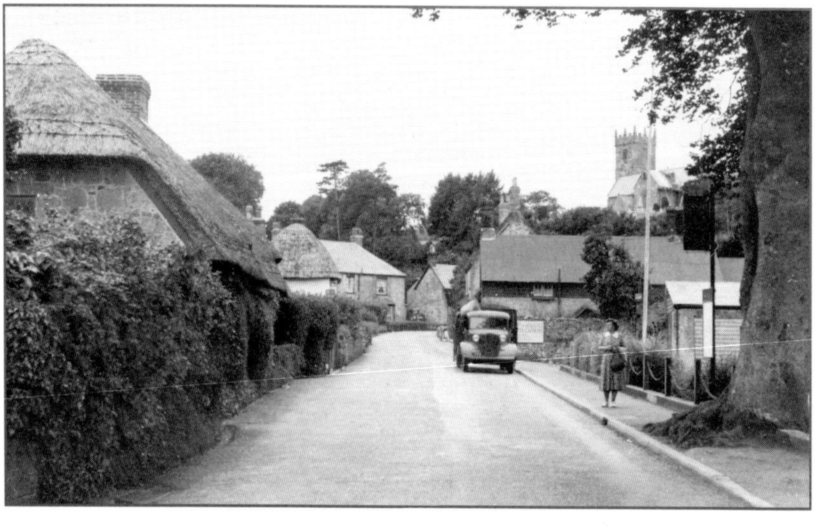

**Godshill, The Village c1950**
G26007
Here we see more traditional thatched cottages, and a neatly dressed lady waiting for the bus in the Shanklin direction. Perhaps she has just left the Hollies Tea Gardens, behind her. A well-loaded truck waits by the kerb - how small they were then! The church looks as if it is keeping watch. The story was that it was going to be built lower down the slope, but the stones were mysteriously moved higher up the hill every night while workmen were trying to start the job.

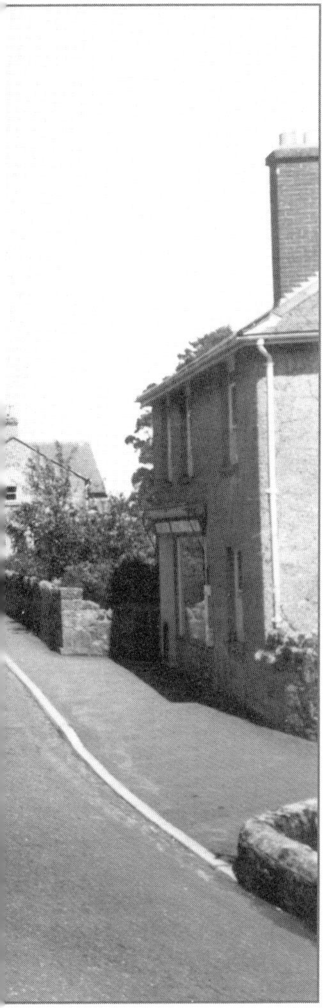

**Godshill, The Village c1950** G26033

The village is strung out along the A3020. A pre-war Ford is parked near the Essex Cottage Tea Rooms. It looks the perfect village, with its own school (the sign is by the corner of the facing thatched cottages). A narrow lane to the left past this cottage leads to the 15th-century church, high on its mound.

**Godshill, The Village c1950** G26019

This is another view of the well-kept properties along the main road. A van is parked dangerously close to the corner, but in those days the traffic did not hurry, and double yellow lines were not needed. In the foreground, somebody is showing off with an American car - so much more stylish than the home-built variety. The tea rooms advertising Hovis under the big tree look inviting.

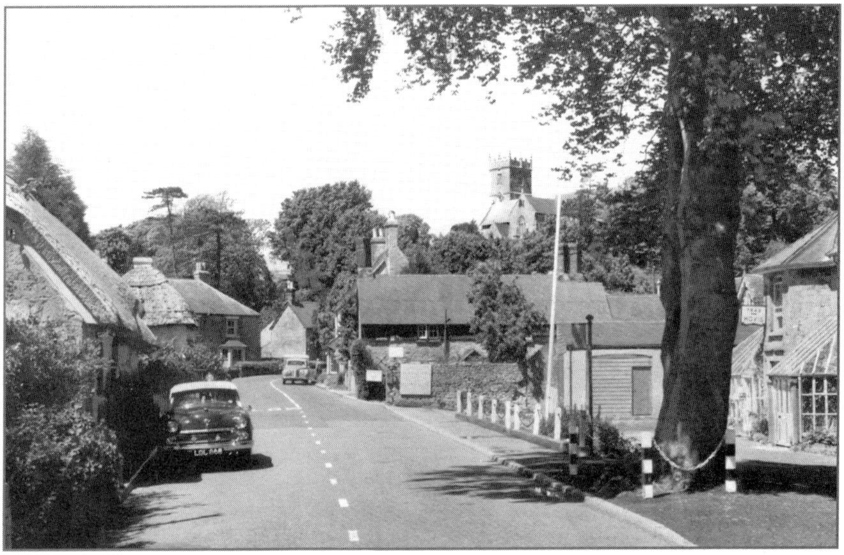

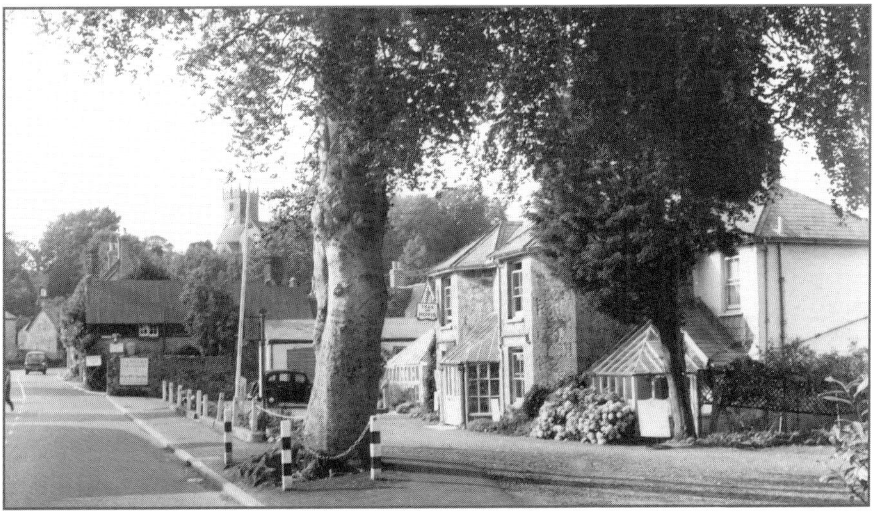

**Godshill, The Hollies Tea Gardens c1955** G26041

Stone built and solid, the tea gardens are very much part of the island's Victorian tradition of tourism. Flowery gardens are among the attractions pulling thousands of tourists here each year.

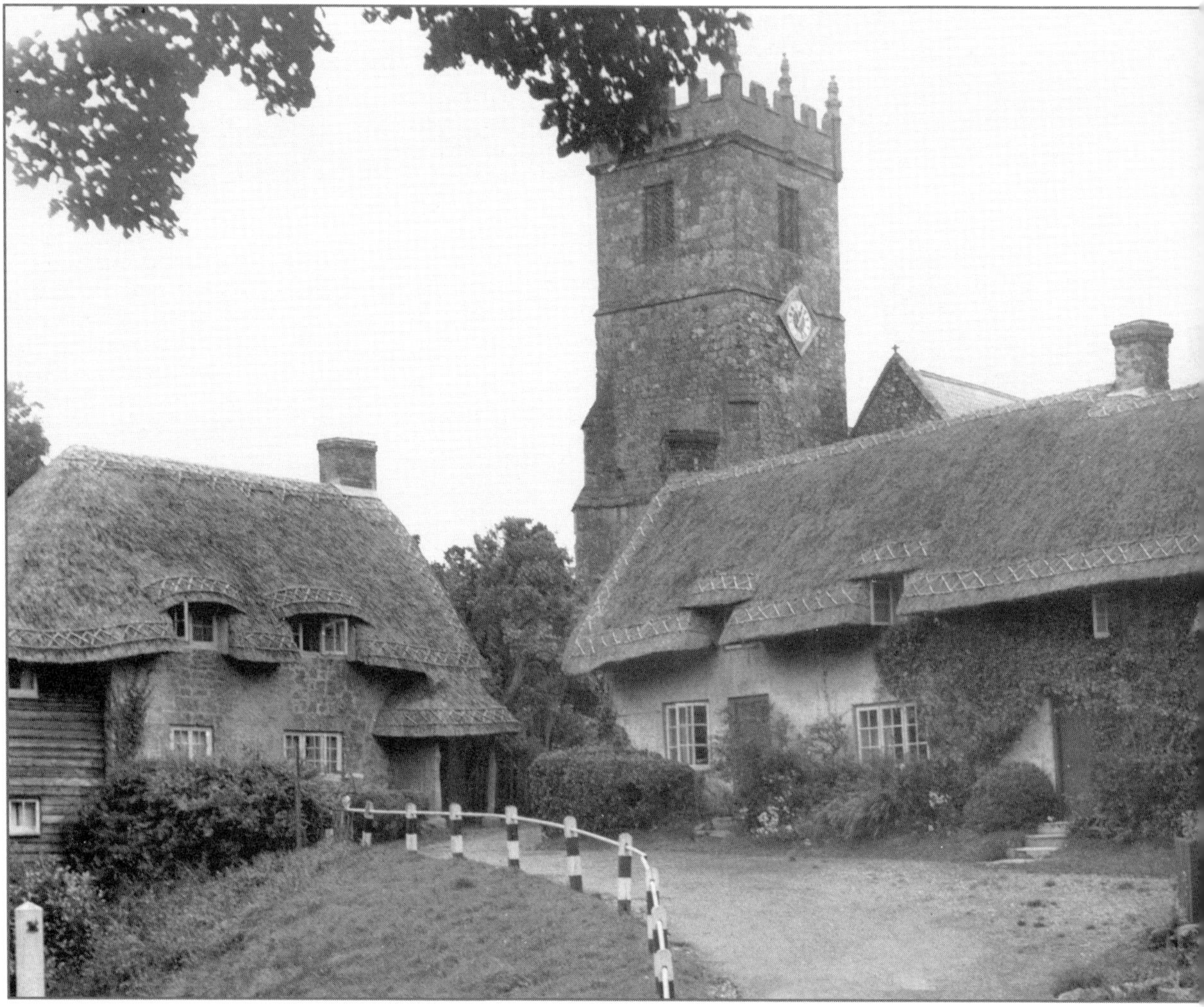

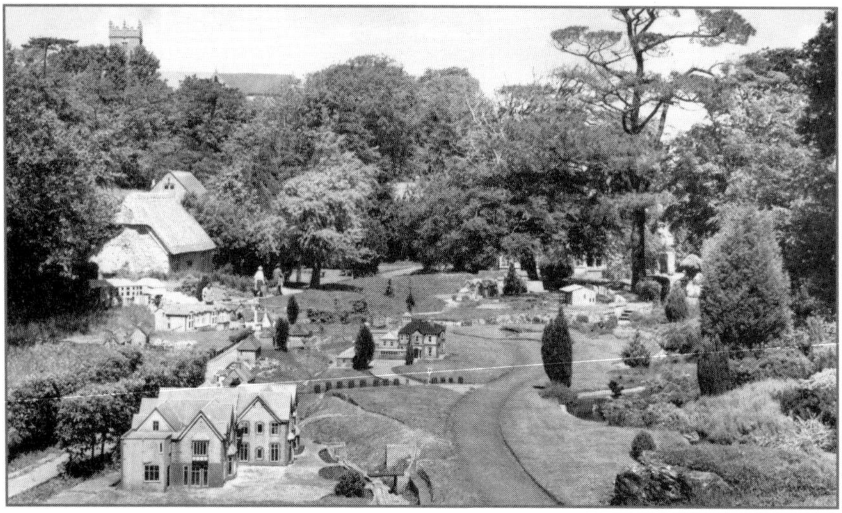

◄ **Godshill, The Model Village c1955** G26022
The village is among many original attractions here. Just west of the church, which we can see above the tree tops, the village is a work of beauty and detail, valued perhaps because it is so much safer and cleaner than reality. It is like a fairy tale among these shrubs and bushes.

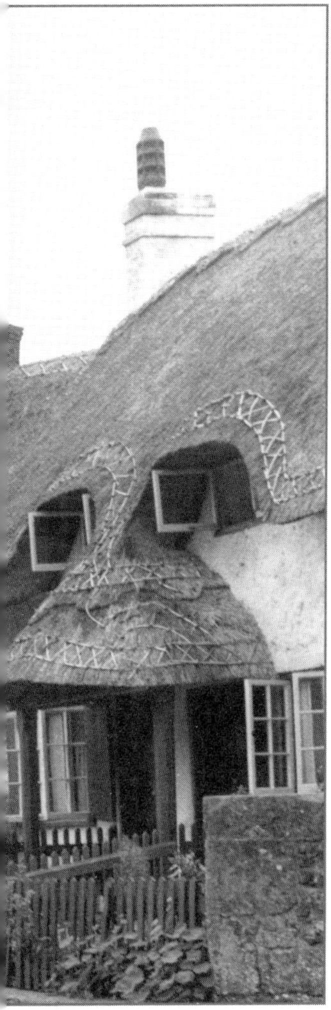

**Godshill, The Church and Thatched Cottages c1955** G26008
This is perhaps one of the most-photographed scenes in England. Godshill's is the largest medieval church on the island. The 1840s Oxford Movement influenced the changes to the interior. The roof is black oak with over half a mile of timbers. There is a 15th- or 16th-century wall painting of a cross on a flowering lily. The church is most remarkable for the tombs in the chancel, which date back to Tudor times; they include the tomb of Sir James Worsley, whose family came over with William the Conqueror. Sir James was page to Henry VII and playmate to Henry VIII, hence the many honours that later came his way.

**Godshill, The Griffin Hotel c1955** G26006
The Worsley's now ruined family home, Appuldercombe, is just south of Godshill. The Griffin Hotel was built by Lord Yarborough, a later owner of Appuldercombe. The griffin was the Worsley family badge.

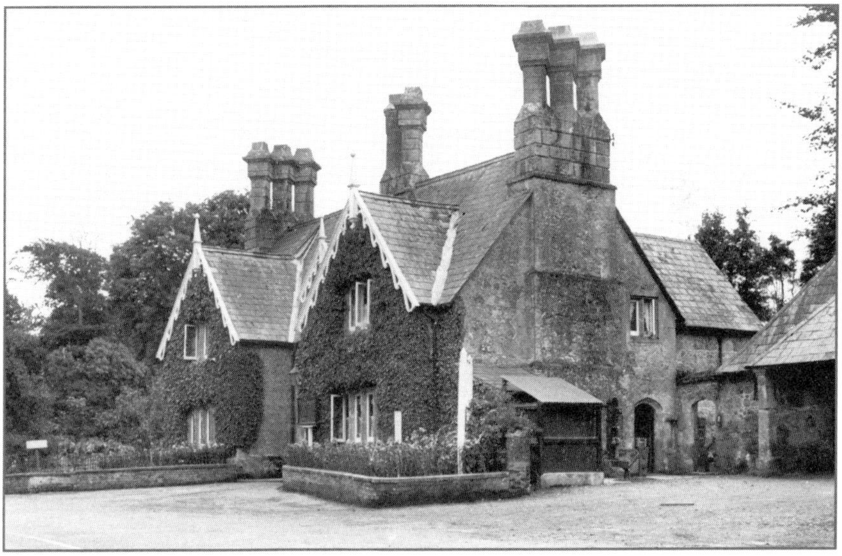

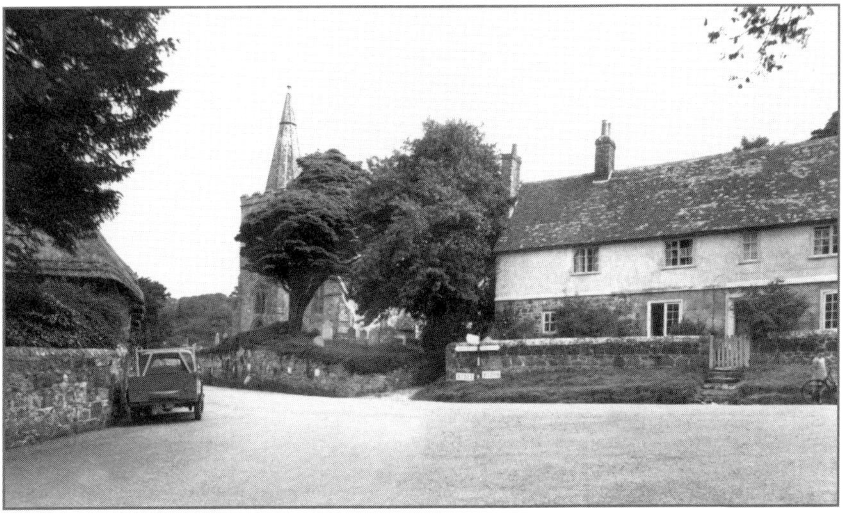

**Shorwell, The Village 1951** S414005
St Peter's spire rises up above the trees, guarding its treasures behind stone walls. The church has a 500-year-old stone pulpit, and among its treasures at the time of this picture was a copy of Cranmer's bible printed in 1541 and a 15th-century wall painting of St Christopher carrying the Christ Child. Looking north, past the church, the sign points along the B3323 to Newport and to the right along the B3399 to Chale and the south coast road.

**▼ Shorwell, The Square c1950** S414003

We are just around the corner from view No S414005. Solidly-built houses testify to the long-term prosperity of old Shorwell, which has three manor houses. The Deputy Governor built Wolverton Manor for £800; it is E-shaped in honour of Queen Elizabeth I.

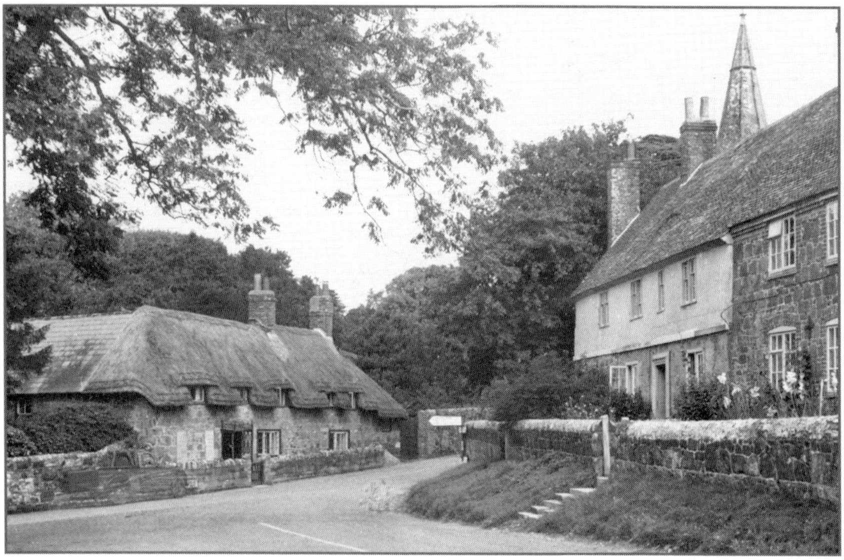

**▼ Shorwell, The Crown Inn c1950** S414004

The Inn is functional in style. With its stream-side garden and hot meals, it was a cosy place to repose. Tucked away under the downs and bowered in trees, it is next to delightful cottages.

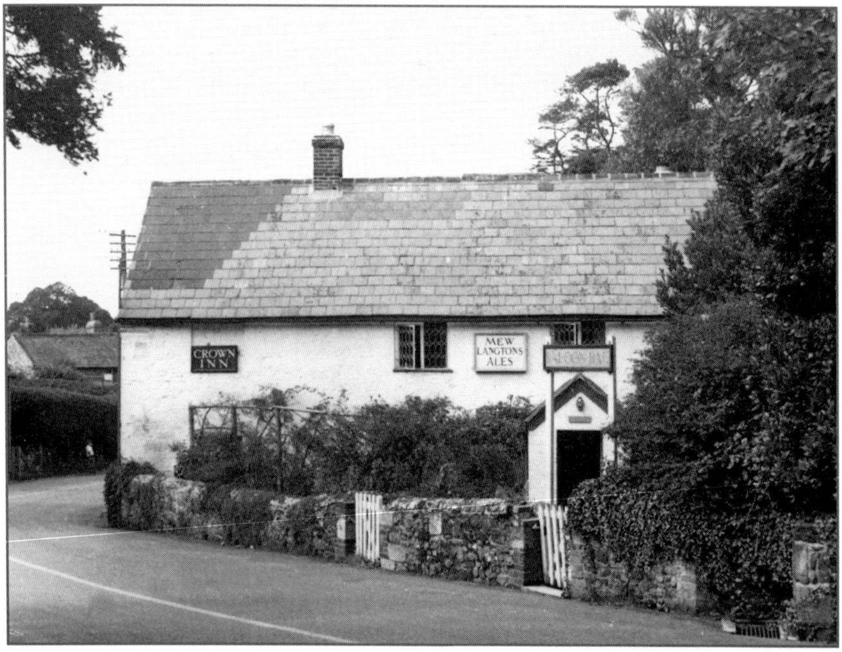


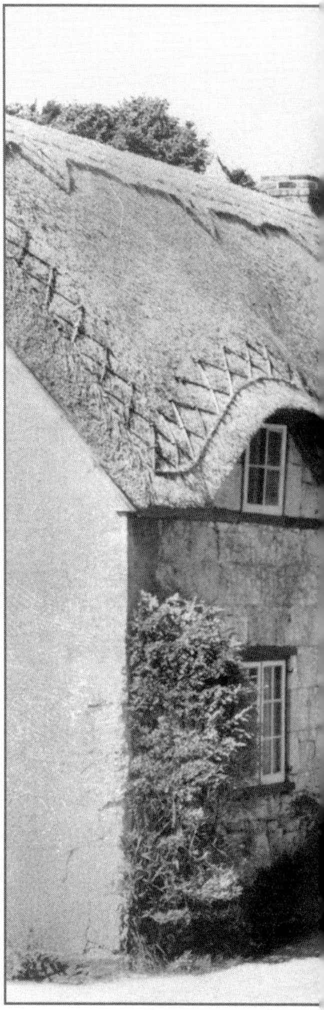

**▲ Brighstone Old Cottages c1960**

B543013

Brighstone- pronounced 'Brixton' locally- shelters under Brighstone Down, which rises to 700 feet; from here the island can be seen almost from end to end. The forest is mainly beech, with displays of spring flowers in its copses; there are ferns and lichens in the older woods, which are alive with red squirrels, foxes and badgers.

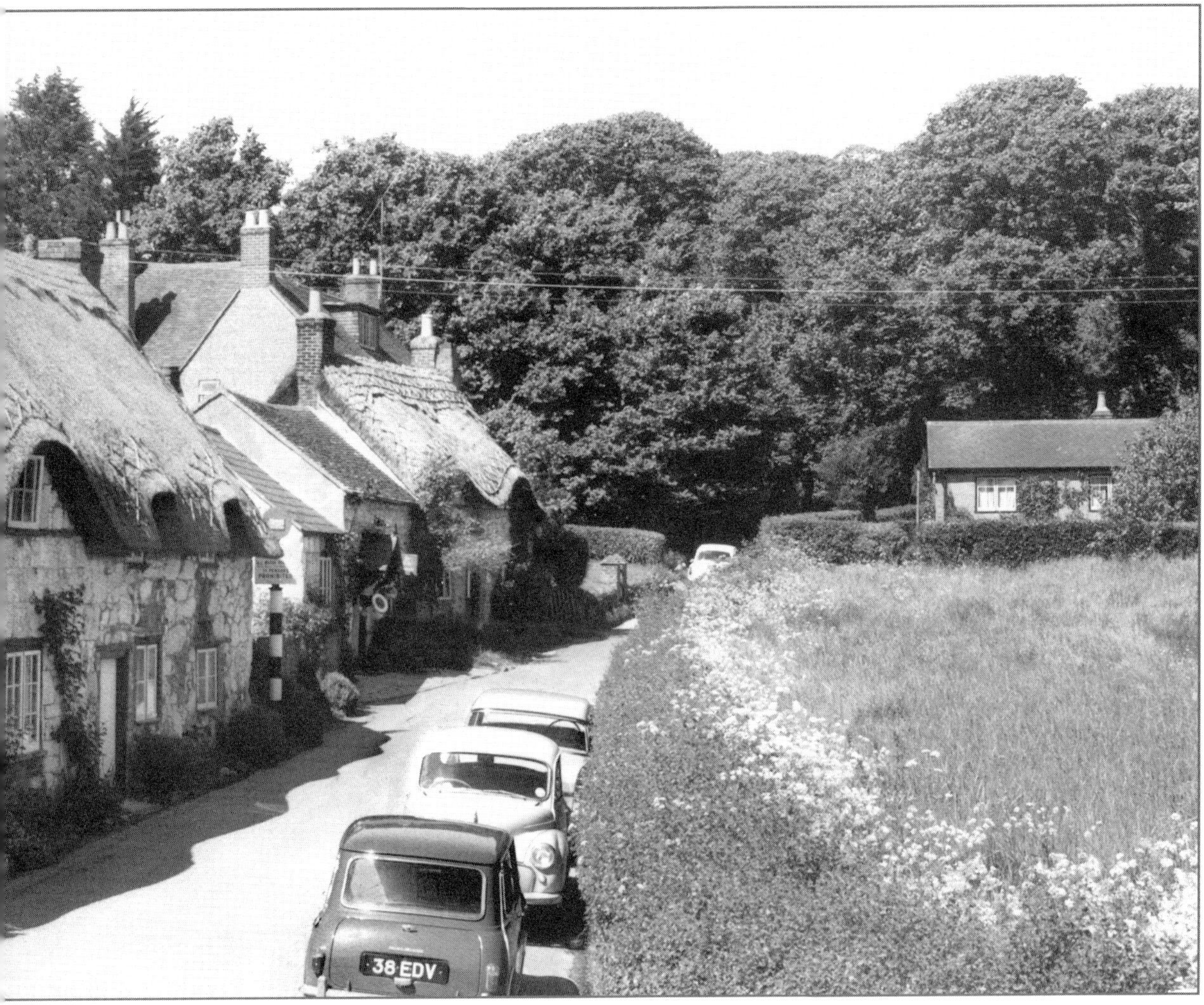


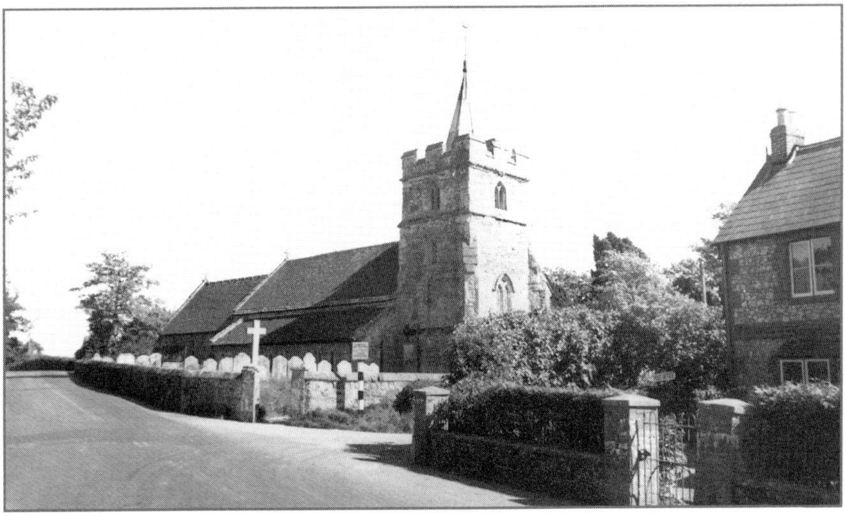

**Brighstone, St Mary's Church c1960** B543016
The church has a Norman arcade and a 13th-century chancel, restored in Victorian times. A sign points to the little cottage which is the post office, but there is not a soul in sight - only those departed in the churchyard. The clergyman Samuel Wilberforce entertained his famous anti-slavery campaigning father William at the Rectory.

▼ **Brighstone, The Village c1955** B543001
The village lies a few miles west of Shorwell on the B3399. Charming little Hillcrest Cottage stands partly hidden among the shrubbery and trees. Properties like this are the essence of the old village.

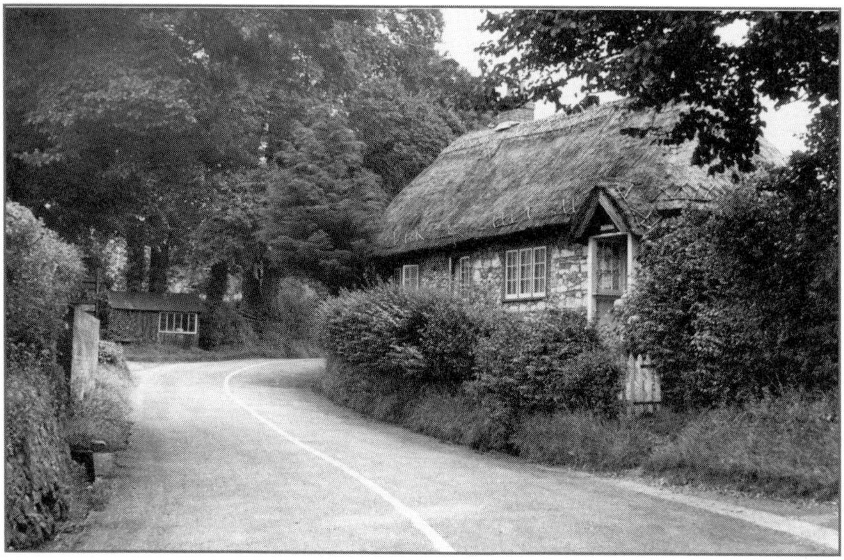

▼ **Brighstone, Old Cottages c1960** B543031
Here is Ye Olde Shoppe, flower-bedecked and beautiful, typical of the village and of the island. The island's beautiful villages draw coachloads of tourists. They are attracted to an ideal which perhaps was never as perfect as it looked, but which can still teach us lessons in living more harmoniously with nature.

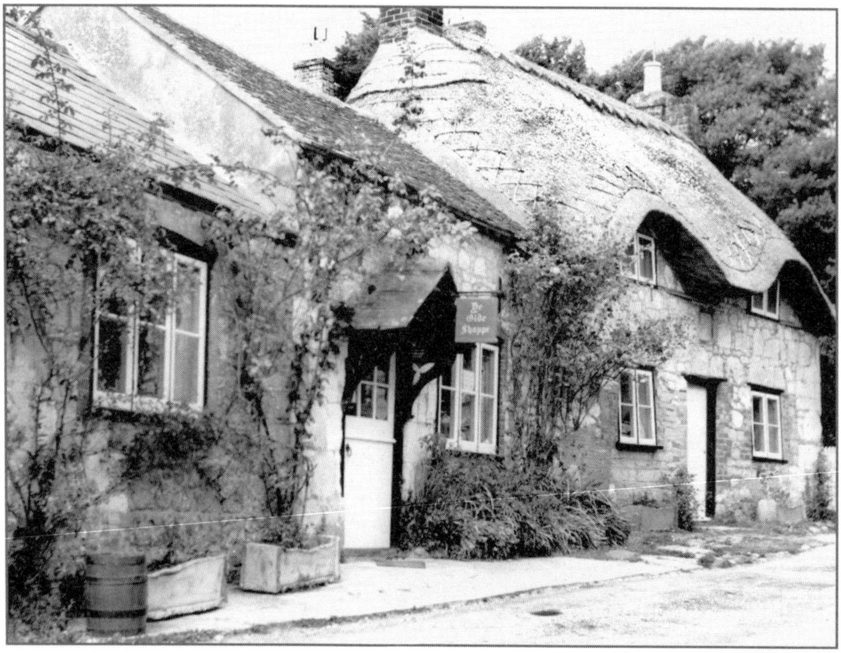

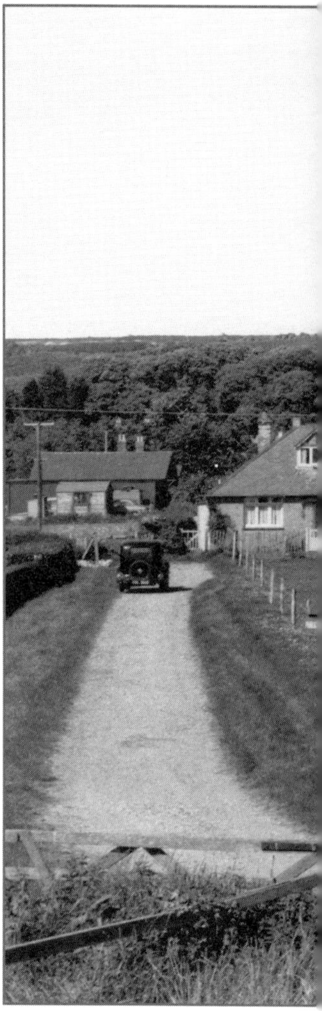

▲ **Brighstone, The Village c1960** B543024
The scenery which has long made the area popular with walkers is well displayed here. The elegant line of the downs and the spire of St Mary's rise over more recent additions to the local housing. The horse in the paddock has got plenty to nibble on, and looks about to tuck in. The artificial horse power parked in the lane looks so much less aggressive than the modern motor.

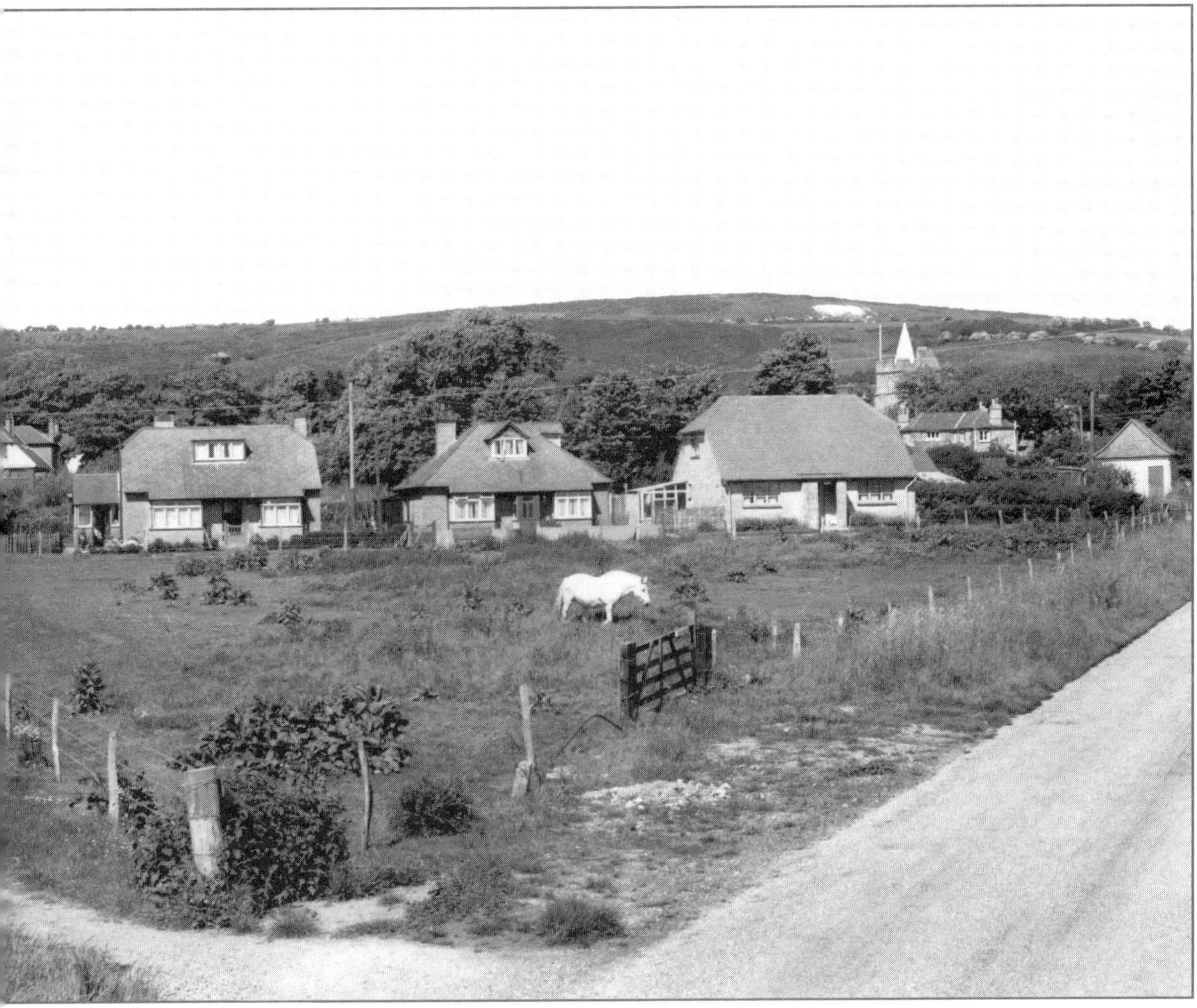

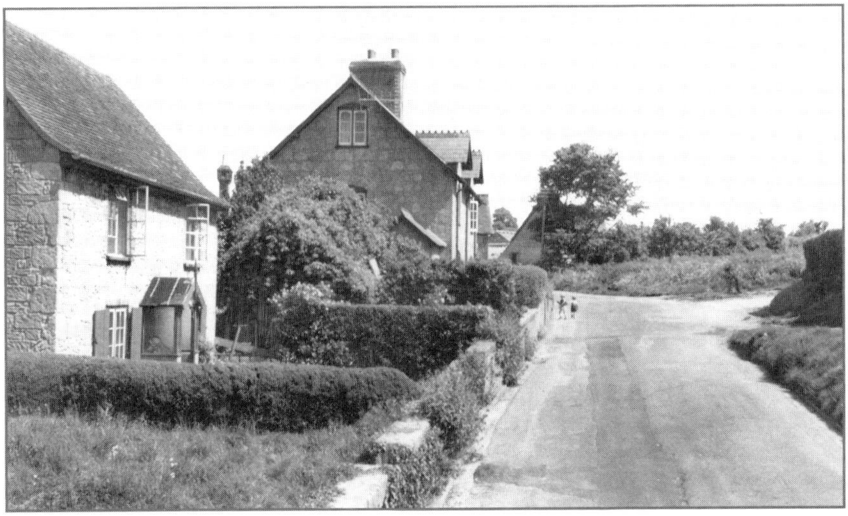

**Calbourne, The Village c1955** C439011
Calbourne lies north beyond Brighstone Forest, around the junction with the B3401. It was once known for its clump of elms; it is still is a delightful place, with a 17th-century water mill in the wooded valley of Caul Bourne stream, which rises in Westover Park. Here the children play free from all the fear of strangers and traffic that cause, so much anxiety today.

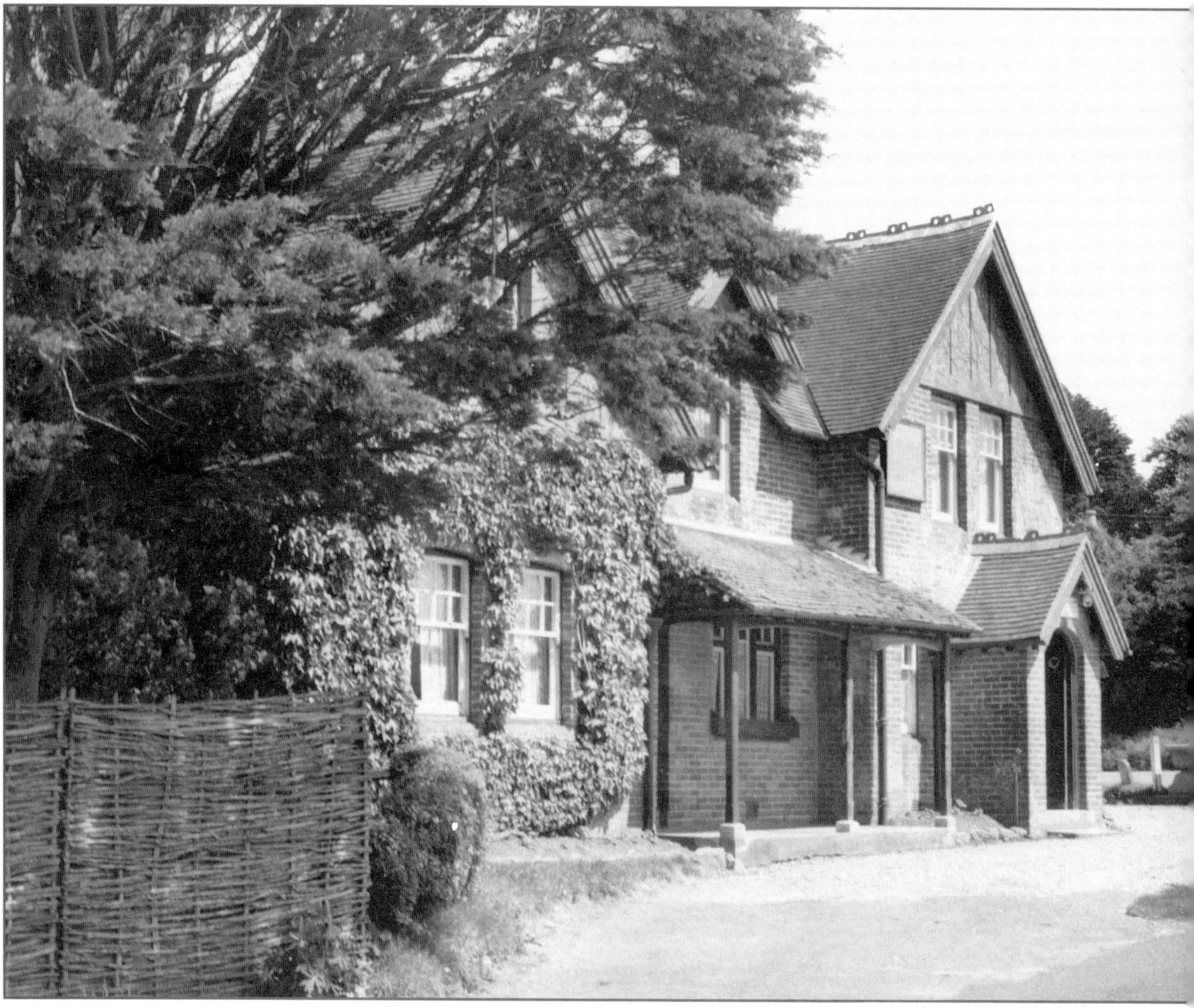

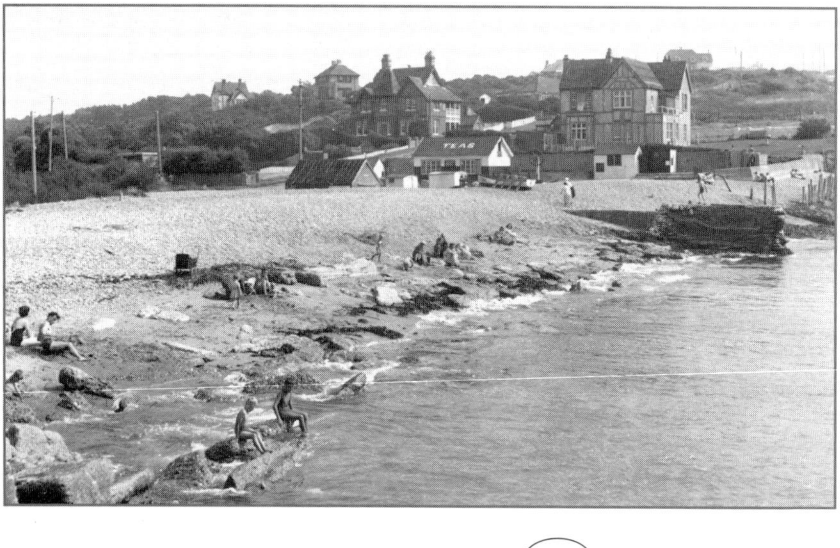


**Freshwater, The Bay c1955** F49001
Turning west along the B3401 at Calbourne, we come to Freshwater and the Bay. The rocky shore is a haven for marine life. It is also a haven for young bathers, and there is even a pram half way up the beach.

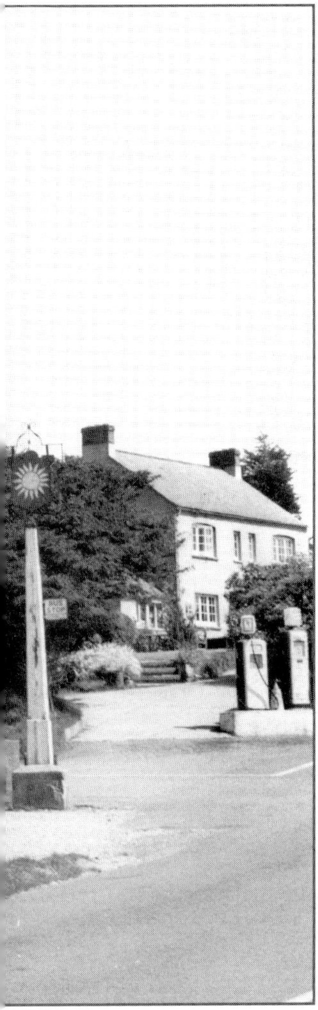

◄ **Calbourne, The Sun Inn c1955** C439019

Those were the days when you could pull up at the roadside and fill the car up at these roadside pumps adjacent to the Sun Inn. Rich in history, the village was the birthplace of William Long, author of a work on Isle of Wight dialect. A brass portrait of a knight in armour commemorates William Montacute, Earl of Salisbury, a 14th-century governor of the island, killed during a jousting match with his father, who placed altar tombs in every village where he held land or houses.

▼ **Freshwater, The Beach c1960** F49002

Freshwater Bay cuts into the white wall of cliff. Note the doorway into the cliffs and steps down to the sea. Victorian anxieties made this area a hive of defence activity, including the military road along the coast. Freshwater Redoubt was built during the 19th century to stop the French landing. All that is forgotten here as holidaymakers have a good time.

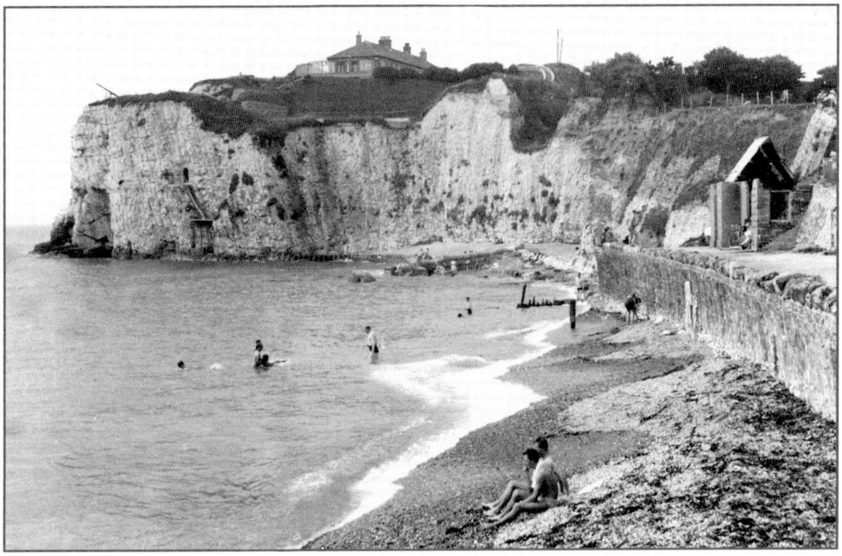

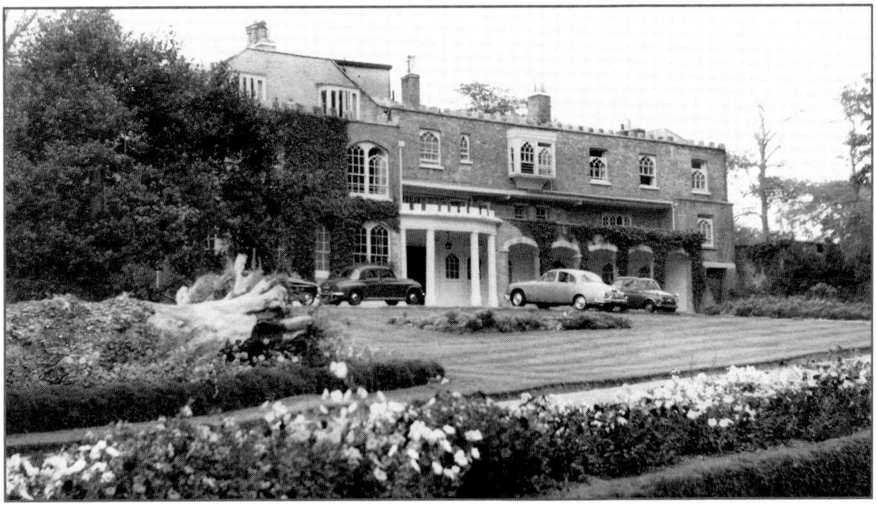

◄ **The Freshwater Hotel Farringford c1965** F49017

This house is well-situated at the end of a long drive; Tennyson rented this property for £2 a week, and bought it 2 years later. He was a familiar figure tramping the downs, black cloak billowing. 'The Charge of the Light Brigade' was composed here, and 1000 copies were distributed to the troops. The poet popularised the bay community.

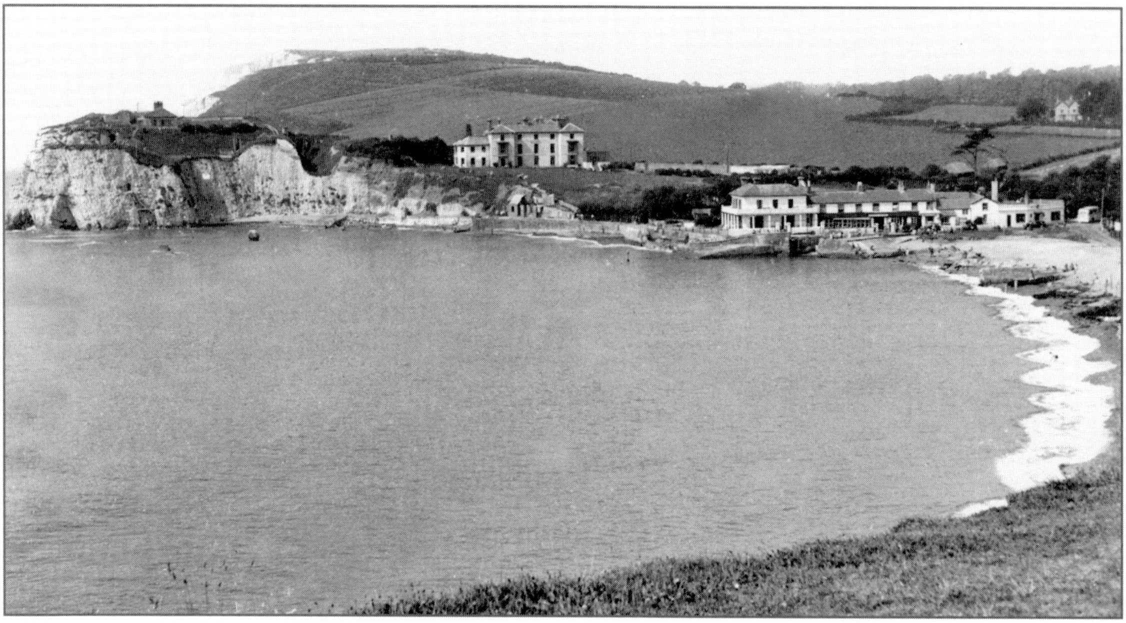

**Freshwater, The Bay c1960** F49008
A bus is dropping off passengers. District nurse and midwife Lois Bown recalled the joys of working in this beautiful part of the island; but long before her days of delivering babies, Robert Hooke, a sickly baby, was born to the local parson. Hooke grew up to be one of the world's greatest scientists, postulating gravity and a theory of flight. Perhaps this scenery inspired him. Tennyson Down rolls away over the hills.

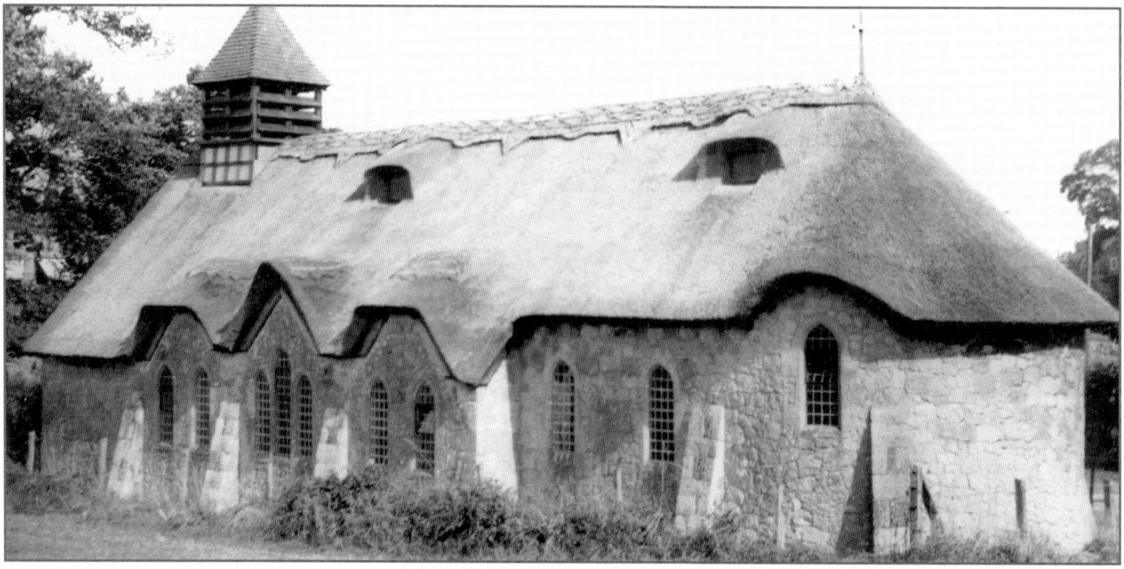

**Freshwater, St Agnes's Church c1960** F49021
Lois Bown's father came to West Wight as curate in 1908. The parish church was 2 miles away, so the locals worshipped in a tin barn, baking in summer and freezing in winter. A meeting was held to consider building something better. Lord Tennyson offered a site, and substantial donations were promised. Wood and iron models were rejected, but luckily someone spotted a water colour of a thatched stone church among a pile of papers. The Rector said it was only his little sketch, but it became the church that we see today. No porch was featured in the sketch, but Lady Tennyson said she would like to donate one in memory of her mother.

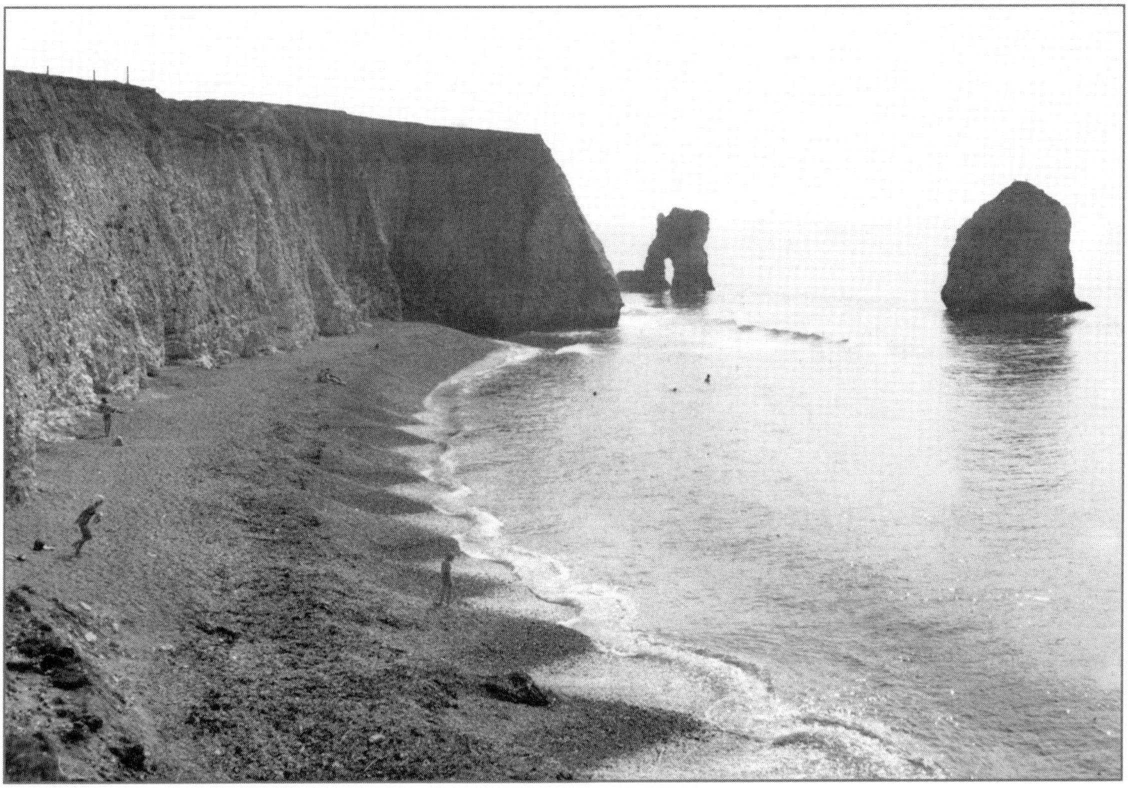

**Freshwater**
**The Beach c1955** F49012
Arch and Stag rocks stand out proudly from the waves. They were severely eroded during the 1990s storms. The beach looks rather exclusive, with just a few people on the beach and bobbing in the waves.

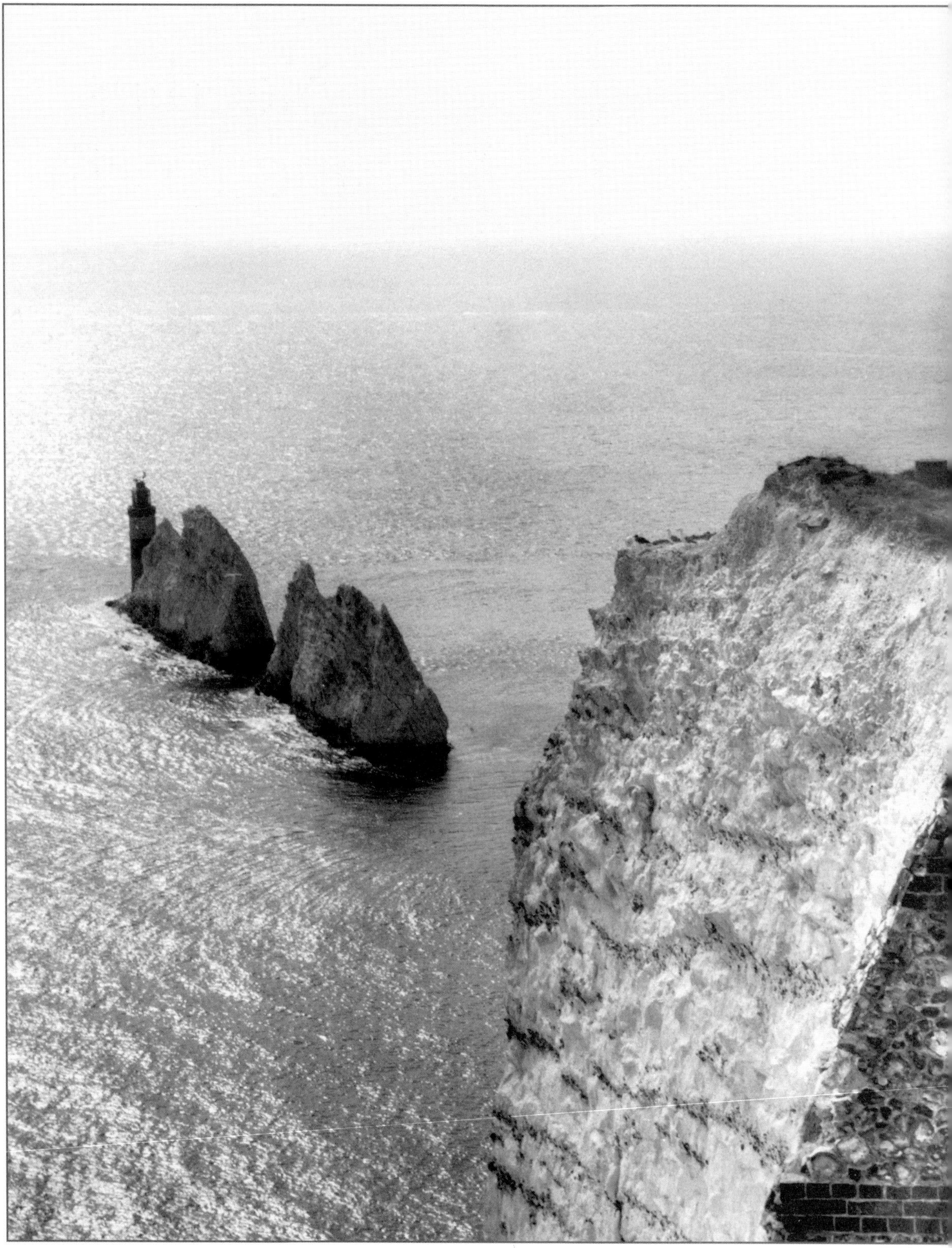

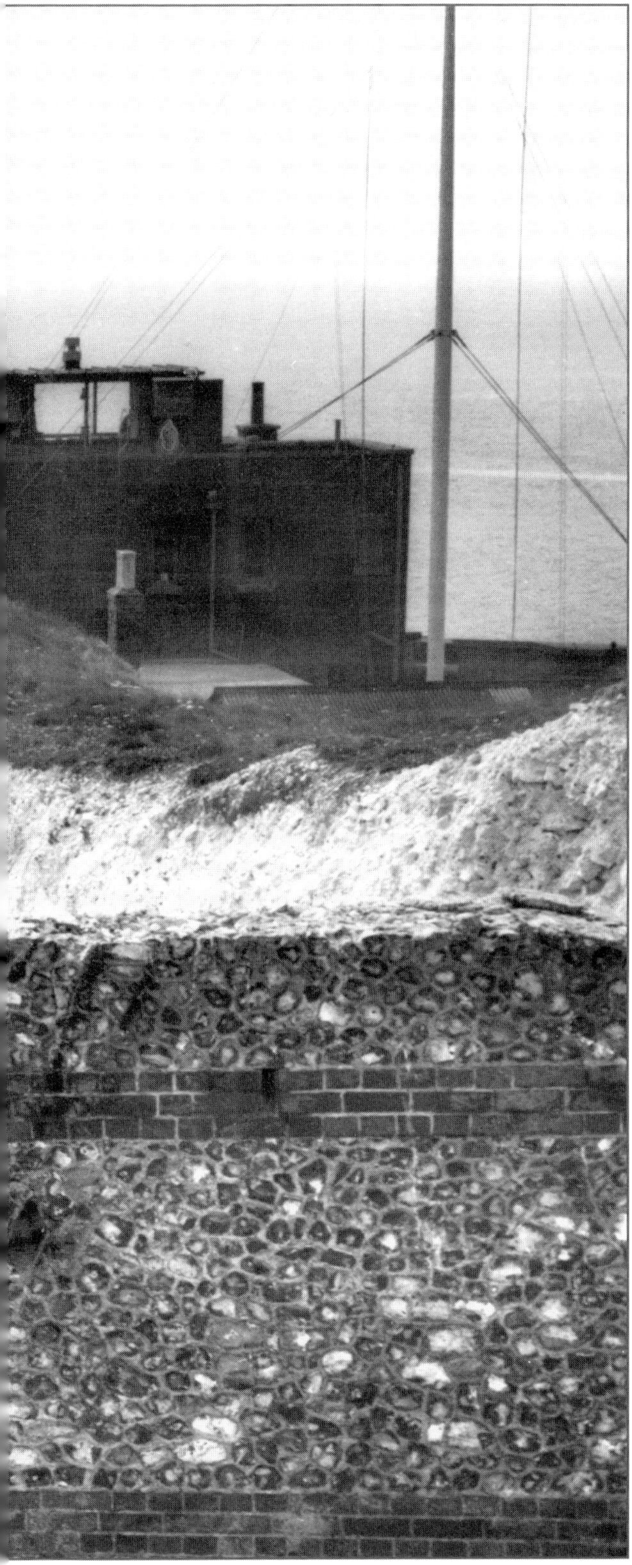

# Needles and North

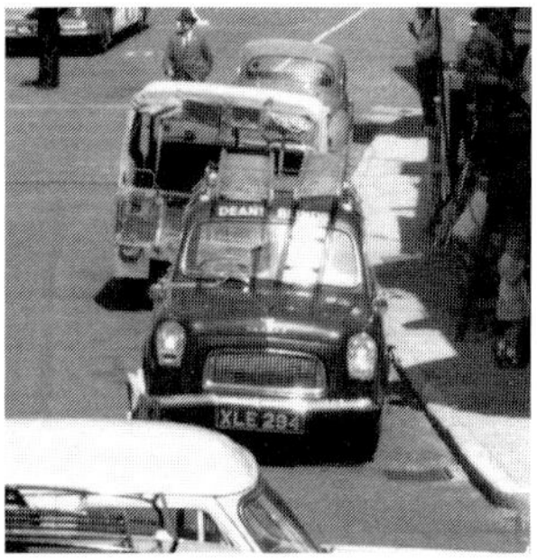

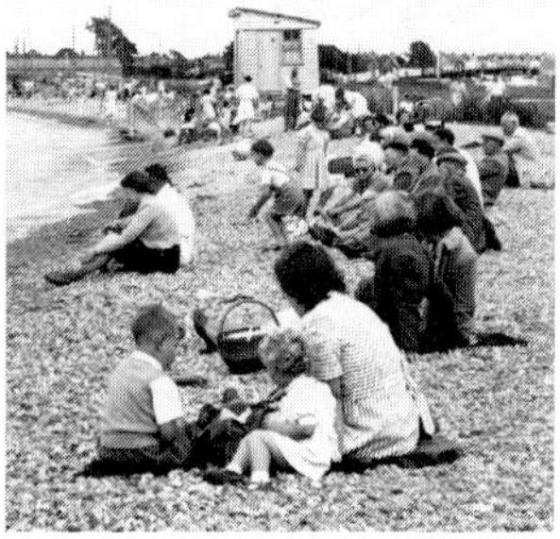

**The Needles, The Coastguard Station c1955**
N7008
This is the island's most westerly point; we are looking across from the cliff top to the Needles and the lighthouse. Needles Old Battery, 1861-3, was a main defence against the French. Two 12-ton guns were hauled up into position, and tunnels through the cliff led to a searchlight station and a parade ground. With its underground facilities, the site has been used in the space race. In 1955, Saunders Roe of Cowes were developing the Black Knight rocket programme, which was thwarted by lack of funds - 22 rockets were launched at Woomera after 3 years of development.

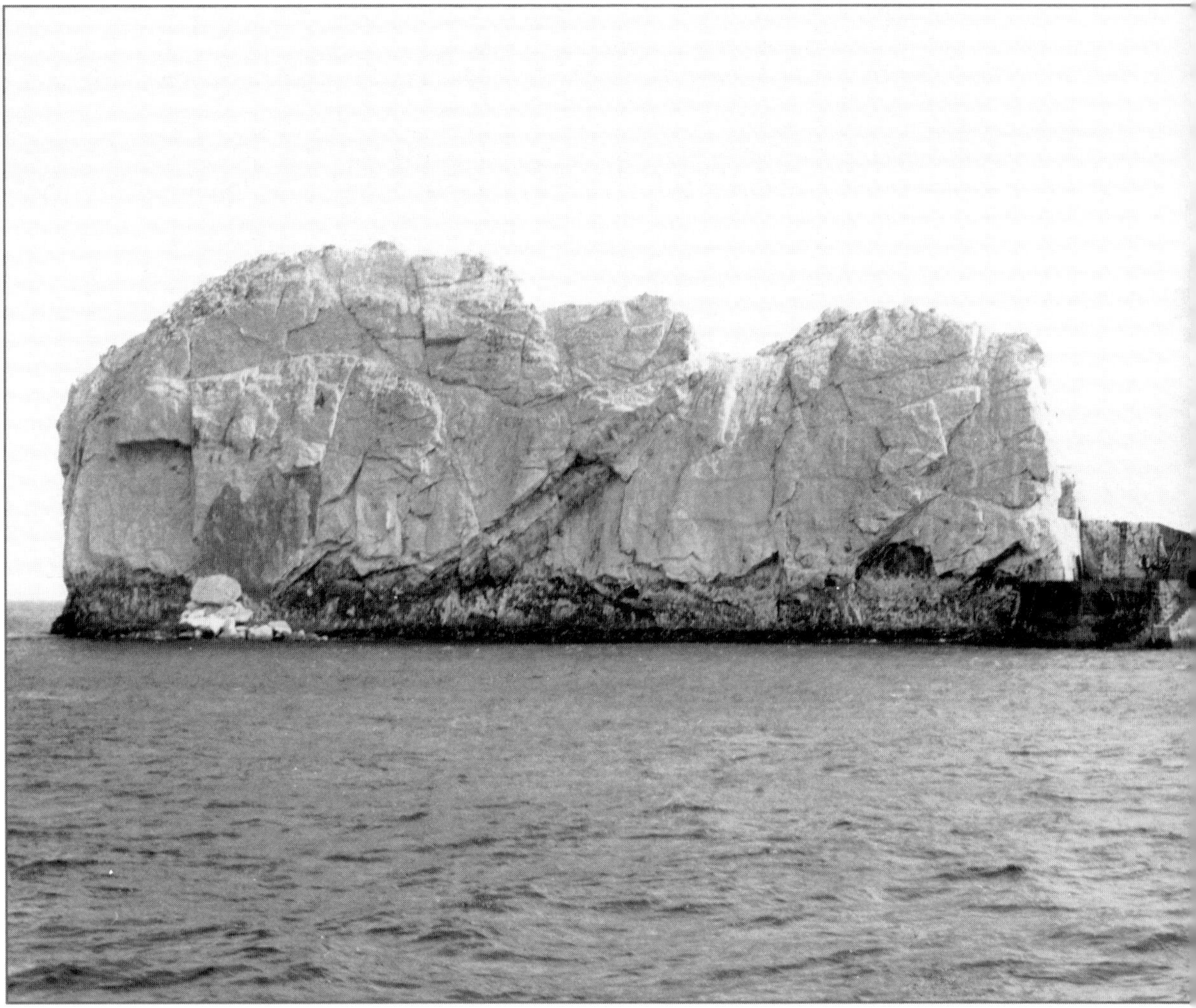

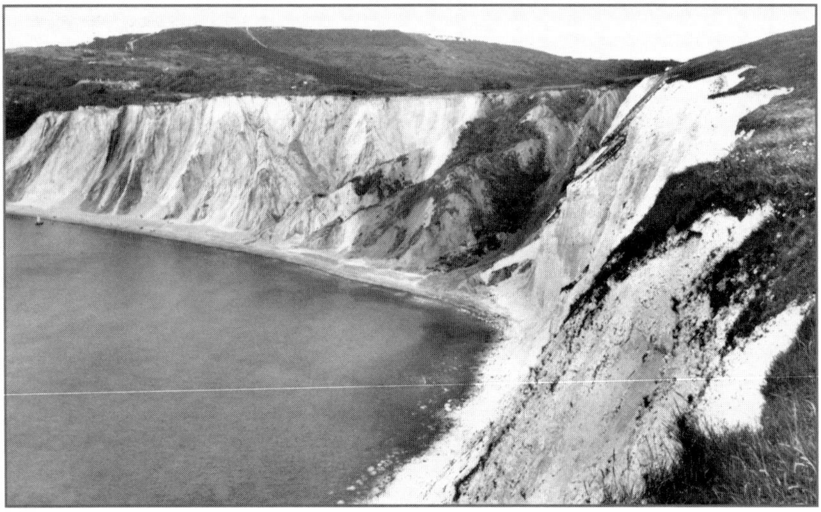

◄ **Alum Bay c1960** A41024
Moving north-eastward, we come to Alum Bay, which lies just beyond the Old Battery. These cliffs are unusual in that they display the famous coloured sands, which are arranged vertically down the cliff face; they are created by water percolating through the surface over thousands of years, depositing chemicals in the process. Alum (sulphate of potassium) was first mined in 1561 for the paper making and tanning industry. The land rises 80 metres to Headon Warren tumuli, with Totland Bay beyond.

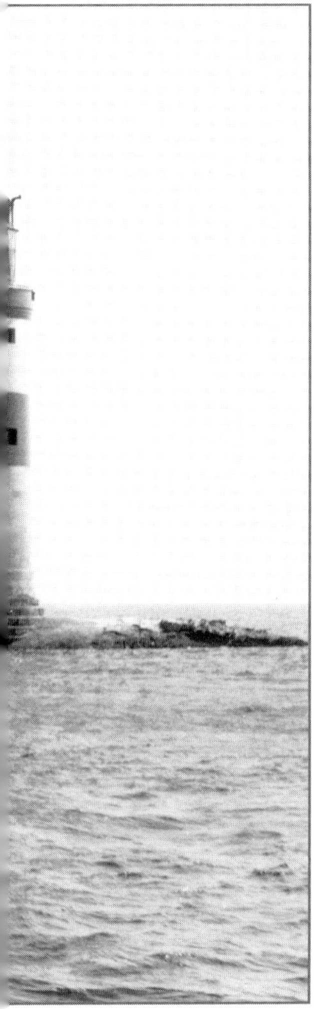

◀ **The Needles The Lighthouse c1955**

N7012

The rocks look like a half-eaten cake with a giant candle. The closest thing they have here to an emergency now is when a foghorn or lamp fails. Today unmanned, the lighthouse is run by computer; 100 ships pass daily.

▼ **Alum Bay, The Royal Needles Hotel c1955**

A41014

Note the set of scales on the veranda: perhaps they are there to check that we have not overeaten after the hot and cold luncheons, ice cream, cups of coffee and cups of tea that are advertised here. The first readable radio signals were transmitted to a steamer in Alum Bay on 6 November 1897. The first permanent wireless station was established nearby on 5 December that year. Marconi first exchanged messages with a tug in Alum Bay, 14 miles away, followed by Bournemouth and Poole, 40 miles away. Lord Kelvin sent the first paid telegram in June 1898.

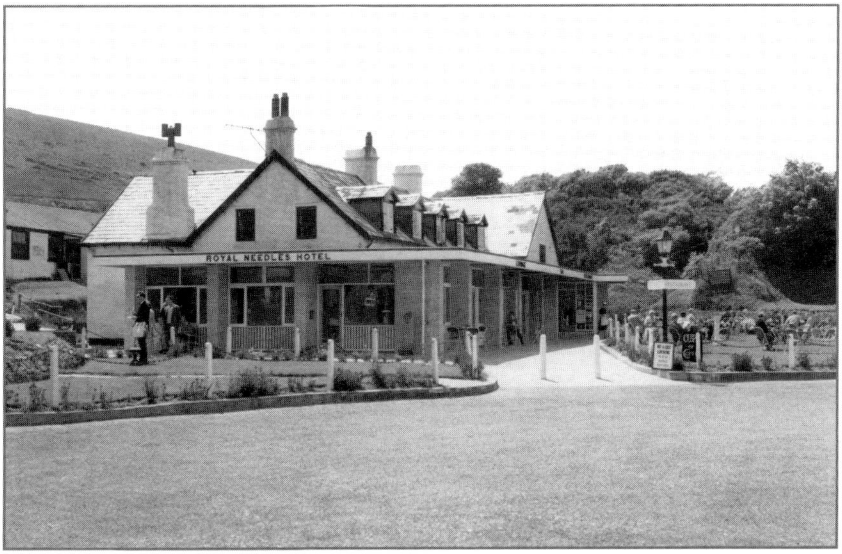


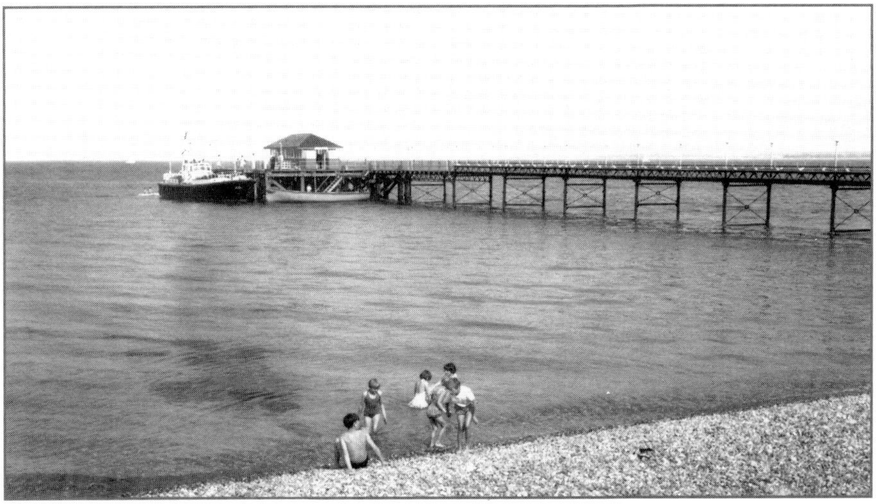

◀ **Totland Bay, The Pier c1955** T65027

Large boats make a pretty picture by the old pier. Totland is among the world's finest resorts, very accessible by the Lymington to Yarmouth ferry - no doubt the way these happy youngsters arrived.

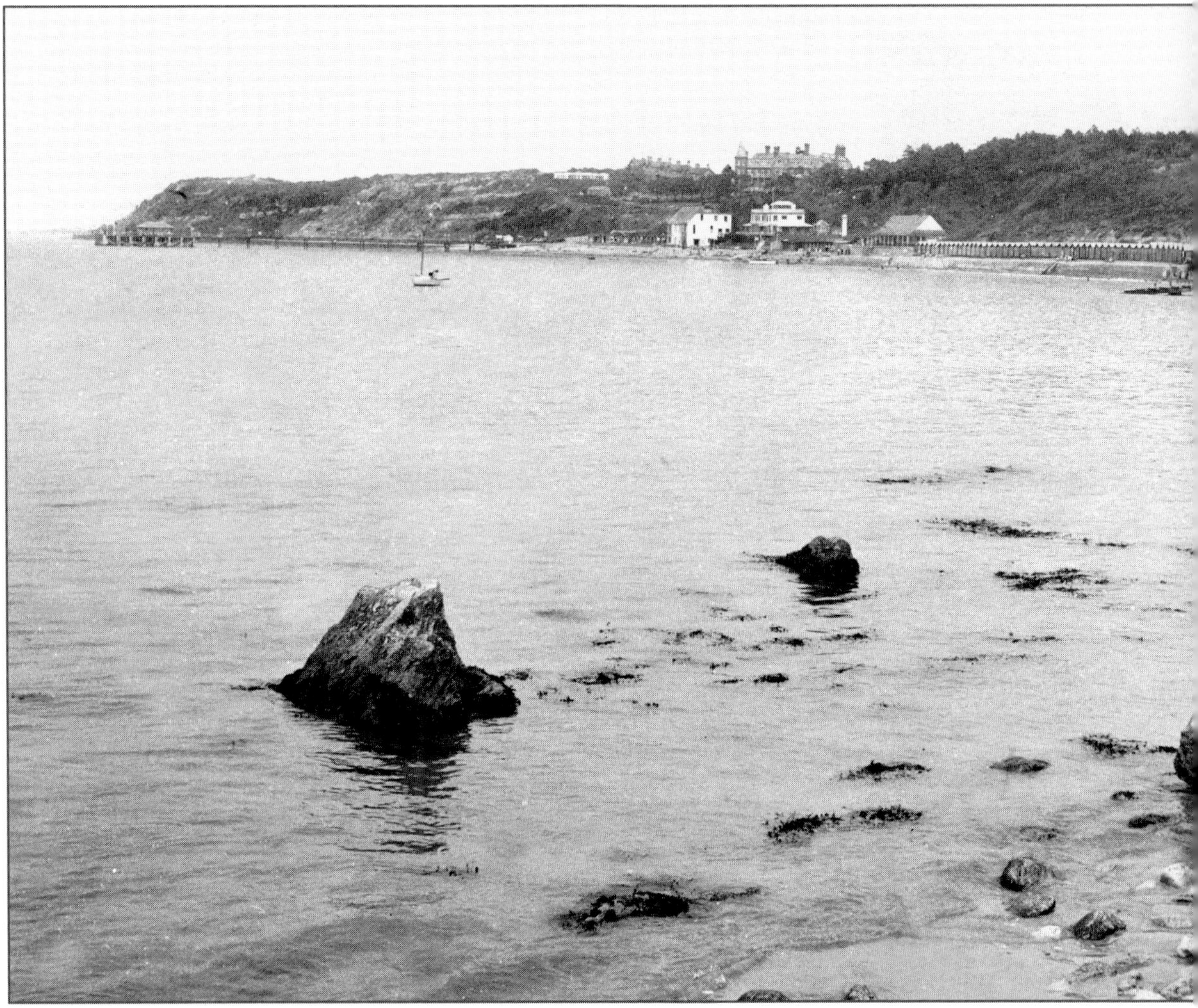

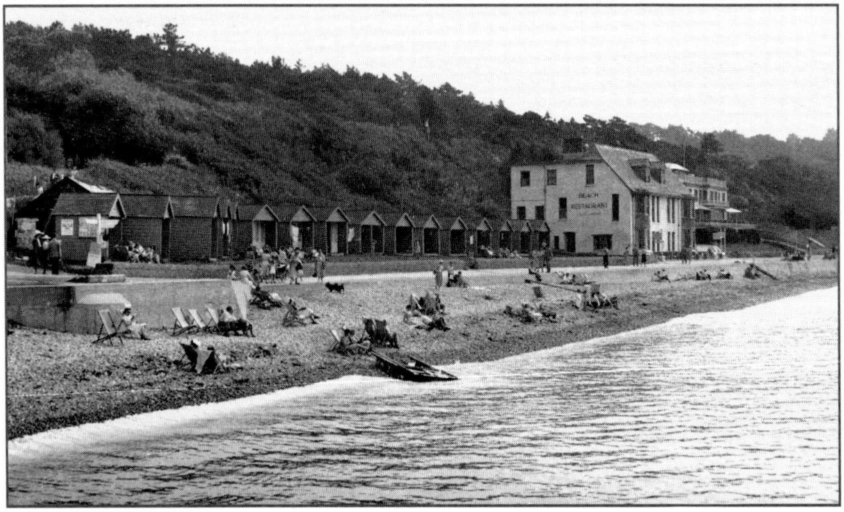

◄ **Totland Bay, The Beach c1955** T65010
Dinky little beach huts in serried ranks are dwarfed by the Beach Restaurant building. One can imagine the hopes and dreams of all those visitors in an early post-war period that promised peace ever after.

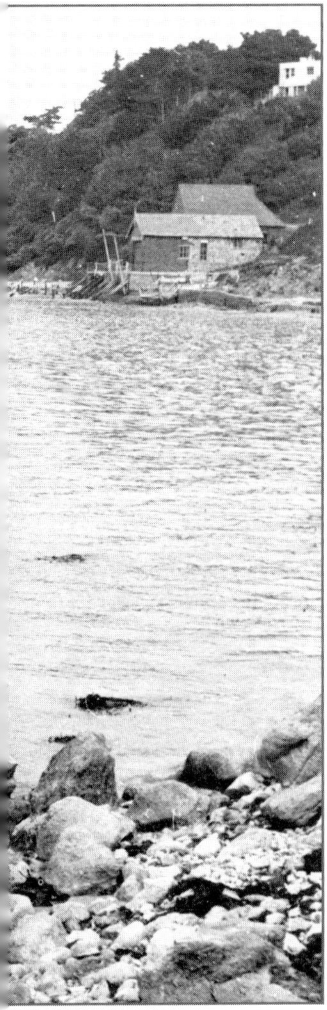

◀ **Totland Bay, General View c1960** T65002
Warden Point reaches out to the sea, and a fine selection of old buildings mark the landscape. Here Weston Manor stands, where Tennyson's esteemed friend, the theologian William George Ward, built a private chapel.

▼ **Colwell Bay c1955** C452004
Fort Albert stands out on the headland, with Hurst Castle on the mainland opposite; these fortifications were designed to defend entry to the Solent. The settlement grew with the defences, and prospered with tourism. A jetty was built to land the big guns for the old Battery. Soldiers camped on the large common during the Napoleonic wars; the common later became popular for gypsy camps. But for the moment defences are down, and these folk get away from it all.

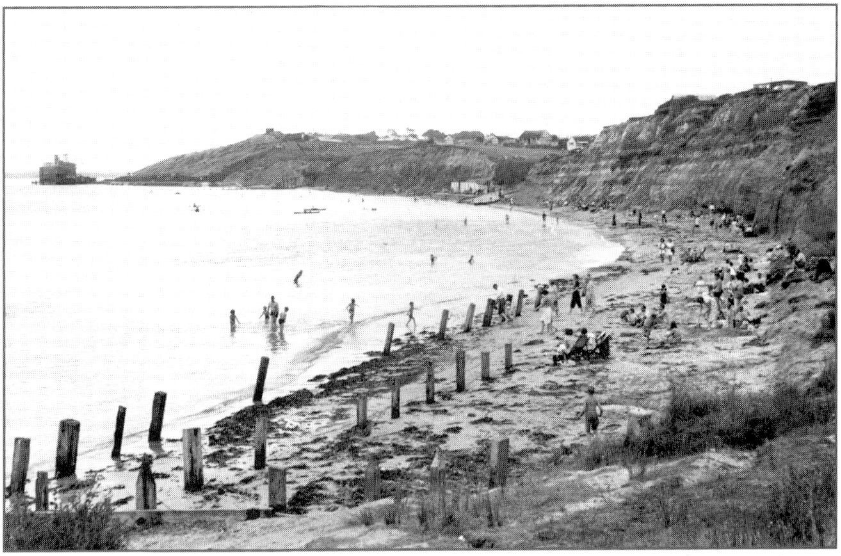

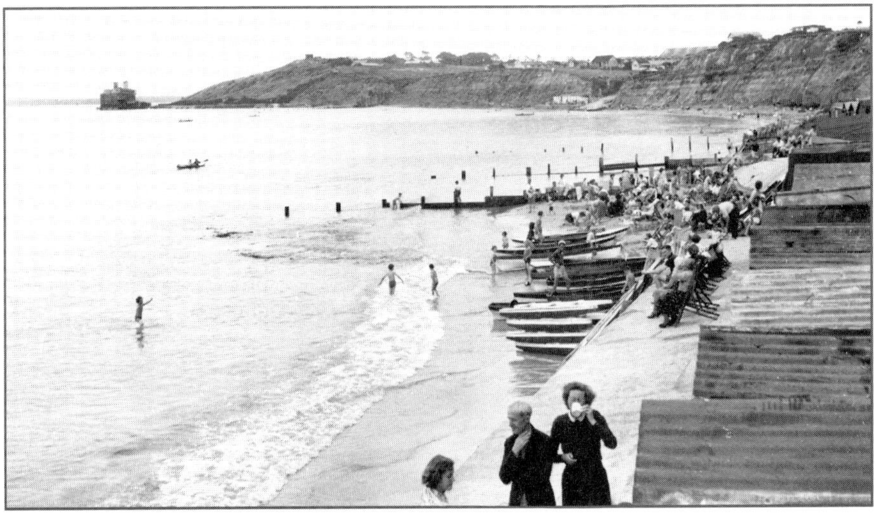

◀ **Colwell Bay The Beach c1955** C452011
In this view of the beach, we see the roofs of no-nonsense bathing huts; the tide is well up the sand, covering the groynes, and boats are ready for the more adventurous. In the foreground a man seems lost in thought, while his companion enjoys a warm drink, probably tea.

▼ **Colwell Bay, The Beach c1955** C452013
Here we have a closer view of some very contented people looking out over the bay. A few of the more adventurous folk are paddling in the waves. In the foreground a mother cuddles her child. The lines of rickety changing huts line up alongside the beach-mat stand, and ices are on sale in a hut at the other end of the path.

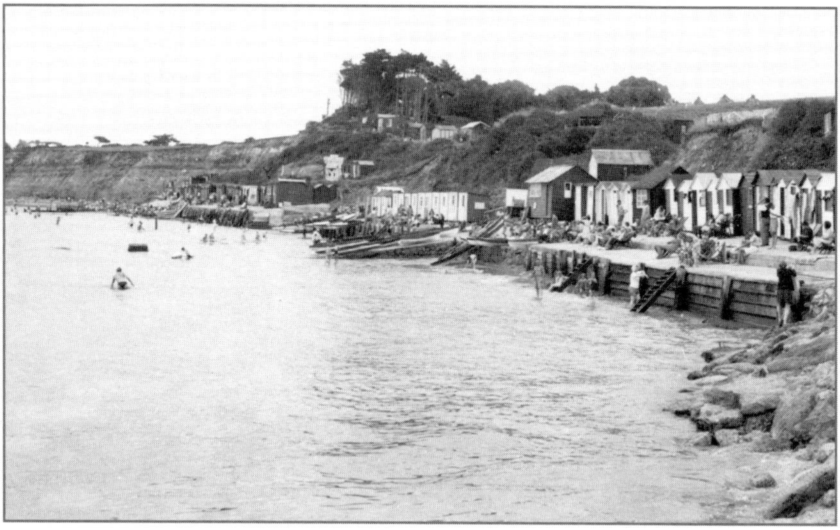

▼ **Yarmouth, The Harbour c1955** Y4023
The ferry from Lymington has docked. Ferries first called here in 1830; before that, passengers arrived by rowing boat, which was no mean feat. Retired Portsmouth policeman Goronwy Wynne Evans recalled: 'We had a police boat house. We rowed over to the island on a pleasure trip. Johnny Stevens was in our crew, and used to work on the ferries. He reckoned this skipper would bring us and the boat back. We jugged up with all these pickled eggs from a pub and were late getting back to the ferry and had to row home.'

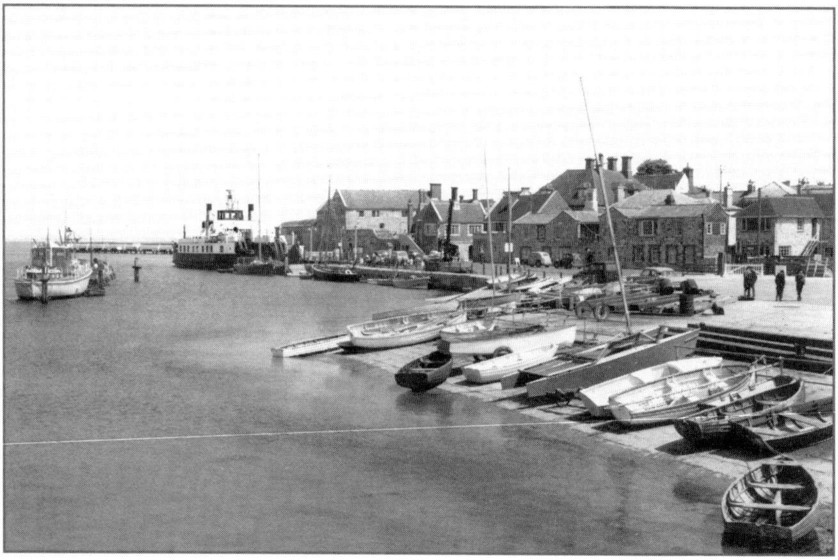

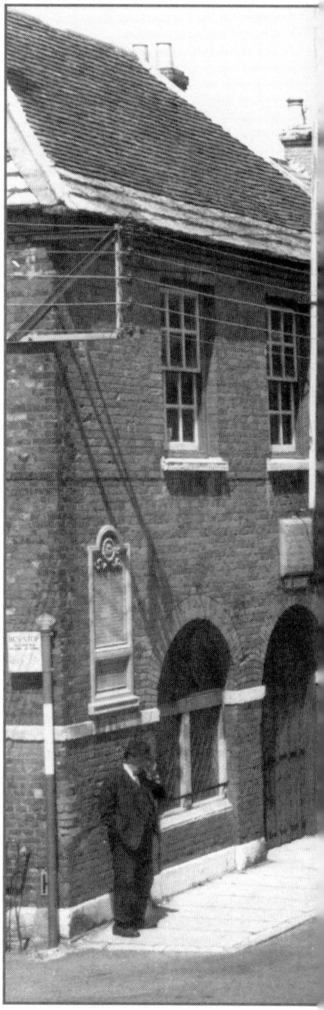

▲ **Yarmouth, The Square c1960** Y4020
Yarmouth is one of the island's oldest towns. At one time the Governor lived here, and the castle was one of Henry VIII's four blockhouses against the French, who twice set the town on fire. Modern times have arrived here in the shape of a few brightly-coloured new cars and a stylish tourist coach. The pier is directly ahead. The old-fashioned Bugle Hotel stands opposite the trendy self-service store.

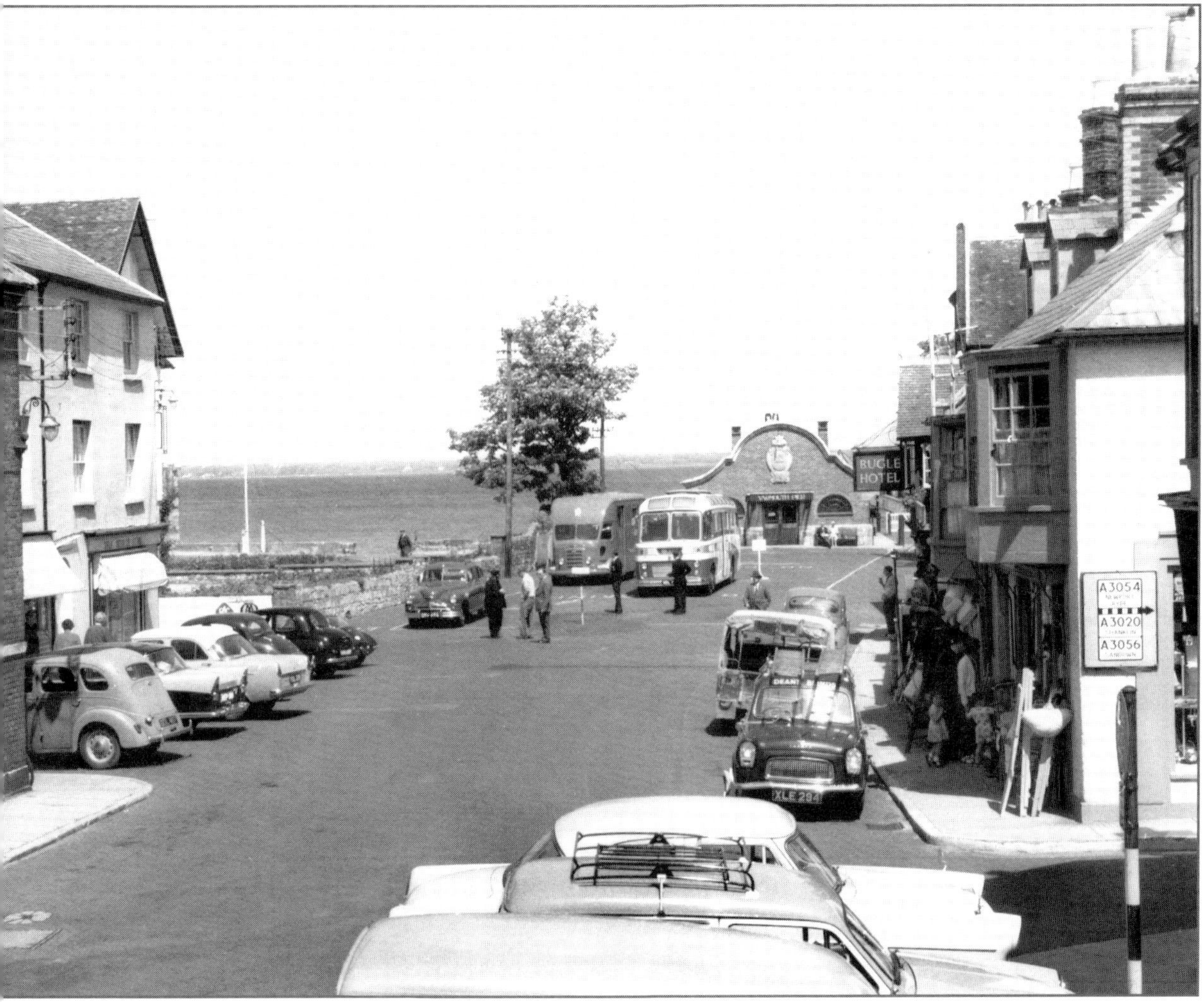


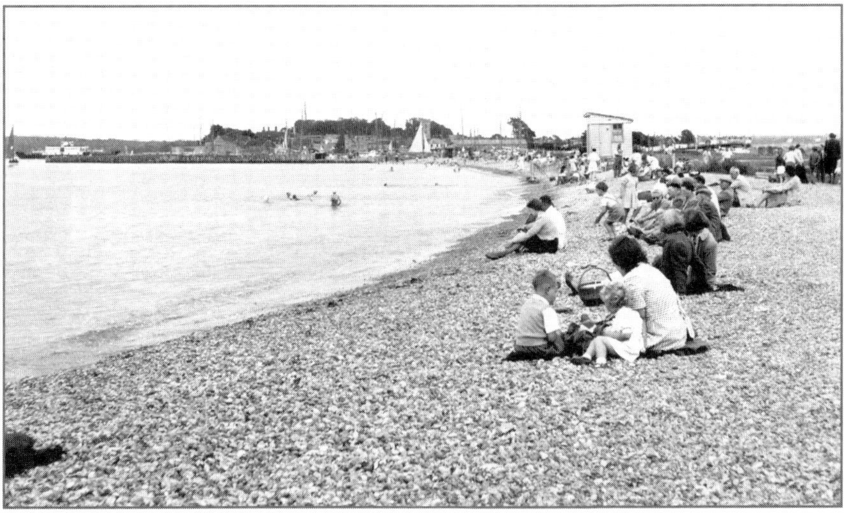

◄ **Yarmouth, The Beach c1955** Y4012
The town is at its best here, with brightly-coloured yachts bobbing around and mesmerising the heat-stricken bathers. The ferry boat looms large in the distance as it departs for Lymington. During the period from 1937 to 1948, the numbers of foot passengers coming to all Isle of Wight ports doubled to 441,000, and the number of cars increased tenfold to 20,000.

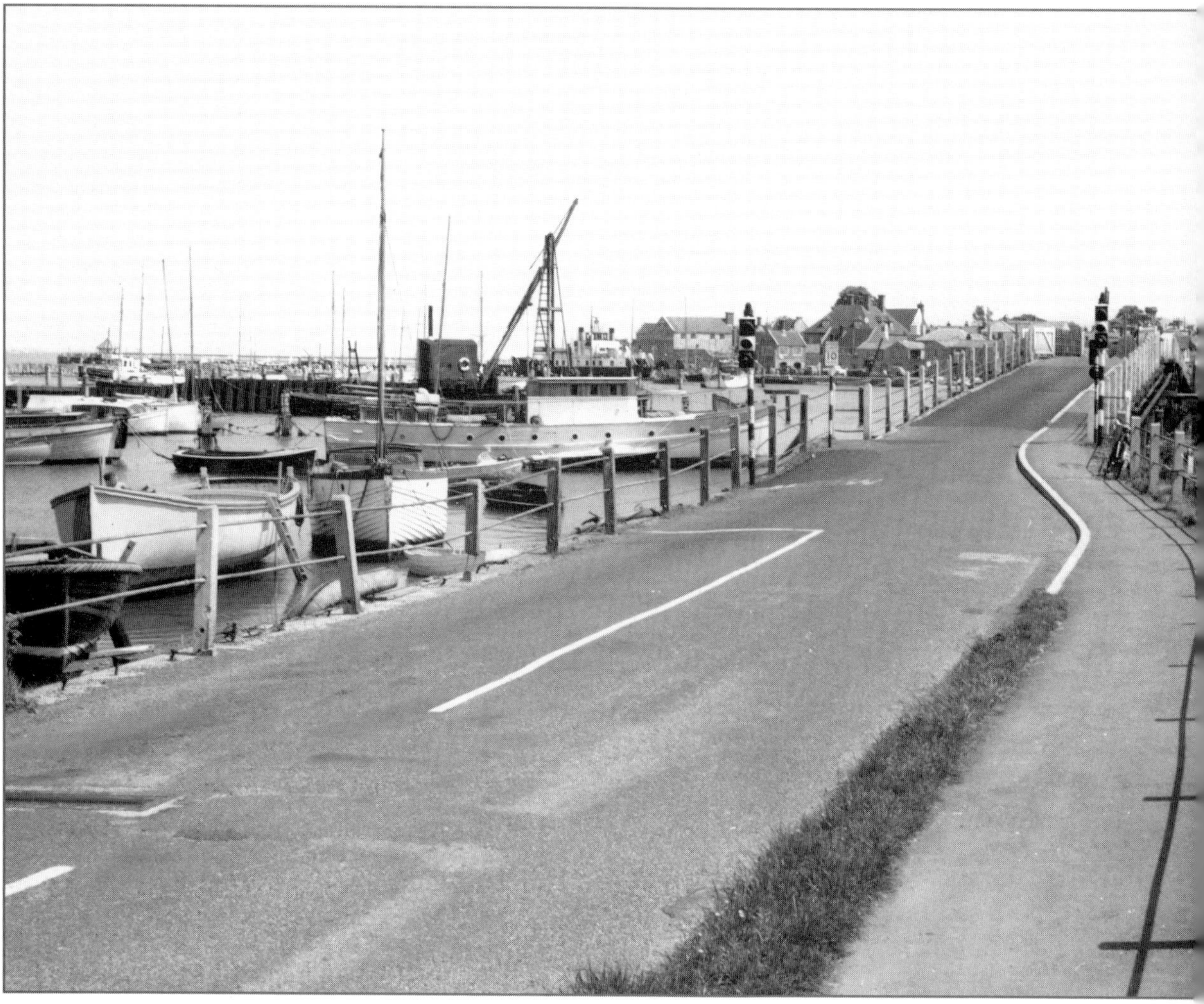

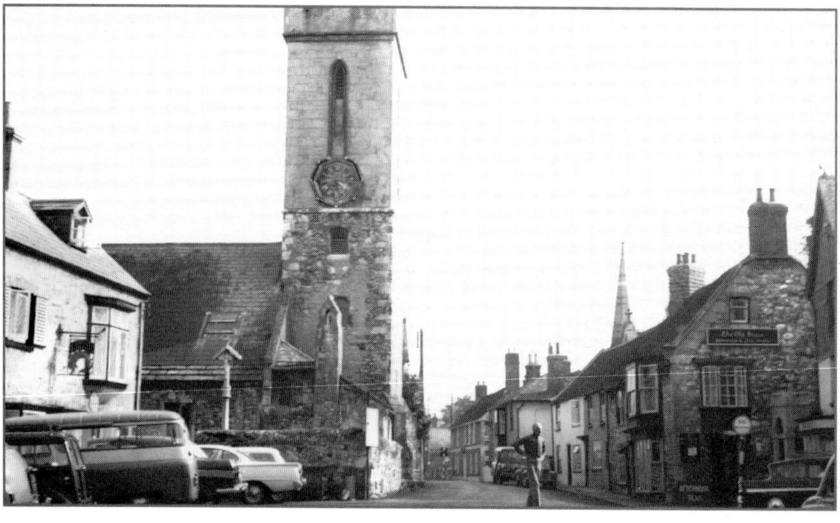

◄ **Yarmouth, The Square c1955** Y4029
The church was rebuilt in 1614-26. The tower is a little unusual. There is a monument (1692) to Sir Robert Holmes, the colourful admiral who twice entertained Charles II. The statue was originally to be a portrait of Louis XIV, and was finished except for the head. The admiral captured it for his memorial, and had a sculpture of his own head made to be added to the figure.

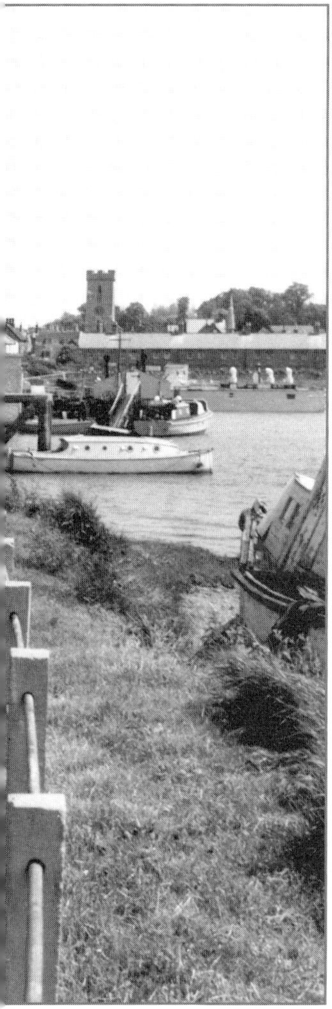

◄ **Yarmouth, The Bridge c1955** Y4024

We are looking north-east over the bridge as it crosses the Yar. Traffic lights are in situ for single track traffic, and the Lymington ferry, ramp down ,is just in view. St James's Church completes the peaceful setting, far right.

▼ **Shalfleet, The Village c1955** S496001

The name of the village means 'shallow creek'. Here the Newport Road crosses the Caul Bourne where it widens into a creek. The tiny village grew around a cross roads, a church, pub, a few houses and a manor. The grey tower of the church looms massively in the background.

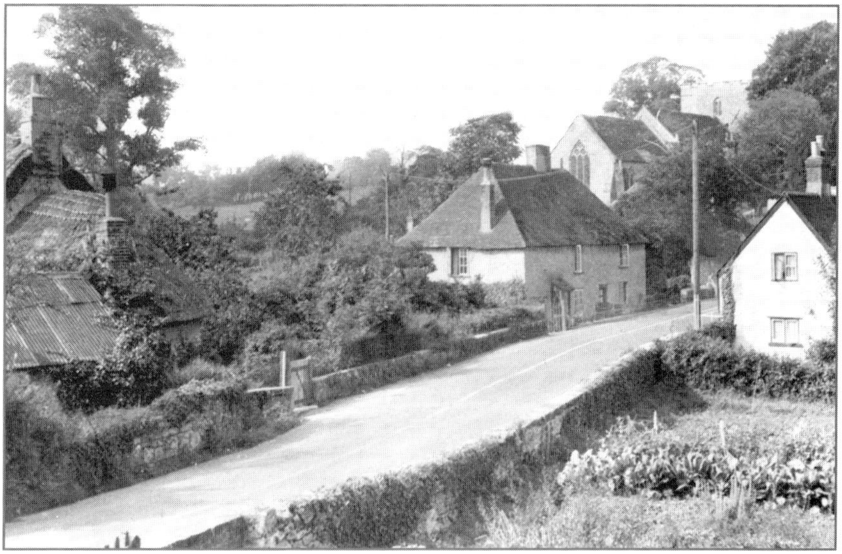

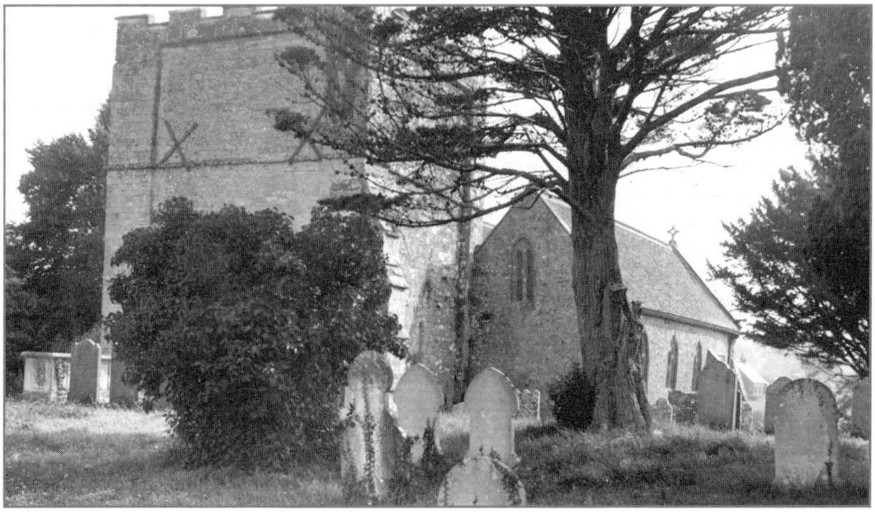

◄ **Shalfleet, The Church c1955** S496003

Huge iron crosses indicate bracing work to keep the old tower stonework steady. This 12th- to 14th-century church has the oldest tower on the island. Originally built on 10 feet of clay and water, the foundations had to be re-laid in concrete.

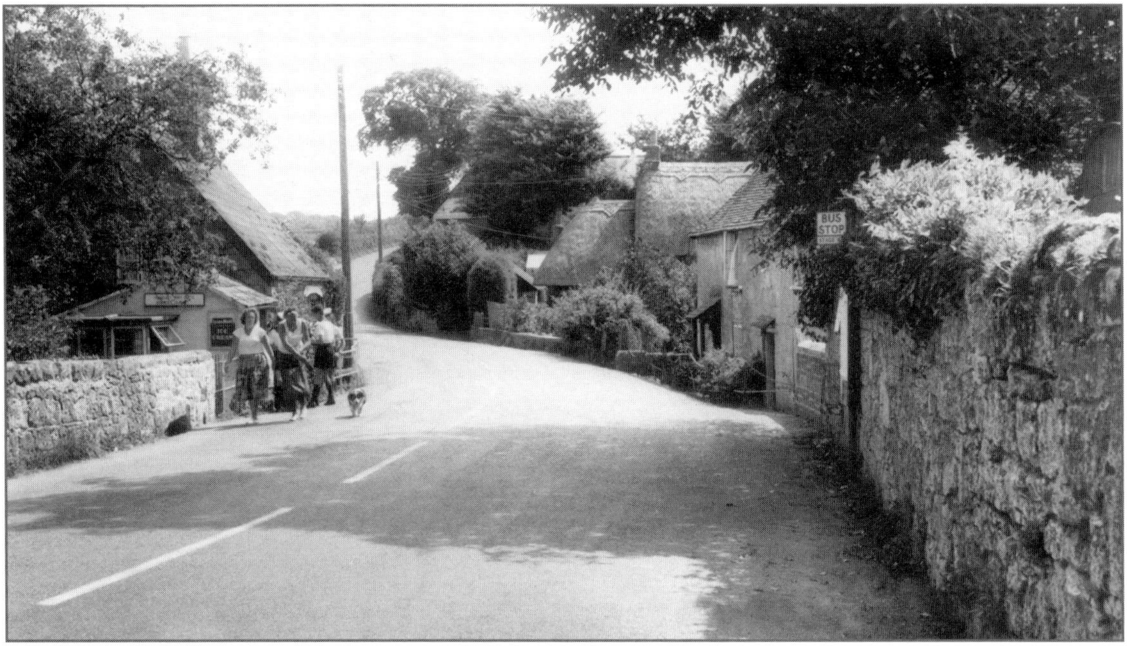


**Shalfleet, The Village c1955** S496020
The village lies in a hollow on the roller coaster A3054 Yarmouth to Newport road. We can feel that it is a nice warm day: the windows are open, and two summer-dressed ladies walk the dog past the little Post Office and General Stores.

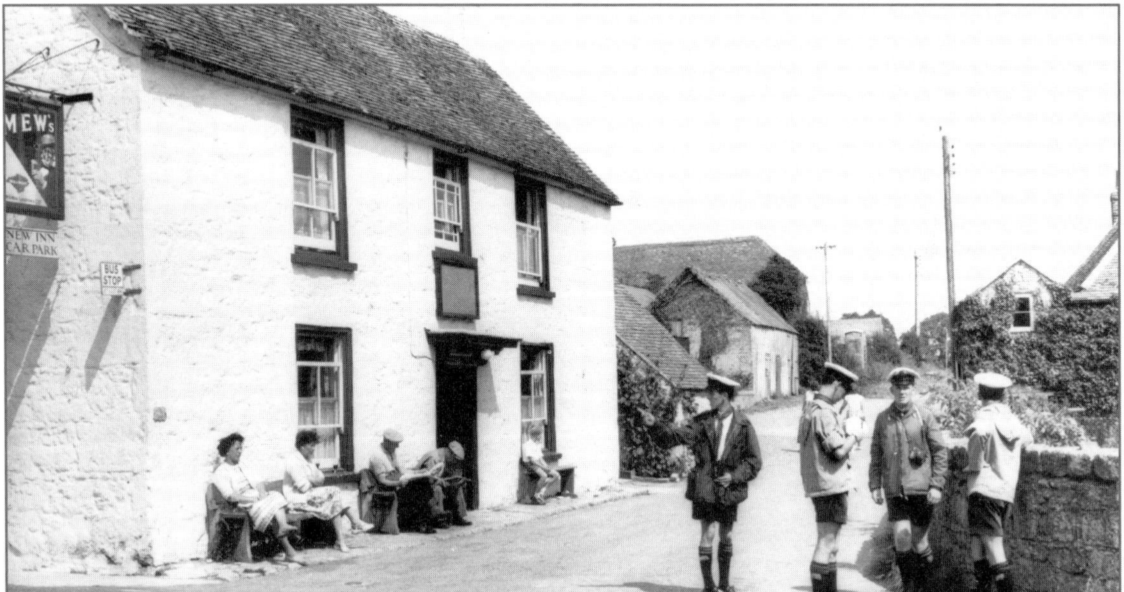


**Shalfleet, The New Inn c1955** S496021
The old pub stands white and bright under the summer sun. A couple of old fellows enjoy their newspapers. The ladies may be waiting for the bus; meanwhile they cast old-fashioned looks at the group of Sea Scouts, who appear to be lost. Or maybe everyone is waiting for the pub to open to enjoy the fresh seafood for which it is famed.

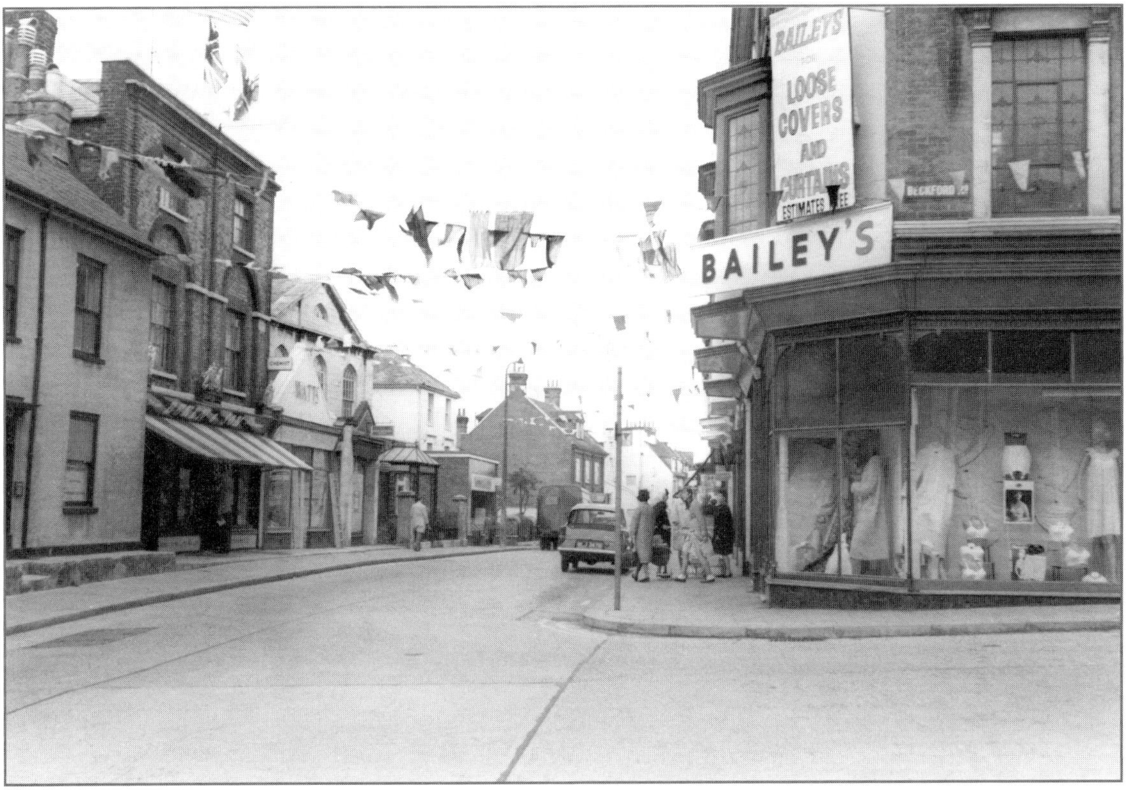


**Cowes**
**Birmingham Road c1965** C173088

We are at the junction with Beckford Road. Few places could be further from Birmingham than Cowes. In the foreground is a fine display of ladies' foundation garments! The Maritime Museum in Beckford Road has fine model ships, many from John Samuel White; this firm built warships on the Medina banks, and yacht designs by Uffa Fox, a friend of Prince Philip.

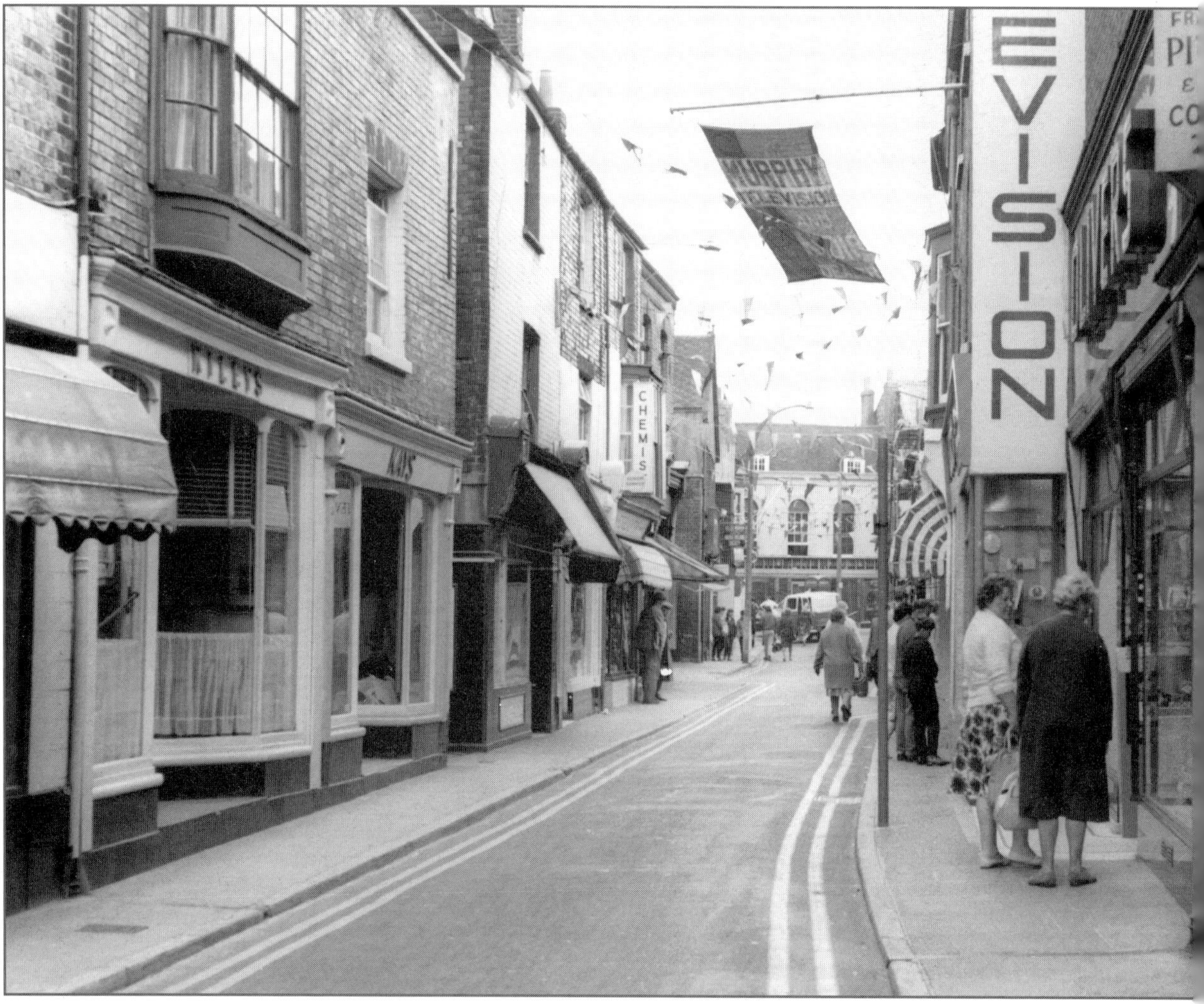


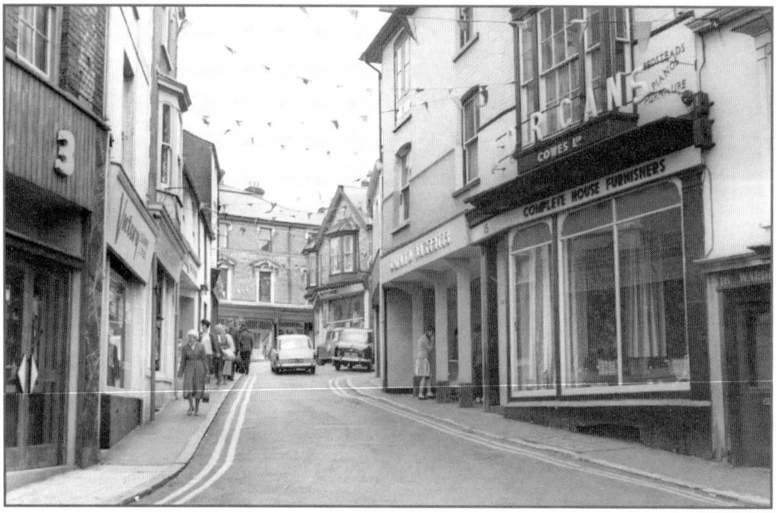


**Cowes, Main Street c1965**

C173087

Here we have a similar slice of the atmosphere of past times further along the narrow Main Street. Double yellow lines signal that another god is taking over modern life, the motor car. A BMC 1100 (which was virtually an enlarged mini with revolutionary hydrolastic suspension) trundles past an Austin and Standard of more bulky 1950s style. The bunting is out, along with the shoppers, who include a girl who appears to be admiring cakes. Morgan's handsome old shop offers all furnishing needs, including the status symbol of a piano.

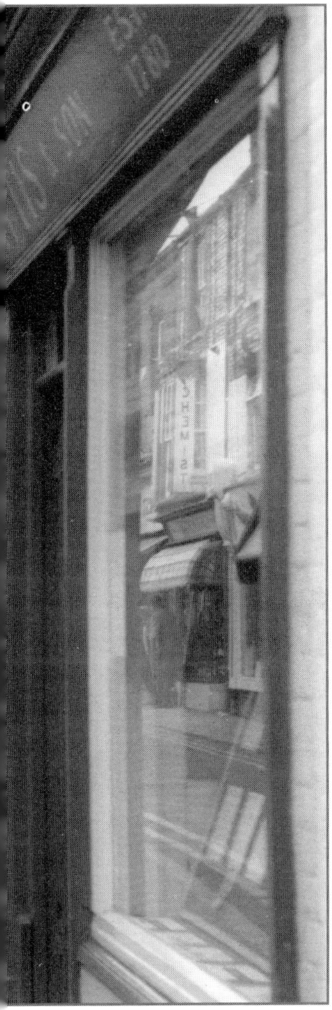

◄ **Cowes, Main Street c1965** C173086
In the foreground is the shop of Francis Pittis & Son, who boast of their establishment in 1780, but this is a modern world: their near neighbours are flying the flag for Murphy televisions (it is ironic, perhaps, that Murphy is among the many British companies that has now disappeared).

▼ **Cowes, Main Street c1965** C173081
Late 50s and early 60s architectural influences can be seen in the street as it slopes down toward the waterside. The outline of the gable end of a demolished old building can be seen in the gap. All the latest in modern motoring is on view: Rootes and Ford Cortina estates are parked near the drab branch of the Westminster Bank, and a trendy Renault stands by Green's restaurant. Two of Ford's older Anglia models are further away from the camera. The bank will soon be merged with the National Provincial as the tide of economic progress keeps bringing in the new and sweeping the old away.

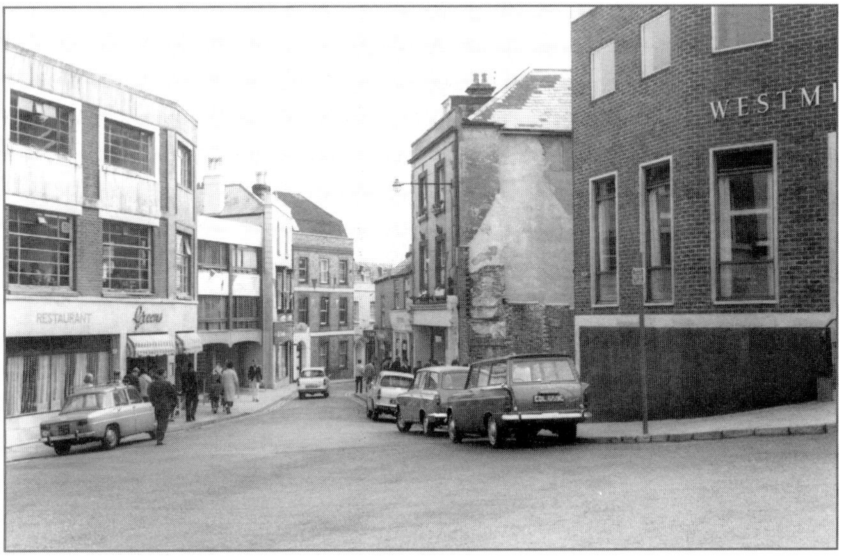


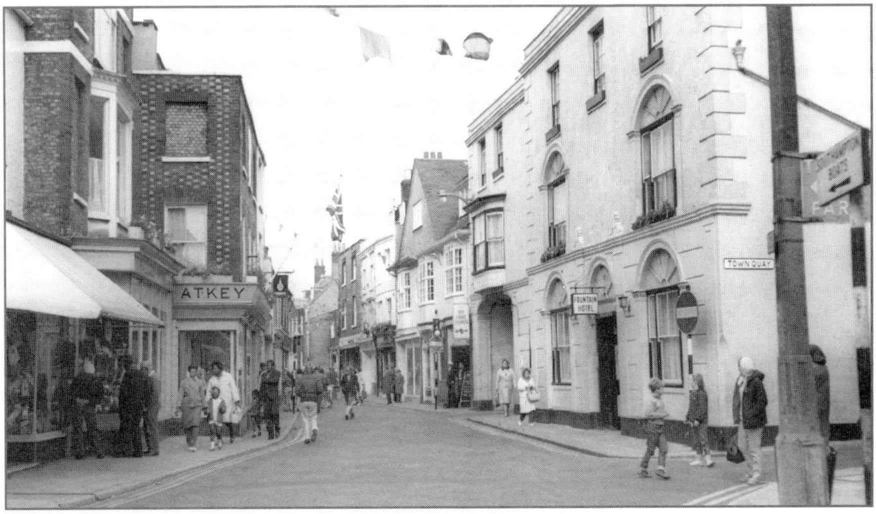


◄ **Cowes, Main Street c1965** C173085
Bunting and flags are out at the bottom of Main Street where it makes a junction with the town quay. The sign pointing to the Southampton boats looks in need of some paint, but the Fountain Hotel with its coaching archway looks in fine order. The railway builder George Stephenson lived near here on Princes's Green in a mansion which later became the Grantham Hotel.

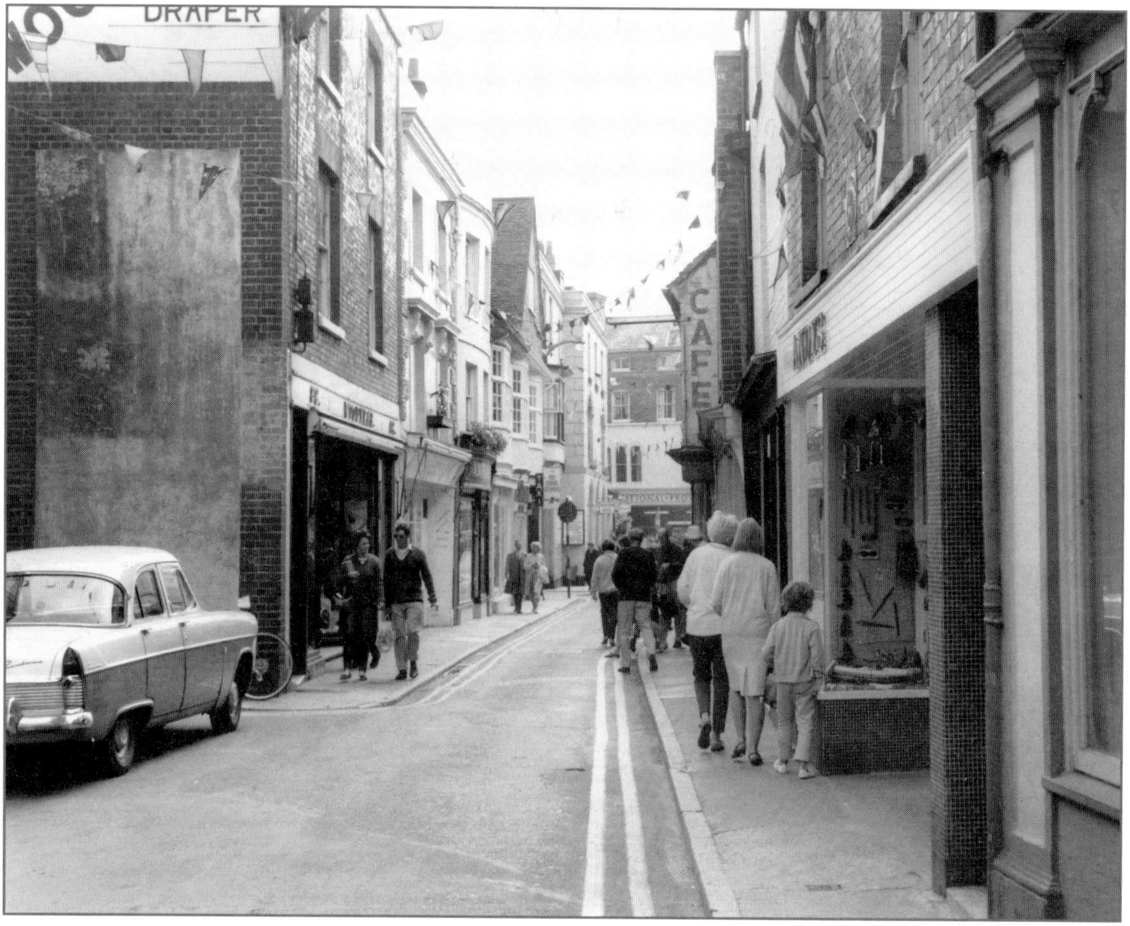


**Cowes**
**High Street c1965** C173082

The parked Ford Zodiac is the most modern artefact along this long narrow stretch of Victorian and Edwardian shops curving along the west front. The National Provincial bank lies straight ahead, and Red Funnel Steamers are signed to the left. Cowes was the birthplace in 1795 of Dr Arnold, headmaster of Rugby School.

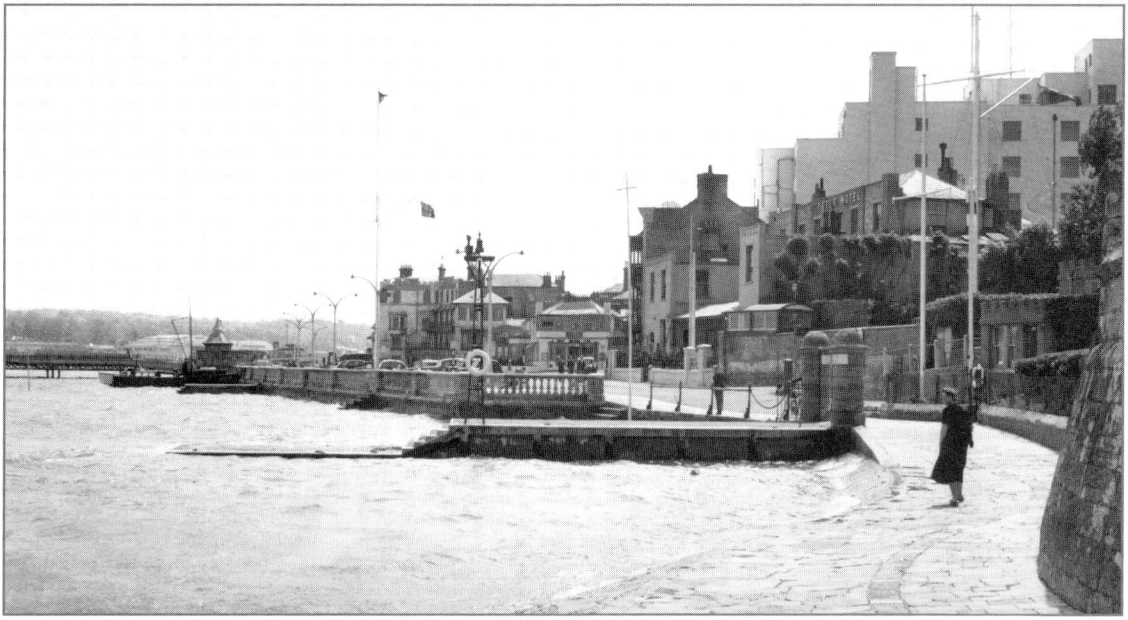

**Cowes, The Parade c1955** C173007
The buildings in the High Street hide the sea. Watch House Lane at the western end, named after the Customs House, leads down to the wide square of the Parade overlooking the Solent. The shelter displays a plaque to the 'Ark and Dove', which sailed to colonise Maryland. Westward the promenade narrows to pass the Royal Yacht Squadron.

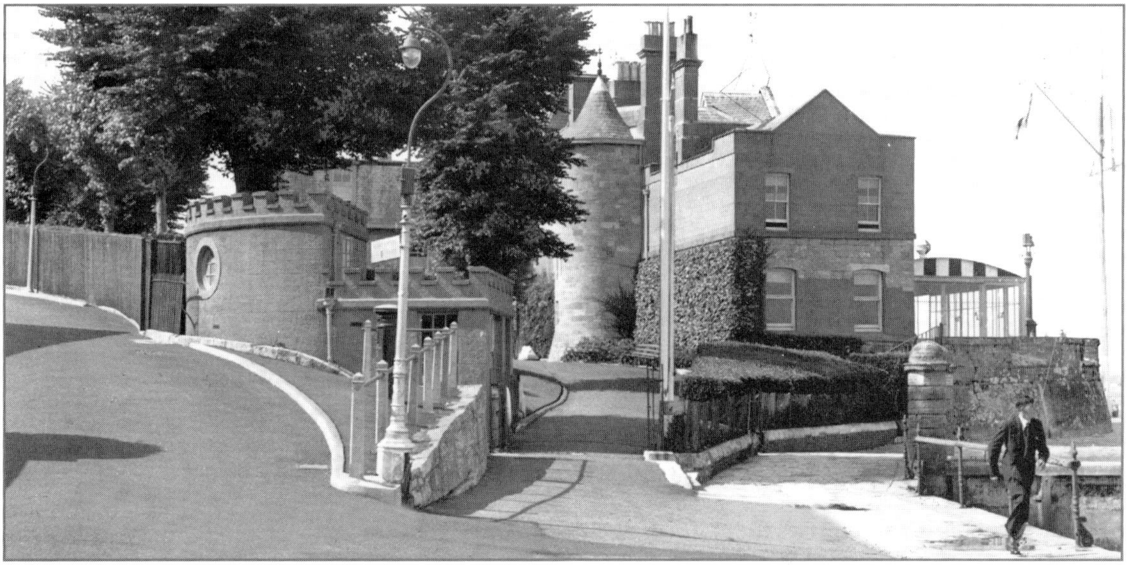

**Cowes, The Royal Yacht Squadron c1955** C173024
It is hard to believe that Cowes was once only a small fishing port. A growth spurt in the 19th century turned it into a premier yachting centre. The Yacht Club was founded in 1815 with 42 upper-crust members. It became the Royal Yacht Club in 1820 and the Royal Yacht Squadron in 1833; in those days, boats were armed. The headquarters is on the site of West Cowes Castle, where only the old semi-circular gun platform survives. Here 22 brass guns from William IV's yacht, the 'Adelaide', are used to start races during Cowes week. Egypt Point, the most northern point of the island, is half a mile west of here.

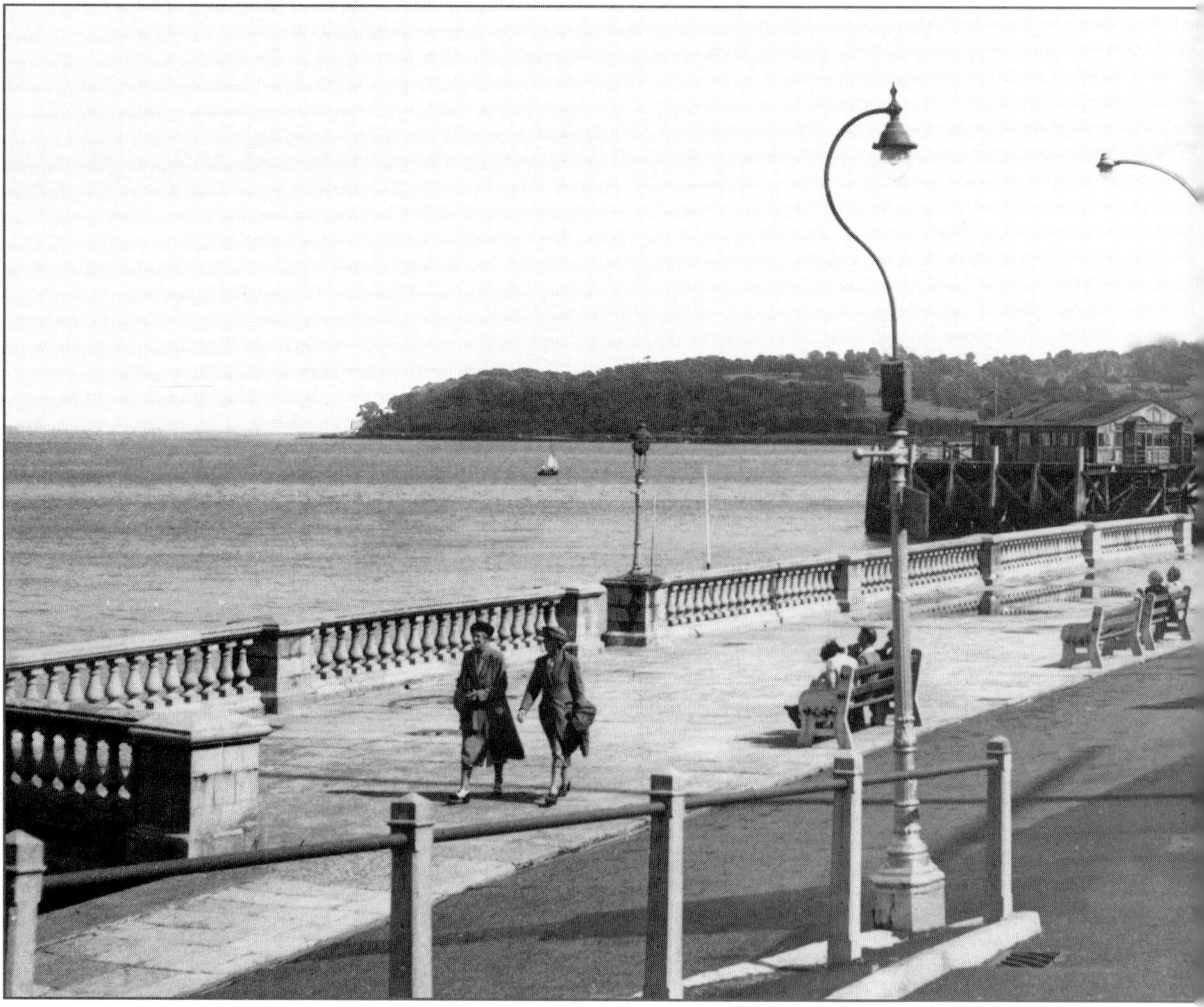

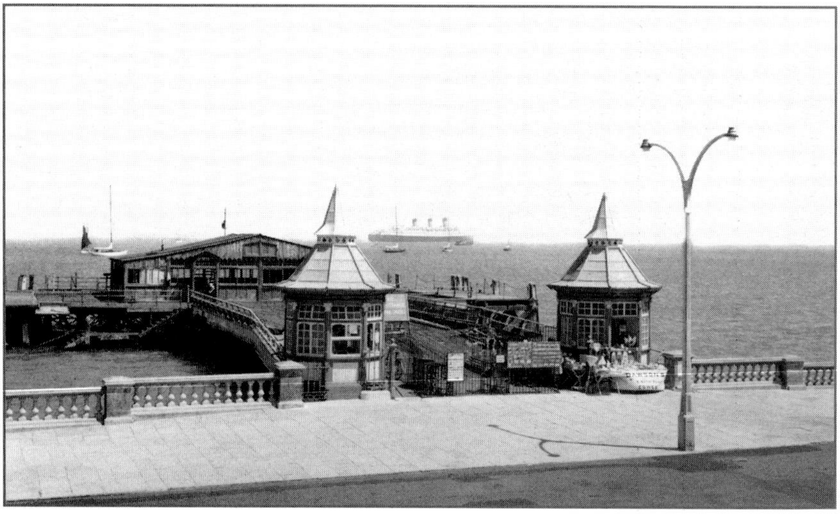

◄ **Cowes, The Old Pier c1950** C173011
This old structure has seen better days and a sign warns of no admittance. That does not stop Dawson's of Bath Road selling gifts and postcards. Meanwhile the 'Queen Mary' sails gracefully past en route from Southampton to New York. Air travel and the increasingly fast pace of life had yet to usurp this gentle giant.

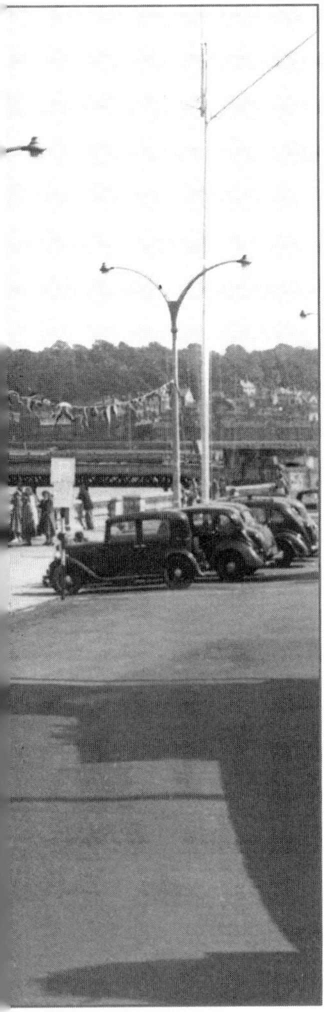

◄ **Cowes, The Esplanade c1950**
C173023
This scene is little changed here since the 1930s, when the Solent was crowded with steamers, and J-Class yachts under 12,000 square feet of sail swooped by like giant butterflies. For the moment all is calm on land and water. People are clustered around the telescope. Behind them, a line of little cars are cosy havens on wheels, rich with the aroma of leather upholstery.

▼ **Cowes, The 'Queen Mary' c1950**
C173012
The Leyland coach shows the destinations Alum Bay and the Needles. It may have brought sightseers to admire the man-made beauty of the 'Queen Mary' and the not unattractive pilot boats. The mighty Cunarder first left her Southampton berth in May 1936, a symbol of national hope. Memories were stirred in May 1996 when recordings of her deep-throated sirens blasted across the dock she had left for the last time on a grey day in 1967.

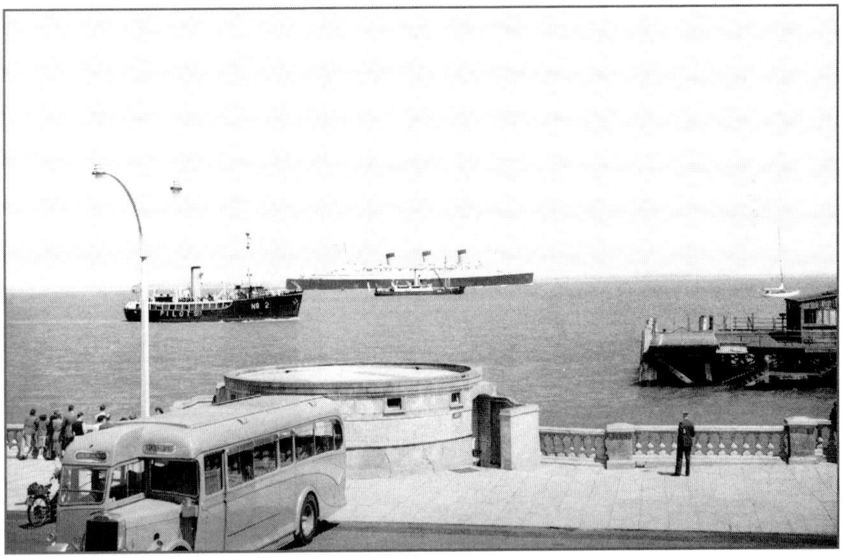

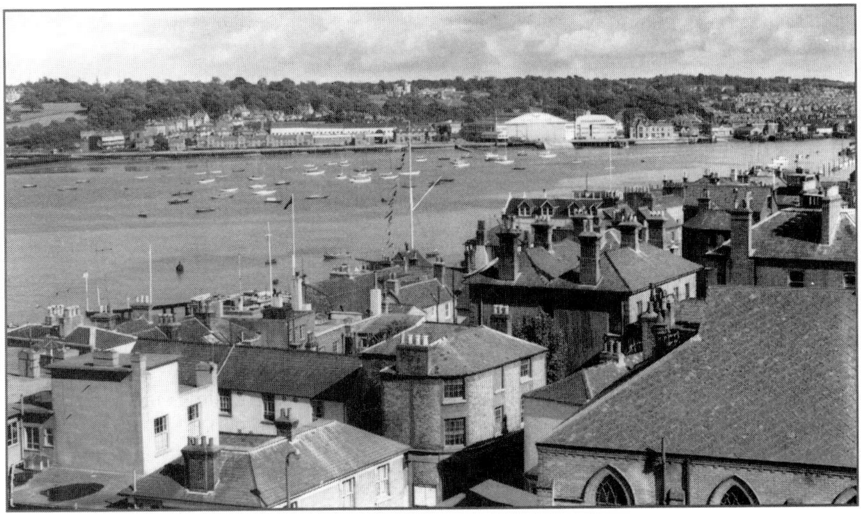

◄ **Cowes, The Harbour c1960** C173061
This photograph gives a clear view across the harbour. Norris Castle is prominent on the wooded skyline. A large hangar and slipway stands out by the waterside. This belonged to Saunders Roe, who at the time were pioneering Sir Christopher Cockerell's hovercraft design. Their SRN 1 first skimmed across to the mainland on its cushion of air in 1959; the first passenger service began in 1965.

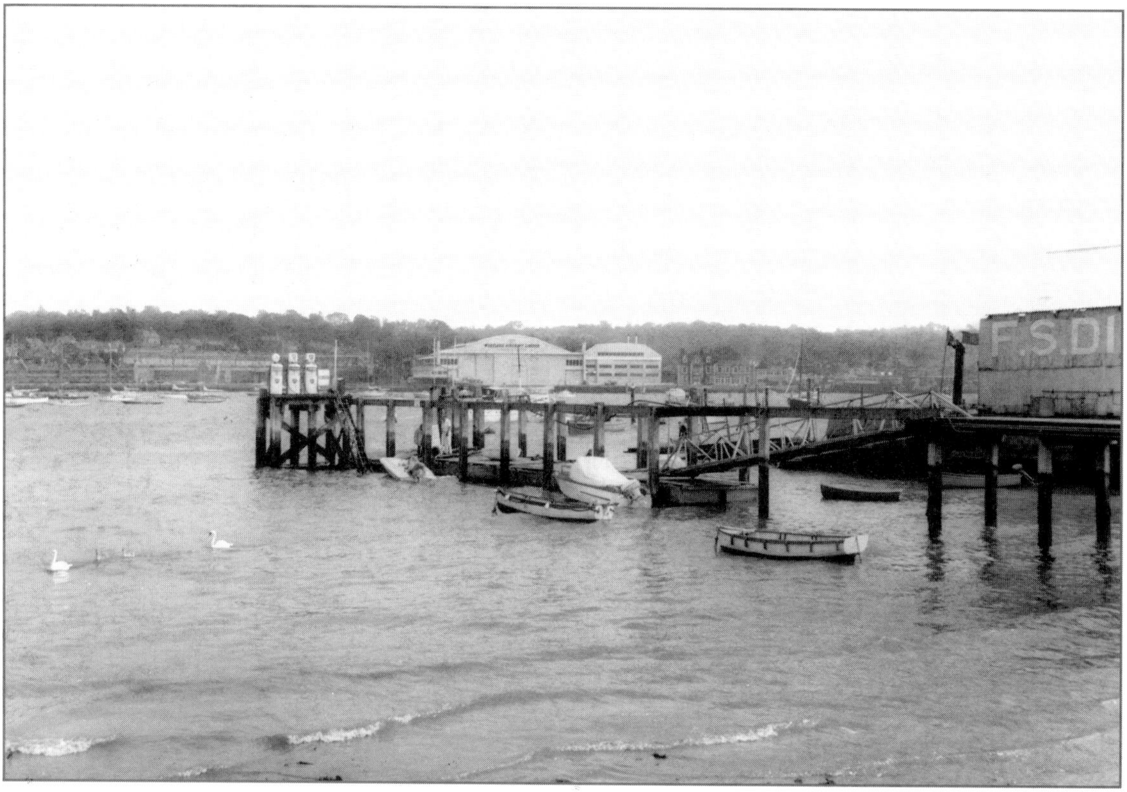


**Cowes**
**The Harbour c1970** C173083
The jetty looks a bit fragile, and the pumps at the end are rather like sentries. However gracefully those boats might float, they cannot compete with the swans in the foreground. By this time Westlands had taken over the hovercraft base; by 1968 it carried the British Hovercraft Corporation logo over its great doors - it is now GKN Westland. 1968 saw the test voyage of the much bigger SRN 4, 'Princess Margaret'. As with everything else, big was about to be beautiful. At least the island is delightfully small, and a place to go if everything else is too much. Let us just hope that those coastal defences are strengthened to stop too much more of the island falling into the sea!

# Index

## Frith Book Co Titles (continued)

| | | |
|---|---|---|
| Liverpool & Merseyside (pb) | 1-85937-234-1 | £9.99 |
| London (pb) | 1-85937-183-3 | £9.99 |
| Ludlow (pb) | 1-85937-176-0 | £9.99 |
| Luton (pb) | 1-85937-235-x | £9.99 |
| Manchester (pb) | 1-85937-198-1 | £9.99 |
| New Forest | 1-85937-128-0 | £14.99 |
| Newport, Wales (pb) | 1-85937-258-9 | £9.99 |
| Newquay (pb) | 1-85937-421-2 | £9.99 |
| Norfolk (pb) | 1-85937-195-7 | £9.99 |
| Norfolk Living Memories | 1-85937-217-1 | £14.99 |
| Northamptonshire | 1-85937-150-7 | £14.99 |
| Northumberland Tyne & Wear (pb) | 1-85937-281-3 | £9.99 |
| North Devon Coast | 1-85937-146-9 | £14.99 |
| North Devon Living Memories | 1-85937-261-9 | £14.99 |
| North Wales (pb) | 1-85937-298-8 | £9.99 |
| North Yorkshire (pb) | 1-85937-236-8 | £9.99 |
| Norwich (pb) | 1-85937-194-9 | £8.99 |
| Nottingham (pb) | 1-85937-324-0 | £9.99 |
| Nottinghamshire (pb) | 1-85937-187-6 | £9.99 |
| Peak District (pb) | 1-85937-280-5 | £9.99 |
| Penzance | 1-85937-069-1 | £12.99 |
| Peterborough (pb) | 1-85937-219-8 | £9.99 |
| Piers | 1-85937-237-6 | £17.99 |
| Plymouth | 1-85937-119-1 | £12.99 |
| Poole & Sandbanks (pb) | 1-85937-251-1 | £9.99 |
| Preston (pb) | 1-85937-212-0 | £9.99 |
| Reading (pb) | 1-85937-238-4 | £9.99 |
| Salisbury (pb) | 1-85937-239-2 | £9.99 |
| St Ives | 1-85937-068-3 | £12.99 |
| Scotland (pb) | 1-85937-182-5 | £9.99 |
| Scottish Castles (pb) | 1-85937-323-2 | £9.99 |
| Sheffield, South Yorks (pb) | 1-85937-267-8 | £9.99 |
| Shrewsbury (pb) | 1-85937-325-9 | £9.99 |
| Shropshire (pb) | 1-85937-326-7 | £9.99 |
| Somerset | 1-85937-153-1 | £14.99 |
| South Devon Coast | 1-85937-107-8 | £14.99 |
| South Devon Living Memories | 1-85937-168-x | £14.99 |
| South Hams | 1-85937-220-1 | £14.99 |
| Southampton (pb) | 1-85937-427-1 | £9.99 |
| Southport (pb) | 1-85937-425-5 | £9.99 |
| Stratford upon Avon | 1-85937-098-5 | £12.99 |
| Suffolk (pb) | 1-85937-221-x | £9.99 |
| Suffolk Coast | 1-85937-259-7 | £14.99 |
| Surrey (pb) | 1-85937-240-6 | £9.99 |
| Sussex (pb) | 1-85937-184-1 | £9.99 |
| Swansea (pb) | 1-85937-167-1 | £9.99 |
| Tees Valley & Cleveland | 1-85937-211-2 | £14.99 |
| Thanet (pb) | 1-85937-116-7 | £9.99 |
| Tiverton (pb) | 1-85937-178-7 | £9.99 |
| Torbay | 1-85937-063-2 | £12.99 |
| Truro | 1-85937-147-7 | £12.99 |
| Victorian and Edwardian Cornwall | 1-85937-252-x | £14.99 |
| Victorian & Edwardian Devon | 1-85937-253-8 | £14.99 |
| Victorian & Edwardian Kent | 1-85937-149-3 | £14.99 |
| Vic & Ed Maritime Album | 1-85937-144-2 | £17.99 |
| Victorian and Edwardian Sussex | 1-85937-157-4 | £14.99 |
| Victorian & Edwardian Yorkshire | 1-85937-154-x | £14.99 |
| Victorian Seaside | 1-85937-159-0 | £17.99 |
| Villages of Devon (pb) | 1-85937-293-7 | £9.99 |
| Villages of Kent (pb) | 1-85937-294-5 | £9.99 |
| Warwickshire (pb) | 1-85937-203-1 | £9.99 |
| Welsh Castles (pb) | 1-85937-322-4 | £9.99 |
| West Midlands (pb) | 1-85937-289-9 | £9.99 |
| West Sussex | 1-85937-148-5 | £14.99 |
| West Yorkshire (pb) | 1-85937-201-5 | £9.99 |
| Weymouth (pb) | 1-85937-209-0 | £9.99 |
| Wiltshire (pb) | 1-85937-277-5 | £9.99 |
| Wiltshire Churches (pb) | 1-85937-171-x | £9.99 |
| Wiltshire Living Memories | 1-85937-245-7 | £14.99 |
| Winchester (pb) | 1-85937-428-x | £9.99 |
| Windmills & Watermills | 1-85937-242-2 | £17.99 |
| Worcestershire | 1-85937-152-3 | £14.99 |
| York (pb) | 1-85937-199-x | £9.99 |
| Yorkshire (pb) | 1-85937-186-8 | £9.99 |
| Yorkshire Living Memories | 1-85937-166-3 | £14.99 |

## Frith Book Co titles available soon

| | | | |
|---|---|---|---|
| 1870's England | Oct 01 | 1-85937-331-3 | £17.99 |
| Amersham & Chesham (pb) | Oct 01 | 1-85937-340-2 | £9.99 |
| Bedfordshire | Oct 01 | 1-85937-320-8 | £14.99 |
| Belfast (pb) | Oct 01 | 1-85937-303-8 | £9.99 |
| Britain Living Memories | Oct 01 | 1-85937-343-7 | £17.99 |
| Chelmsford (pb) | Oct 01 | 1-85937-310-0 | £9.99 |
| Gloucester (pb) | Oct 01 | 1-85937-417-4 | £9.99 |
| Oxfordshire (pb) | Oct 01 | 1-85937-430-1 | £9.99 |
| Picturesque Harbours | Oct 01 | 1-85937-208-2 | £17.99 |
| Romford (pb) | Oct 01 | 1-85937-319-4 | £9.99 |
| Worcester (pb) | Oct 01 | 1-85937-165-5 | £9.99 |
| Villages of Sussex (pb) | Sep 01 | 1-85937-295-3 | £9.99 |

**See Frith books on the internet www.francisfrith.co.uk**

# Frith Products & Services

Francis Frith would doubtless be pleased to know that the pioneering publishing venture he started in 1860 still continues today. A hundred and forty years later, The Francis Frith Collection continues in the same innovative tradition and is now one of the foremost publishers of vintage photographs in the world. Some of the current activities include:

### *Interior Decoration*

Today Frith's photographs can be seen framed and as giant wall murals in thousands of pubs, restaurants, hotels, banks, retail stores and other public buildings throughout the country. In every case they enhance the unique local atmosphere of the places they depict and provide reminders of gentler days in an increasingly busy and frenetic world.

### *Product Promotions*

Frith products are used by many major companies to promote the sales of their own products or to reinforce their own history and heritage. Frith promotions have been used by Hovis bread, Courage beers, Scots Porage Oats, Colman's mustard, Cadbury's foods, Mellow Birds coffee, Dunhill pipe tobacco, Guinness, and Bulmer's Cider.

### *Genealogy and Family History*

As the interest in family history and roots grows world-wide, more and more people are turning to Frith's photographs of Great Britain for images of the towns, villages and streets where their ancestors lived; and, of course, photographs of the churches and chapels where their ancestors were christened, married and buried are an essential part of every genealogy tree and family album.

### *Frith Products*

All Frith photographs are available Framed or just as Mounted Prints and Posters (size 23 x 16 inches). These may be ordered from the address below. From time to time other products - Address Books, Calendars, Table Mats, etc - are available.

### *The Internet*

Already twenty thousand Frith photographs can be viewed and purchased on the internet through the Frith websites and a myriad of partner sites.

For more detailed information on Frith companies and products, look at these sites:

www.francisfrith.co.uk
www.francisfrith.com
*(for North American visitors)*

**See the complete list of Frith Books at:**
***www.francisfrith.co.uk***
This web site is regularly updated with the latest list of publications from the Frith Book Company. If you wish to buy books relating to another part of the country that your local bookshop does not stock, you may purchase on-line.

***For further information, trade, or author enquiries please contact us at the address below:***
**The Francis Frith Collection, Frith's Barn, Teffont, Salisbury, Wiltshire, England SP3 5QP.**
Tel: +44 (0)1722 716 376 Fax: +44 (0)1722 716 881 Email: sales@francisfrith.co.uk

**See Frith books on the internet www.francisfrith.co.uk**

## TO RECEIVE YOUR FREE MOUNTED PRINT

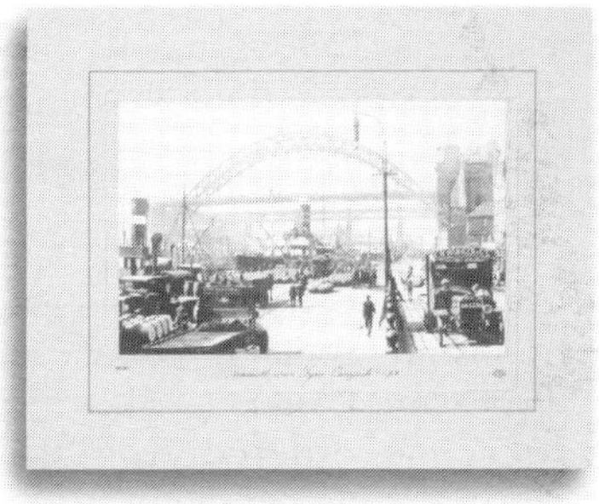

**Mounted Print**
*Overall size 14 x 11 inches*

*Cut out this Voucher and return it with your remittance for £1.95 to cover postage and handling, to UK addresses. For overseas addresses please include £4.00 post and handling.*
*Choose any photograph included in this book. Your SEPIA print will be A4 in size, and mounted in a cream mount with burgundy rule line, overall size 14 x 11 inches.*

**Order additional Mounted Prints at HALF PRICE (only £7.49 each*)**
If there are further pictures you would like to order, possibly as gifts for friends and family, purchase them at half price (no additional postage and handling required).

**Have your Mounted Prints framed***
For an additional £14.95 per print you can have your chosen Mounted Print framed in an elegant polished wood and gilt moulding, overall size 16 x 13 inches (no additional postage and handling required).

*** IMPORTANT!**
**These special prices are only available if ordered using the original voucher on this page (no copies permitted) and at the same time as your free Mounted Print, for delivery to the same address**

## Frith Collectors' Guild

*From time to time we publish a magazine of news and stories about Frith photographs and further special offers of Frith products. If you would like 12 months FREE membership, please return this form.*

*Send completed forms to:*
**The Francis Frith Collection, Frith's Barn, Teffont, Salisbury, Wiltshire SP3 5QP**

## *Voucher* for FREE and Reduced Price Frith Prints

| Picture no. | Page number | Qty | Mounted @ £7.49 | Framed + £14.95 | Total Cost |
|---|---|---|---|---|---|
| | | 1 | **Free of charge*** | £ | £ |
| | | | £7.49 | £ | £ |
| | | | £7.49 | £ | £ |
| | | | £7.49 | £ | £ |
| | | | £7.49 | £ | £ |
| | | | £7.49 | £ | £ |

*Please allow 28 days for delivery*   * **Post & handling** **£1.95**

**Book Title** . . . . . . . . . . . . . . . . . **Total Order Cost** **£**

***Please do not photocopy this voucher. Only the original is valid, so please cut it out and return it to us.***

I enclose a cheque / postal order for £ . . . . . . . . . . .
made payable to 'The Francis Frith Collection'
OR please debit my Mastercard / Visa / Switch / Amex card
***(credit cards please on all overseas orders)***

Number . . . . . . . . . . . . . . . . . . . . . . . . . . . . . . . . . . . . . . . . . . . .

Issue No (Switch only) . . . . . . . Valid from (Amex/Switch) . . . . . . .

Expires . . . . . . . . . . . Signature . . . . . . . . . . . . . . . . . . . . . . . .

Name Mr/Mrs/Ms ..................................................................

Address ..............................................................................

..............................................................................

..............................................................................

.................................................. Postcode ...............................

Daytime Tel No .................................... Valid to 31/12/02

## The Francis Frith Collectors' Guild

Please enrol me as a member for 12 months free of charge.

Name Mr/Mrs/Ms ..................................................................

Address ..............................................................................

..............................................................................

..............................................................................

.................................................. Postcode ...............................

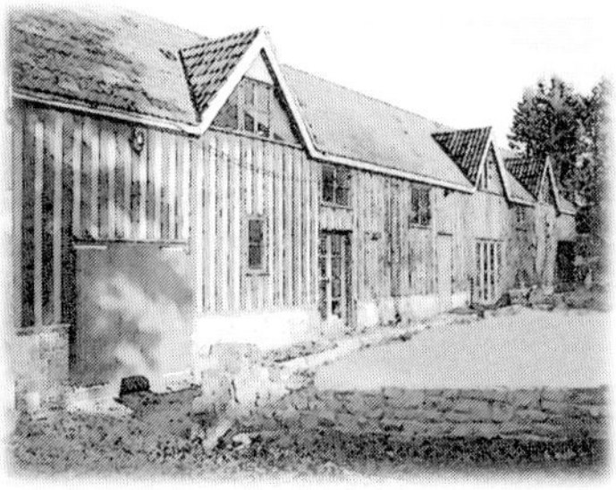

**Would you like to find out more about Francis Frith?**

We have recently recruited some entertaining speakers who are happy to visit local groups, clubs and societies to give an illustrated talk documenting Frith's travels and photographs. If you are a member of such a group and are interested in hosting a presentation, we would love to hear from you.

Our speakers bring with them a small selection of our local town and county books, together with sample prints. They are happy to take orders. A small proportion of the order value is donated to the group who have hosted the presentation. The talks are therefore an excellent way of fundraising for small groups and societies.

**Can you help us with information about any of the Frith photographs in this book?**

We are gradually compiling an historical record for each of the photographs in the Frith archive. It is always fascinating to find out the names of the people shown in the pictures, as well as insights into the shops, buildings and other features depicted.

If you recognize anyone in the photographs in this book, or if you have information not already included in the author's caption, do let us know. We would love to hear from you, and will try to publish it in future books or articles.

**Our production team**

Frith books are produced by a small dedicated team at offices in the converted Grade II listed 18th-century barn at Teffont near Salisbury, illustrated above. Most have worked with the Frith Collection for many years. All have in common one quality: they have a passion for the Frith Collection. The team is constantly expanding, but currently includes:

Jason Buck, John Buck, Heather Crisp, Isobel Hall, Rob Hames, Hazel Heaton, Peter Horne, James Kinnear, Tina Leary, Eliza Sackett, Terence Sackett, Sandra Sanger, Shelley Tolcher, Susanna Walker, Clive Wathen, Jenny Wathen and Douglas Burns.